THE INDEPENDENT TRAVELLER

SIR PETER USTINOV
Actor, Dramatist, Film Director and British G...
interviewed by Sarah Tucker

"I don't really have a favourite hotel in Europe. When you travel as much as I do, you don't have a favourite hotel in each country – you have one in each town. Ones I go to regularly and I know I can trust. I always try to meet the owner or manager – usually the same person in smaller hotels – and cultivate a good rapport. They get to know my little ways.

"I prefer the smaller, more intimate hotels. I feel like a person and not just another cover in the restaurant, or another cheque in the cash register. When I go into a hotel and they ask for my credit (sic) card before I have even put down my suitcase, I feel as if they don't trust me. Not a good start.

"It is in smaller hotels, where you'll find personal touches and quaint old ways that give a hotel character. Some hotel chains seem to take all the fun out of staying in a hotel – and destroy the character by mass standardisation and expansion. When will they learn that bigger isn't necessarily better?

"I love hotels which make that much more of an effort. Where every room is decorated differently and beautifully. And perhaps where they make the most of the grounds. There's a hotel in Germany I stay in regularly and which boasts a wonderful swimming pool – which seems to overflow only when I get into it. The view is wonderful.

"As for service, the Italians are so gifted at giving good service – I think its in their culture. They genuinely seem to enjoy it. In England service seems rather below everybody. It dates back to Henry VIII when he first played tennis. Deeming it was beneath his dignity to put the first ball into play, he asked one of his servants to start the game, hence 'service'. Some hoteliers in England still seem to feel like that about running a hotel. They are of course the exceptions.

"I discovered an interesting fact about Italian hotels not long ago. In Italy many of the former hotels are now prisons and buildings which were prisons have been turned into hotels. I don't think that that would or could happen in many other countries in Europe.

"As for hotels which change their schedules to suit the customer, rather than themselves – well the Spanish are probably the most accommodating. If I wanted something to eat mid morning, mid afternoon or the middle of the night – I could probably get it. In Switzerland, lunch is served between 12 noon and 1.30 pm. Not before and not after. Service is punctual and perfect – but immovable as a rock.

"And the most interesting experience I have ever had in a hotel? Well I can tell you one of the most amusing ones. Many years ago, I was staying at a rather grand hotel in Monte Carlo. I was given a suite at the very top and views from the balcony were spectacular. One of the windows from my room overlooked another balcony and in this room I saw two women standing naked talking, laughing, wonderfully oblivious of my eyes. They then closed their curtains and I thought I had been discovered – not that I was looking for naked ladies of course. When they opened the curtains again, They were dressed in swimsuits and appeared ready for a day of serious sunbathing.

"That afternoon, they returned to the room again, closing the curtains to get changed and opening them – again to be revealed in their birthday suits. I don't know if they ever knew I had watched them, but found it most unusual and perhaps a little charming, that they should seek privacy to change while they were happy to expose themselves to the rest of the world when they had nothing but their perfume to cover their modesty."

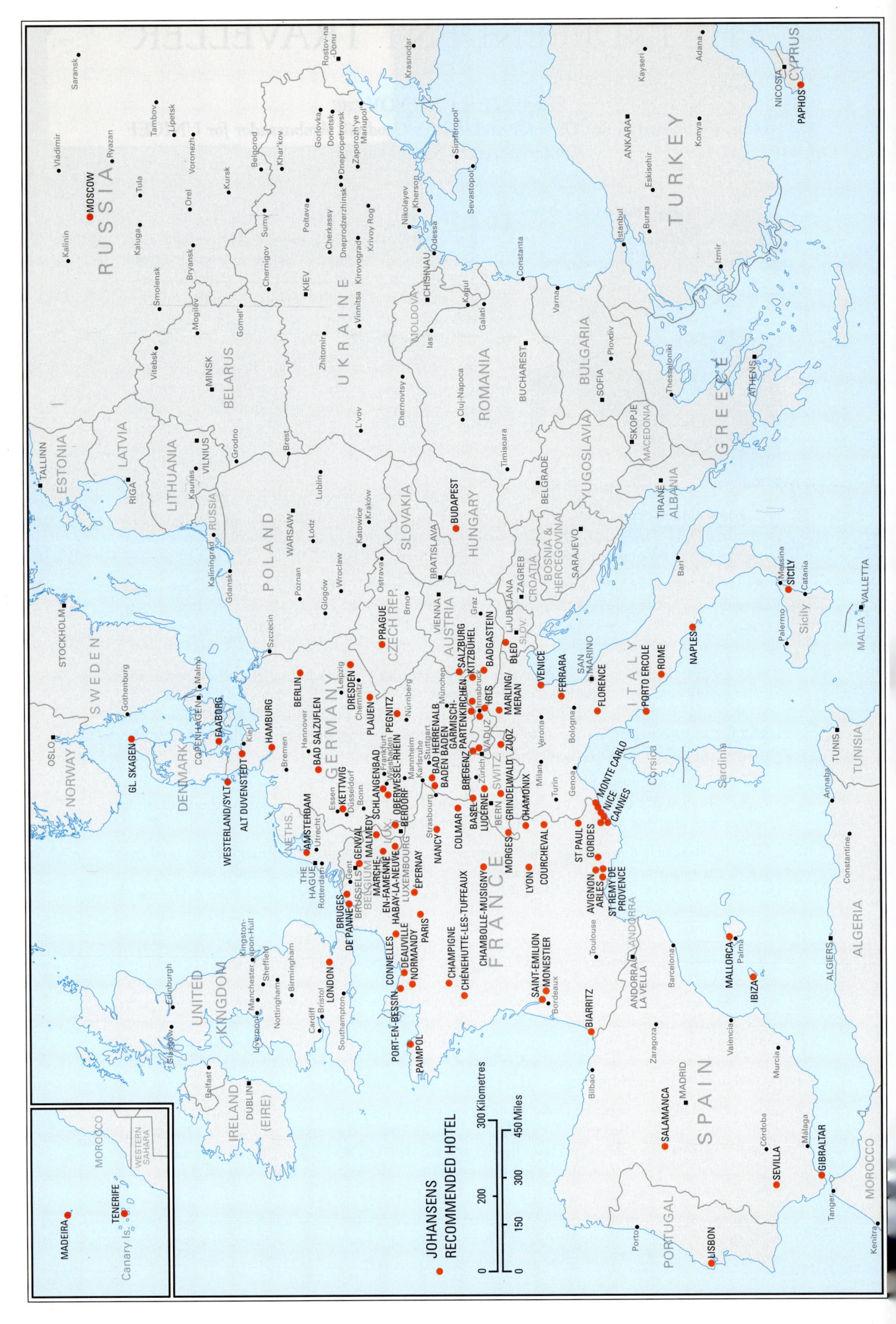

JOHANSENS RECOMMENDED HOTEL

CONTENTS

*Cover Picture: Château Grand Barrail,
Saint-Emilion, France (see page 93).*

Introduction by Sir Peter Ustinov CBE	1
Map of Europe	2
How to use this guide	4
Key to symbols	6
Austria	9
Belgium	21
British Isles	33
Cyprus (Southern Cyprus)	43
Czech Republic	45
Denmark	47
France	50
Germany	100
Gibraltar	119
Hungary	121
Italy	123
Luxembourg	139
Monaco	141
The Netherlands	143
Portugal	145
The Russian Federation	148
Slovenia	150
Spain	152
Switzerland	158
Index	164
Mini Listings of all Johansens Recommendations in The British Isles	165
Johansens Guides Order Forms and Guest Survey Reports	167

In association with MasterCard

INTRODUCTION BY THE EDITOR

Johansens guides, now in their 15th year, have developed from one single hotel guide into what this year is a set of five – Recommended Hotels, Recommended Inns with Restaurants, Recommended Country Houses and Small Hotels, Recommended Business Meetings Venues and now, for the first time, Johansens Recommended Hotels in Europe. The market place has grown and we have grown with it. Our principles, nevertheless, have remained constant. The annual inspection of candidates for inclusion in our guides reinforced by the thousands of reports from Johansens guide-users sustains our criterion of excellence.

We are publishers and as such we form the link between two groups of clients: hoteliers who, if accepted for membership, pay an annual fee and their guests, who are in many cases purchasers of our guides. We value both these relationships hoping

In association with MasterCard

Published by
Johansens, 175-179 St John Street, London EC1V 4RP
Tel: 0171-490 3090 Fax: 0171-490 2538
Find Johansens on the Internet at: http://www.johansen.com

Editor:	Rodney Exton
Copywriter:	Sally Sutton
Style Editor:	Sarah Tucker
Publishing Director:	Andrew Warren
P.A. to Publishing Director:	Angela Franks
Associate Publisher:	Peter Hancock
Secretary to Associate Publisher:	Carol Sweeney
Executive Inspectors:	Diana Davis
	Jolyon Harris
Research:	David Rauch
Special Projects Manager:	Fiona Patrick
Locations:	Joanna Falcon
Production Manager	Daniel Barnett
Production Controller:	Kevin Bradbrook
Designer:	Matthew Davis
Assistant Designer:	Matthew Cleveland
Sales and Marketing Manager:	Mike Schwarz
Marketing Executive:	Juliet Brookes
Marketing Assistant:	Rebecca Ford
Managing Director:	Martin Morgan

Whilst every care has been taken in the compilation of this Guide, the publishers cannot accept responsibility for any inaccuracies or for changes since going to press, or for consequential loss arising from such changes or other inaccuracies, or for any other loss direct or consequential arising in connection with information describing establishments in this publication. Recommended establishments pay an annual subscription to cover the costs of inspection, the distribution and production of copies placed in hotel bedrooms and certain membership services.

No part of this publication may be copied or reproduced, stored in a retrieval system or transmitted, in any form or by any means, electronic, mechanical, photocopy, recording or otherwise, without the prior permission of the publishers.

The publishers request readers not to cut, tear or otherwise mark this Guide except Guest Reports and Mail Coupons. No other cuttings may be taken without the written permission of the publishers.

Copyright © 1995 Johansens
Hobsons Publishing plc,
a subsidiary of the Daily Mail and General Trust plc
ISBN 1 86017 128 1
Printed in England by St Ives plc
Colour origination by Graphic Facilities

Distributed in the UK and Europe by Biblios PDS Ltd, Partridge Green, West Sussex, RH13 8LD. In North America by general sales agent: SunWelcome, INC., Clearwater, Florida (direct sales) and The Cimino Publishing Group, INC. New York (bookstores). In Australia and New Zealand by Bookwise International, Findon, South Australia.

HOW TO USE THIS GUIDE

If you want to identify a Hotel whose name you already know, look for it in the indexes on pages 164.

These indexes are arranged by Country.

If you want to find a Hotel in a particular area,
- Turn to the map of Europe on page 2, which will show you the Countries in which there are Johansens recommended hotels.
- Turn to the title page of the Country that you want, where you will find a Map. The location of each Hotel appears in red on the Map with a number corresponding to the page on which the Hotel entry is published.

The Countries and place names appear in alphabetical order throughout the guide.

Mini Listings pages 165–166: The names, locations and telephone numbers of all Johansens recommendations in the British Isles are listed. The Johansens guides in which these recommendations appear are fully described on the outside back cover. Copies of these guides are obtainable direct from Johansens by calling 44 990 269397 or by using the order coupons on page 168.

The prices, in most cases, are a guide to the cost of one night's accommodation with breakfast, for two people. Prices are shown for single occupancy. These rates are correct at time of going to press but they should always be checked.

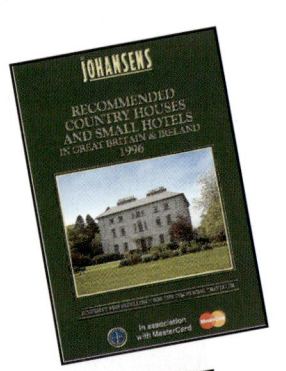

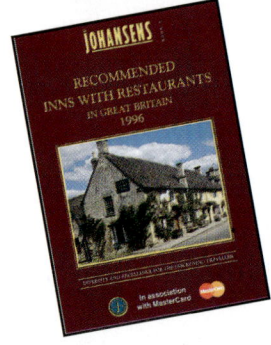

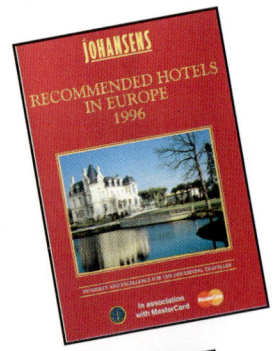

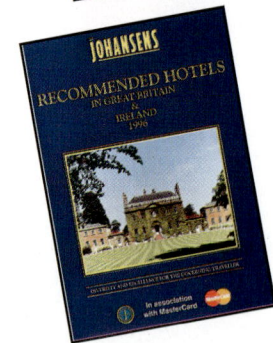

Harrods
KNIGHTSBRIDGE

WHEN IT COMES TO MEN'S FASHION,
WE'VE GOT A FIRST IN CLASSICS.
HARRODS MENSWEAR, GROUND FLOOR

In association with MasterCard

KEY TO SYMBOLS

	English		French		German
13 rms	Total number of rooms	13 rms	Nombre de chambres	13 rms	Anzahl der Zimmer
MasterCard	MasterCard accepted	MasterCard	MasterCard accepté	MasterCard	MasterCard akzeptiert
VISA	Visa accepted	VISA	Visa accepté	VISA	Visa akzeptiert
AMERICAN EXPRESS	American Express accepted	AMERICAN EXPRESS	American Express accepté	AMERICAN EXPRESS	American Express akzeptiert
	Diners Club accepted		Diners Club accepté		Diners Club akzeptiert
	Quiet location		Un lieu tranquille		Ruhige Lage
	Access for wheelchairs to at least one bedroom and public rooms		Accès handicapé		Zugang für Behinderte
20	Meeting/conference facilities with maximum number of delegates	20	Salle de conférences – capacité maximale	20	Konferenzraum-Höchstkapazität
8	Children welcome, with minimum age where applicable	8	Enfants bienvenus	8	Kinder willkommen
	Dogs accommodated in rooms or kennels		Chiens autorisés		Hunde erlaubt
	Cable/satellite TV in all bedrooms		TV câblée/satellite dans les chambres		Satellit-und Kabelfernsehen in allen Zimmern
	Direct-dial telephone in all bedrooms		Téléphone dans les chambres		Telefon in allen Zimmern
	No-smoking rooms (at least one no-smoking bedroom)		Chambres non-fumeurs		Zimmer für Nichtraucher
	Lift available for guests' use		Ascensrur		Fahrstuhl
	Indoor swimming pool		Piscine couverte		Hallenbad
	Outdoor swimming pool		Piscine de plein air		Freibad
	Tennis court at hotel		Tennis à l'hôtel		Hoteleigener Tennisplatz
	Croquet lawn at hotel		Croquet à l'hôtel		Krocketrasen
	Fishing can be arranged		Pêche		Angeln
	Golf course on site or nearby, which has an arrangement with hotel allowing guests to play		Golf		Golfplatz
	Shooting can be arranged		Chasse		Jagd
	Riding can be arranged		Chevaux de selle		Reitpferd
(H)	Hotel has a helicopter landing pad	(H)	Hélipad	(H)	Hubschrauberlandplatz

For restaurant location, see maps on pages 180–186

JOHANSENS demand the highest standards

So we've taken a leaf out of their book.

An entry into Johansens is greatly coveted and hard to achieve.

Not only do levels of service have to be second to none, but the hotels and their surroundings must mirror that commitment to excellence.

Which is where we come in.

Knight Frank & Rutley's Hotel Department reflects those standards. We specialise in acquisitions, disposals, valuations and all other aspects of Hotel Property.

We are dedicated to providing the best hotel property service, tailor-made to your needs.

Knight Frank & Rutley. Is it any wonder we're in Johansen's?

THE EUROPEAN

THE WEEKLY NEWSPAPER FOR EUROPE

Europe depends on where you view it from

- News ■ Analysis ■ Sport

- Business ■ Economics
- Finance ■ Company Profiles
- Country Trends ■ Stockwatch

- The European MagAZine –
an A-Z Guide to the Best of Culture,
Entertainment and Lifestyle
in Europe

What's *your* view?

Every week in *The European*

For subscription information telephone 01708 386865 or fax 01708 340132

AUSTRIA

Austria, the land of the waltz, lingers in the mind long after you leave its borders. Views over the Austrian Alps rival any in the world, and when juxtaposed with medieval walled cities, the experience is memorable. Sweeping Alpine valleys, ornate churches, mountain top castles, and people that owe their existence to the land. The Danube – not as blue as one might hope – is still beautiful – meandering past gloomy castles and industrial towns, vineyards and apricot and apple orchards, rising in Germany's Black Forest – emptying into the Black Sea.

Austria's vineyards – spread out over the northern and eastern countryside – offer a good excuse to see areas far from the beaten tourist track. The countryside is relaxed and rolling in the north, rather more dramatic if you decide to head south.

The northern reaches of the Tyrol and the western parts of Upper Austria border on Germany and possess a more robust character than the eastern and southern provinces – of which there are nine. Although the majestically beautiful city of Salzburg, capital of rugged Salzburg province, perches right on the German border, Austrian traditions, folk customs and the music of Mozart flourish more so here than in any other part of the country.

The old centre of Salzburg is small but brims over with history – from remnants of Roman city, Juvavum, to the churches, palaces and squares constructed during Salzburg's thousand years under the powerful prince-archbishops. Towering over the city is the medieval fortress, symbol of the power politics and religion that ruled the town. The other quality that shapes Salzburg is music, and there is music everywhere – in the churches, palaces, castles and concert halls.

Innsbruck, another glorious city and the capital of the Tyrol is one of the loveliest towns of its size anywhere in the world owing much of its fame and charm to its unique setting. To the north, the steep, sheer sides of the Alps rise like a glacial blue and white wall, literally from the edge of the city – an impressive backdrop for the mellowed green domes and red roofs of the baroque town tucked beneath. To the south, the peaks of Tuxer and Stubai form hazy purple steps fading into the distance.

And Vienna. A city in love with its past. Inspiration for Haydn, Mozart, Beethoven, Schubert, Brahms, Strauss, Mahler – you hear their music playing from every restaurant, supermarket and corner shop, surpassing the most popular of 20th century melodies. Like an architectural waltz, the capital's baroque buildings are frozen in time and present the same artful synthesis of licence.

The architecture is magnificent. Baroque mansions dominate the streets of the Stephansdom Quarter, while outside the centre you'll find the grand summer palaces where the Habsburg emperors and aristocracy lived during the warmer months.

Stroll through Vienna's streets and marvel at the beautifully preserved historic buildings, from former imperial residences to humbler burghers' dwellings. The majority date from the 17th and 18th centuries and illustrate the various phases of baroque architecture.

Viennese cooking could be described as hearty and filling – more suited to the meat eater than the vegetarian – and to a cold winter than a hot summer. Lots of potatoes, rice, meat and cabbage. In the more expensive restaurants, you'll find more variety and a tendency to nouvelle cuisine – which ironically is wonderful in the summer but leaves you wanting more after the meal in the winters – which are bitter.

Viennese pastries are the best in the world. The Viennese enjoy cakes mid morning or afternoon, and they set time aside for between-meal snacks – the afternoon coffee breaks being known as Jause. You'll be as fascinated by the pastry shop windows as children are by their first experience of toys.

AUSTRIA (Bad Gastein)

HOTELDORF GRÜNER BAUM
KÖTSCHACHTAL 25, BAD GASTEIN 5640, AUSTRIA
TEL: 43 64 34 25 16 0 FAX: 43 64 34 25 16 25

This is not a hotel, but a hotel village! The original building a 19th century hunting lodge in the Gastein valley, the complex now has five buildings, all blending into the surrounding countryside. It offers something for everyone – a skilful combination of a health spa, sportsman's haven and a family hotel. Many of the flower-filled rooms have panelled walls and traditional rustic furniture. The delightful bedrooms – all en suite – echo this comfortable simplicity. The bar is a focal point of the 'village', with its sunny terrace. Typical mountain fare such as venison and trout and many Bohemian dishes are served together with a selection of regional wines. Outdoor life dominates the choice of activities – skiing in the winter and in summer guests congregate round the pool, stroll in the meadows, play tennis or golf, fish, hunt or go hiking. Sometimes the hotel organises a gourmet picnic! The healing spa treatments and beauty salon play an important part in the lifestyle at Grüner Baum. The thermal pool and superbly equipped treatment rooms and gymnasium in the Kösslerhaus together with the beauticians, who pamper the guests, equate to the house philosophy of health, vitality and beauty. **Directions:** From Salzburg take the A10 through St Johann and Schwarzach into the Gastein valley. Price guide: Single öS800–öS1500; double/twin öS900–öS1500; suites öS1200–öS1900.

10

In association with MasterCard

AUSTRIA (Bad Gastein)

THERMENHOTEL HAUS HIRT

KAISERHOFSTRASSE, 14 BAD GASTEIN, AUSTRIA
TEL: 43 64 34 27 97 FAX: 43 64 34 27 97 48

The Haus Hirt is ten minutes walk from the centre of the spa resort of Bad Gadstein. It is in a lovely park, one of the sunniest places in the area, peaceful and verdant, with breathtaking views over the Gastein valley to the mountains. There are pleasant rooms in which to relax, and a superb terrace frequented by sunbathers. Al fresco eating is also encouraged and many of the delightful bedrooms have balconies. A whole floor is dedicated to health and reducing stress. Guests indulge themselves with thermal cures, mud-baths, hydrotherapy, aromatherapy, saunas and steam baths, massage, the solarium and beauty salon, The energetic take exercise classes or dive into the large, scenic indoor pool. The versatile restaurant, with attractive rustic furniture and overlooking the valley, prepares delicious, imaginative meals, both for those who are hungry and those on special diets. Fine wine is listed, and there is a cocktail party once a week. The hotel is well situated for first-class skiing, with many lifts and cablecars, and spectacular pistes. Après-ski includes a visit to the Casino. In summer, golf and riding are popular. **Directions:** From Salzburg, exit at Bischofshofen to Schwarzach and the Gastein Valley. On reaching the town centre, follow the Kaiser Wilhelmstrasse to the Haus Hirt. Price guide: Single öS780–öS1040; double/twin öS1640–öS2780.

AUSTRIA (Bregenz)

In association with MasterCard

DEURING SCHLÖSSLE
EHRE-GUTA-PLATZ 4, 4-6900 BREGENZ, AUSTRIA
TEL: 43 55 74 47800 FAX: 43 55 74 47800-80

Covered in red creeper, with its onion domed tower, this spectacular hotel is high on a hill above the Bodensee, Lake Constance, surrounded by a beautiful park full of flowers. The interior of the 'little castle' is magnificent, the salons filled with exquisite inlaid 18th century furniture. Brilliant rugs cover the polished floors and the lighting is discreet. The Armoury houses a superb collection of swords and sabres. The delightful bedrooms overlook either the Bodensee or Bregenz, while the opulent suites in the octagonal tower have views in all directions! The pride of this hotel is its restaurant and its wine cellar. Panelled walls, candle-light and graceful furniture are the setting for sumptuous meals. Fish from the lake, game from the hills, mushrooms from the forests, fruits from the gardens and other delicacies are presented in great style and Bernadette, the sommelier, advises on the selection of the best of French and Austrian wines. There is a marvellous timbered hall which is ideal for seminars and private functions. Concerts take place here occasionally. Sailing on the lake, relaxing in the hotel grounds, enjoying music festivals or feasting during one of the gourmet weekends are pleasant occupations. **Directions:** Leave A14 Bregenz exit, take Bahnhof Strasse, Kirchstrasse, then Thalbach Strasse towards the Old City. Price guide: Single öS1000–öS1270; double/twin öS900–öS1485; suites öS1925–öS2800

In association with MasterCard

AUSTRIA (Ellmau)

HÔTEL DER BÄR
KIRCHBICHL 9, A-6352 ELLMAU, TIROL, AUSTRIA
TEL: 43 53 58 23 95 FAX: 43 53 58 23 95 56

A delightful hotel, purpose-built with families in mind, in the pretty Tyrolean village of Ellmau – a marvellous ski resort in winter and wonderful in summer too. Special provisions are made for children, with a supervised play area, during the holidays, their own ski school and more outdoor fun when the snow has gone. Guests receive a warm welcome in reception, which leads to comfortable lounges. The bedrooms have smart modern furniture and spectacular views of the Wilder Kaiser mountains. There are also apartments and suites – some are in the chalet adjacent to the 'Bär'. The Grizzly Bar is lively. Dining in the elegant restaurant is by candle-light. The chefs prepare international dishes and regional specialities. The cellar holds excellent Austrian, French and Italian wines. On sunny days meals are alfresco by the pool. In winter families enjoy Ski-World, with something for everyone, great pistes, curling, skating and tobogganing. The Tyrol is beautiful in summer, meadows full of flowers, cowbells tinkling in the distance. While parents play golf or tennis, children are supervised in the mini club (during holidays). **Directions:** From Innsbruck leave A12 at Wörgl-Ost exit, taking the B312 to Ellmau. Price guide per person incl. half-board: Single öS1350–öS2030; double/twin öS1165–öS1930; suites öS1565–öS2470.

AUSTRIA (Igls)

In association with MasterCard

SCHLOSSHOTEL IGLS

VILLER STEIG 2, A-6020 IGLS, TIROL, AUSTRIA
TEL: 43 512 37 72 17 FAX: 43 512 37 86 79

Igls, on a sunny terrace above Innsbruck, is the beautiful tree-lined site for the Schlosshotel, an enchanting Tyrolean castle with turrets and spires. Glistening white with snow in the winter, in summer the hotel parkland becomes flower-filled gardens leading out to brilliant green pastures. The Schloss has deserved its award of five stars. The interior of the hotel is exquisite, with the most lovely festooned curtains and co-ordinating wallpapers, graceful period furniture, clever use of colour and discreet lighting. The bedrooms and suites are charming, with views across the countryside to the Patscherkofel Mountains. The spacious reception area is welcoming and the bar, with its baroque fireplace, very convivial. Guests linger in the elegant dining room, appreciating the fine food and wines served by attentive staff. The hotel has an indoor/outdoor swimming pool, steam room, saunas and solarium. Skiing is for Olympians, families, beginners and those who enjoy cross-country. Bobsleigh, skating and curling are alternative winter sports. In summer, tennis, walking in the 'old park' and golf on nearby courses are the principal activities. Nearby Innsbruck has theatres, concerts, exhibitions and museums. **Directions:** Leave Innsbruck on the Inntal highway, following signs to Igls. Price guide: Single öS1800–2300; Double/twin öS1650–␣S2150; suites öS1950–öS2450.

In association with MasterCard

AUSTRIA (Igls)

SPORTHOTEL IGLS

HILBERSTRASSE 17, A-6080 IGLS, TIROL, AUSTRIA
TEL: 43 512 37 72 41 FAX:43 512 37 86 79

In Igls, on its sunny terrace above Innsbruck, stands this élite chalet-style hotel offering traditional Austrian hospitalilty all the year – in winter when Igls is a premier ski resort and in summer when visitors enjoy the many sporting activities and walking through the scenic countryside. It is also an exceptional venue for conferences. Fine pieces of Austrian period furniture can be found in the hall and the spacious elegant salon. The bedrooms, suites and apartments are very comfortable. Guests relax in the winter garden, take apéritifs in the lounge or join friends in the Tyrolean dance-bar. Dinner is by candlelight in the handsome restaurant, a feast of New Austrian Cuisine which has won many awards. Marvellous buffets appear for occasions and conference guests enjoy superb banquets in the private dining hall. The excellent wine list is cosmopolitan. The leisure centre is magnificent – a large indoor/outdoor pool with a poolside bar, saunas, solariums, gymnasium, whirl-pools and a beauty parlour. Winter sports include skiing, skating, curling and tobogganing. In summer guests play golf, tennis and bowls, explore the countryside on bikes or on foot and climb the mountains. Innsbruck offers theatres, music, and museums. **Directions:** Leaving Innsbruck on the Inntal highway, follow signs to Igls. Price guide: Single öS1100–1520; double/twin öS950–1370; suites öS1420–1840.

AUSTRIA (Kitzbühel)

ROMANTIK HOTEL TENNERHOF
6370 KITZBÜHEL, GRIESENAUWEG 26, AUSTRIA
TEL: 43 5356 3181 FAX: 43 5356 318170

Once a farmhouse, now a first-class hotel, the Tennerhof is a most attractive chalet-style building, with flower bedecked balconies, standing in beautifully kept grounds – snow-covered in winter and much enjoyed by summer guests. The reception rooms are charming, the spacious lounge with its elegant furnishings and the more traditional stone-floored sitting-room with its fireplace. Bridge players have their own corner and there is a smart, well-stocked bar. The bedrooms, many with panelled walls, beamed ceilings and traditonal painted furniture include highly romantic suites. There are two restaurants, one slightly more formal, and a popular terrace for alfresco dining. The chefs prepare gourmet international specialities, using home-grown vegetables. Well-chosen wines are listed. Other facilities within the hotel are a well-equipped conference room, and a leisure complex with a palatial pool surrounded by plants and spectacular murals, a sauna and steam-room. A second, outdoor pool is a focal point in summer. In winter Kitzbühel is a famous ski-resort, and when the snows go there are three golf courses. The hotel also arranges excursions with wonderful picnics. **Directions:** Take A12 from Innsbruck, exit at Wörgl, take the B312, then B161 to Kitzbühel. Price guide: öS1700–öS2420; double/twin öS1530–öS2300; suites öS1980–öS3500.

In association with MasterCard

AUSTRIA (Salzburg)

HOTEL AUERSPERG

AUERSPERGSTRASSE 61, A-5027 SALZBURG, AUSTRIA
TEL: 43 662 88 944 FAX: 43 662 88 944 55

The Hotel Auersperg is a traditional family run hotel near the right bank of the river Salzach. Just five minutes walk from the fascinating Old City in which Mozart was born. The hotel has beautiful green and sunny gardens, a wonderful place to relax after a long day's sightseeing. The guest rooms and suites are delightful, with comfortable modern furniture, big windows and chinz covers – each individually decorated in harmonious colours. A fitness centre with a sauna and steam-bath occupies the top floor, together with a roof-terrace which has spectacular views. The welcoming spacious reception hall, with its marble floor and 19th century moulded ceiling, leads into the drawing room, filled with antiques and period furniture. The smart library-bar is convivial, informal meals being available in the dining area. International dishes and local specialities are served in the restaurant, and some of the wine is from the region. Salzburg is famous for its music, major festivals taking place regularly. Many historic old buildings, museums and the castles wait to be explored. Pleasant days can be spent driving to the mountains and lakes, including the famous Wolfgangsee. **Directions.** Take the Salzburg North exit from the Autobahn. Auerspergstrasse runs east off Schwarzstrasse by Kongress Haus. The hotel has car parking. Price guide: Single öS1250; double/twin öS2060; suites öS2780.

AUSTRIA (Salzburg)

In association with MasterCard

HOTEL SCHLOSS MÖNCHSTEIN

MÖNCHSBERG PARK, 26, CITY CENTER, A-5020, SALZBURG, AUSTRIA
TEL: 43 662 84 85 55 0 FAX: 43 662 84 85 59

This enchanting castle, awarded as 'The urban sanctuary of the world' by Hideaway Report, has offered hospitality since the 14th century. It stands on the Mönchsberg, a small mountain in the heart of Salzburg, surrounded by the most beautiful gardens, an ivy-clad haven far above the city and yet part of it. The interior is majestic with antiques from many periods of history, brilliant chandeliers and elegant wall coverings. The intimate Paris Lodron Restaurant, 'the best restaurant in the city of Mozart' – awarded by Gault Millau 1992/95, has the finest reputation in Salzburg, founded on the exquisite table settings with the view over the old city, impeccable staff and, above all, the imaginative presentation of Austrian dishes and a connoisseurs' wine list. Guests meet in the friendly Cocktail Bar, divine pastries in the Schloss Salon or on the Apollo Terrace. Romantics exchange vows in the Wedding Chapel followed by a banquet. Music is very important in Salzburg and there is a rich programme throughout the year. The castle itself holds chamber concerts twice a week. **Directions:** On reaching Salzburg, take the Müllner Hauptstrasse, the Augustiner Gasse and follow the signs for the Mönchsberg Hill. Price guide: Single öS1800–öS4500; double/twin öS2400–öS6200; suites öS4900–öS22,000.

In association with MasterCard

AUSTRIA (Schwarzenberg im Bregenzerwald)

ROMANTIK HOTEL GASTHOF HIRSCHEN
HOF 14, 6867 SCHWARZENBERG, AUSTRIA
TEL: 43 55 12/29 44 0 FAX: 43 55 12/29 44 20

The Gasthof Hirschen, in Schwarzenberg, one of the prettiest villages in the Vorarlberg, has offered hospitality since 1757. Still with baroque detail, it is now a delightful hotel in surroundings that are snowclad in winter and verdant in summer. The spacious and elegant lounge, with its big fireplace, is also the bar. The restaurant, with its carved ceiling, stone floors and traditional furniture, faces an attractive courtyard with a fountain. The menu is Austrian/cosmopolitan, and the wine list extensive. Bedrooms in the Gasthaus are cosy and rustic, with fabulous views across to the Arlberg. A second house, once the old farmhouse, just 30 metres from the hotel, has been converted into a contemporary annex. Other facilities include a sauna, steam room and underground parking. In winter this is a skiers' hotel, with superb skiing made especially pleasant by the many ski huts along the pistes. Summer is the time for walkers and climbers to explore the Bregenzerwald. Nearby Bregenz has many attractions, the old town with historic buildings and the new with its shops and casinos, boat trips on Lake Constance and superb music at festival time. **Directions:** Leave the A14 at the Dornbirn Nord exit, driving through Dornbirn to Bödele and Schwarzenberg, the Gasthof is in the square. Price guide: Double/twin öS1080–öS1500; suites öS1800–öS2850.

AUSTRIA (Seefeld)

In association with MasterCard

HOTEL VIKTORIA
GEIGENBÜHELWEG 589, A-6100 SEEFELD/TIROL, AUSTRIA
TEL: 43 52 12 44 41 FAX: 43 52 12 44 43

Visitors enjoy a stay in Seefeld, both in winter and summer. Perhaps best known as a ski-resort, it is also a marvellous centre for summer holidays. The Hotel Viktoria is a very modern chalet, utterly luxurious, the interior designers having used an enormous amount of glass and marble, creating an impression of immense space and reaching towards the Millenium. The bedrooms are categorised as suites, apartments or duplexes, all having two bathrooms and often an additional shower-room. All are individually decorated and very modern with spectacular views over the mountains. The cosmopolitan dining room, with its impeccable staff, serves suberb food and has an impressive wine list. The bar is very friendly and well-stocked. Leisure facilities include a well-equipped gymnasium, sauna, solarium and steam room. There is also an enormous Jacuzzi but no pool as yet. Winter sports occupy guests from December to March, and when the snows have gone in April the Viktoria re-opens for tourists coming up from Innsbruck, perhaps en route for Salzburg. They enjoy the walking in the flower-filled meadows, mountaineering, fishing in the lake or playing the nearby golf courses. **Directions:** A12 from Innsbruck to the centre of Seefeld, then turn left at the station. Car parking is available. Price guide per person: Single from öS1,400; double/twin from öS1,400 per person; suites from öS2,000.

Belgium

The Channel Tunnel now operates between London, Waterloo and Brussels, Midi, taking the traveller 3¼ hours to reach the heart of Belgium. It will be interesting to watch to what extent the new link opens up the country to the British during the next few years.

Good things come in small packages. Belgium, which occupies the stretch of land bordering the North Sea between France and Holland, measures just over 150 miles from Ostend in the west to the German border, in the east and less than 100 miles from Antwerp in the north to the French border in the south.

With more than 10 million people, Belgium is the second most densely populated country in the world. Belgium has a distinctive culture, or rather two – Flemish and Walloon. The Flemish, who speak Dutch (Flemish) inhabit the northern half of the country and account for over half of the population. The French speaking Walloons live in the other half. The capital, Brussels, is officially designated a dual-language area.

Brussels stands in the very centre of the country. A booming, expanding and often expensive city, it is now the capital of Europe. Here the European Community has its headquarters.

Brussels is an odd mixture of the provincial and the international. Underneath the bureaucratic surface, the city is a subtle meeting of the Walloon and Flemish cultures. As the heart of the ancient Duchy of Brabant, Brussels retains its old sense of identity and civic pride. In the shade of the steel and glass towers, there are cobble streets, canals where old barges still discharge their cargo, and forgotten spots where the city's eventful and romantic past is plainly visible through its 20th century veneer.

The south of the country is a wild, wooded area, with mountains rising to more than 2,000 feet. In the Dutch-speaking north, in contrast, the land is flat and heavily cultivated, as it is in neighbouring Holland. Here stand the medieval Flemish cities of Ghent and Bruges, with the celebrated carillons and canals – not to mention 42 miles of sandy beach that makes up the country's northern coastline. Due north of Brussels lies Antwerp, the country's dynamic seaport. This city, where the painter Rubens lived, is now the world's leading diamond cutting centre.

Antwerp, lying on the Scheldt River over 30 miles north of Brussels, is the world's fifth largest port and the main city of Belgium's Flemish region. Its name, according to legend, is derived from 'handwepen' or hand throwing. A Roman soldier cut off the hand of a malevolent giant and flung it into the river – his feat is commemorated by a statue on the Grote Markt. Antwerp is also a world leader in the diamond trade.

If you can't afford a girl's best friend, then good quality lace is available in several shops in Brussels – but not in cheap souvenir shops. It is recommended that you visit Bruges before making your final choice. Similarly, if you are interested in fashion, the avant-garde boutiques in Antwerp are among the most select in Europe.

If your visit includes Liège, go first to the Val St Lambert factory shop before buying crystal elsewhere.

And chocolate. Vying with Switzerland as the chocolate capital of Europe, some of the best brands – Godiva, Neuhaus, Daskalides – are produced here. If you buy chocolate, buy some just before you leave Belgium – otherwise you will be tempted to eat the lot before your departure!

The Belgians, in general, take dining seriously and are discerning about fresh produce and innovative recipes. As in France, nouvelle cuisine has meant a liberation of creative spirits, and the standards have improved greatly over the past few decades. More recently, the trend has been back to regional and traditional dishes, and now you can enjoy old-fashioned recipes with a modern twist in many restaurants.

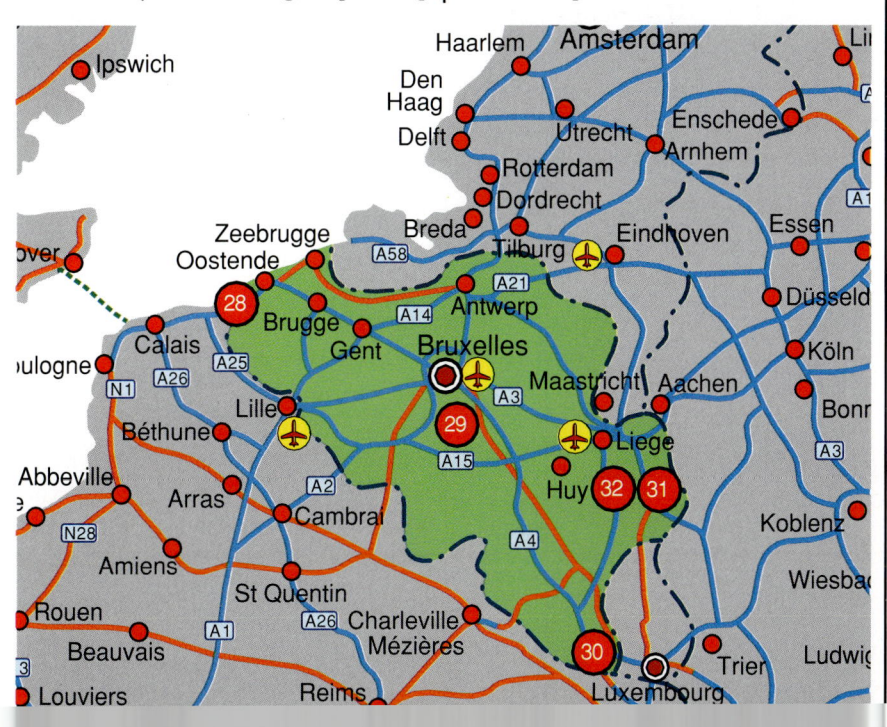

BRUGES

Bruges – also known by its Flemish name Brugge – is an exquisitely preserved medieval town. Europe's first stock exchange was established here, and it was here that oil painting was invented by Jan Van Eyck, causing the arts to flourish in the city. But at the end of the 15th century, disaster struck when the waterway silted up and Bruges was left behind the times. This misfortune created Bruges's present glory for the city has become a perfectly preserved medieval museum. Little has changed in this city interlaced with canals, overhung with humped back bridges and adorned with weeping willows.

Bruges – and twin town of Ghent – are the art cities of Flanders that represented the flowering of the late middle ages. The North Sea Coast provided irresistible sandy shores on which the Vikings beached their long boats, and it was to fend off these marauders that Baldwin of the Iron Arm – and the impressive name – first Count of Flanders, built the original fortifications at Bruges. The city came to prominence as a centre of the cloth trade. Flemish weavers had been renowned since the days of the Romans, but it was in the Middle Ages that they began to use the finest wool from England, Scotland and Ireland, and their products became genuinely superior.

Thus the English acquired an interest in keeping Flanders from the French. This early form of industrialisation also prepared the ground for communal strife, pitting common weavers against patrician merchants.

The centre of Bruges is best seen on foot. The winding streets may confuse your sense of direction, but if you look up, there's always the Belfry to guide you back to the Markt or market square. The Market is a good place from which to start exploring Bruges. In the middle stands the statue of the city's medieval heroes, Jan Breydel and Pieter De Coninck, who led the commoners of Flanders to their short lived victory over the aristocrats of France. The Belfort – Belfry tower above it, rises to a height of 200 feet – commanding the city and surrounding countryside with more power than grace. The octagonal lantern which crowns the tower, added in the 15th century, contains the 47 bells of the remarkable Bruges carillon.

Breidelstraat, on the left of the Belfry, leads directly to the Burg. It is an enchanted square, never more so than when completely floodlit after dark. The Burg derives its name from the fortress built by heroic Baldwin.

Bruges has been a centre for lace making since the 15th century, and such intricate variations on the art as the rose pattern and the fairy stitch, which requires more than 300 bobbins, were developed here. Most tourists buy lace as a souvenir costing a few hundred francs, and you can find it in a great many souvenir shops. Hand made lace in intricate patterns, however, takes a very long time to produce, and this is reflected in the price. for work of this type you should be prepared to part with 10,000 Belgian Francs or more. The best shop for the serious lace lover is Apostelientje, across the street from the Lace Museum.

A road to the small, very pretty town of Damme, just 4½ miles north of Bruges, follows a canal lined with tall and slender poplars, all slightly bent by the constant breeze. You can ride a bike along the top of the levee, and if the return trip seems too daunting, you can take the bike aboard a miniature paddle steamer, the Lamme Goedzak.

In 1134 a tidal wave opened an inlet of the sea from the Zwin in the neighbourhood of Bruges, whose people were quick to build a canal to link up with it. Damme started life as a fishing village at the junction. It became an important port that held exclusive rights to import such varied commodities as wine from Bordeaux and herring from Sweden, and the Maritime Law of Damme became the standard for Hanseatic merchants. Damme is worth a visit if you are staying in Bruges. Bruges is worth a long visit wherever you happen to be.

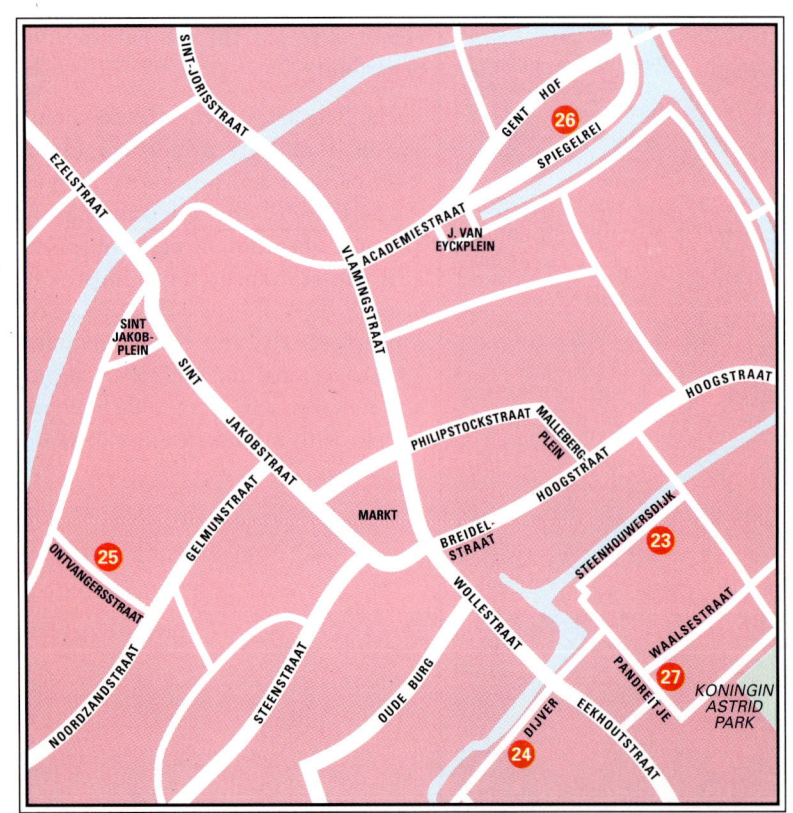

In association with MasterCard

BELGIUM (Bruges)

Die Swaene

STEENHOUWERSDIJK, 8000 BRUGES, BELGIUM
TEL: 32 50 34 27 98 FAX: 32 50 33 66 74

Swans are legendary symbols in Bruges. Die Swaene, dating back to the 15th century, once the home of city elders, has been brilliantly transformed into the most magnificent hotel, romantically situated by a pretty canal and surrounded by historic buildings. Guests enter into luxury on a grand scale – lovely antiques, gleaming chandeliers, large mirrors, baskets of fruit and bowls of fresh flowers, indoor plants and statuary abound. The drawingroom is reminiscent of Louis XV. There is a terraced garden where guests enjoy apéritifs on fine evenings and gracious dining areas where spectacular candlelit dinners and champagne lunches take place. The menu offers classical and contemporary dishes and the large cellar houses some rare vintage wines. The bedrooms are opulent, with exotic festoons over ornately carved beds, although there are some simpler rooms available. Facilities include a well equipped conference room, fitness centre, indoor pool and private car park. Guests enjoy exploring Bruges, taking the canal tours arranged by the hotel. **Directions:** Enter Bruges from Katelijnepoort, taking Katelijnestraat, turn right along Gruuthusestraat, and follow the canal, keeping it on the left, along Dyver and then left at Vismarkt into Steenhouversdijk. Price guide: Single Bf4150; double/twin Bf5100–Bf6350; suite Bf8500–Bf10400.

BELGIUM (Bruges)

In association with MasterCard

HOTEL DE TUILERIEEN

DYVER, 8000 BRUGES, BELGIUM
TEL: 32 50 34 36 91 FAX: 32 50 34 04 00

This exquisite small hotel, a 15th century mansion in the old city, overlooks one of the fascinating canals. The charming interior combines Flemish history with luxurious comfort. Period wall coverings and drapery, family portraits, harmonious flower arrangements and fine porcelain all create a warm ambience, enchanced by the lively proprietress, Madame Béatrix Geeraert, who ensures that her multi-lingual staff provide impeccable service. Our inspector wrote that excellence here means perfection! While a delicious breakfast is offered, including tempting fresh fruit such as melon with strawberries; there is no dining room, so guests enjoy sampling the nearby bistros and restaurants. Residents congregate in the bar, perhaps following a session in the pool, sauna or solarium. The bedrooms are spacious, pretty, and superbly equipped. Seminar facilities are available. Some participants stay at the sister Hotel de Orangerie across the canal, not so lavish but with the same high standards. Travellers will find Bruges a beautiful city with its waterways and historic buildings. It is very accessible from Ostend and from Brussels Airport, both by train or by road – the hotel has a large carpark. **Directions:** Enter Bruges by Katelijnestraat, turn right at the Gruuthuse into Dyver; the hotel is on the right. Price guide: Single Bf6950–Bf7950; double/twin Bf7950–Bf8950; suite Bf11,950.

In association with MasterCard

BELGIUM (Bruges)

HOTEL PRINSENHOF

ONTVANGERSSTRAAT 9, 8000 BRUGES, BELGIUM
TEL: 32-50-34 26 90 FAX: 32-50-34 23 21 FAX FROM USA TOLL FREE 1 800 710 7984

This 20th century Flemish mansion, in the very heart of Bruges, having been renovated with great flair, is now a superb small hotel hidden down a side street. A member of Relais du Silence, it is family run, the ambience is warm, with a feeling that guests are all-important. The interior decoration, in the style of Burgundy, is rich with chandeliers, moulded ceilings and antiques, polished floors and marvellous rugs. The breakfast room is charming, where an excellent buffet is served in the mornings, but there is no restaurant, although drinks are available from the licensed bar. Many interesting places to dine can be found nearby. The bedrooms are peaceful, double glazing keeping out noise, beautifully furnished in traditional style and having particulary elegant drapery. A discreet mini-bar completes the many comforts provided. Businessmen find the central location ideal, and tourists enjoy wandering through the maze of small streets, along the canal banks and exploring the many museums and fascinating shops. **Directions:** Approaching Bruges from Zeebrugge or Ostend, leave the ring road at Ezelpoort, taking Ezelstraat, forking left into St Jakobstraat, right into Geldmunstraat to Noordzandstsraat, with a right turn into Prinsenhof and left in front of the castle leading finally to Ontvangersstraat. Price guide: Single 2900Bf–3300Bf; double/twin 3800Bf; suite 4500Bf–6500Bf.

BELGIUM (Bruges)

In association with MasterCard

RELAIS OUD-HUIS AMSTERDAM

SPIEGELREI 3, 8000 BRUGES, BELGIUM
TEL: 32-50-34 18 10 FAX: 32-50-33 88 91

This hotel is in the heart of Bruges, an extremely elegant building alongside one of the canals – a peaceful haven created from imaginative reconstruction of two 17th century gentlemen's houses into the graceful building of today. A unique feature is the terraced garden at the back, with attractive cane furniture, and filled with exotic shrubs and floodlit at night. The Oud-Huis is beautifully decorated in traditional style, and justifiably proud of its bar, with its antiques and large leather chairs. While a delicious breakfast is offered, there is no formal restaurant although meals may be arranged. However most guests enjoy the opportunity to explore the local restaurants. The handsome bedrooms are roomy, and with the luxurious bathrooms they provide all modern amenities. Small meetings can be hosted in the stylish boardroom overlooking the garden. Visitors will appreciate the excellent map of Bruges provided by the hotel listing the 'Musts' and 'Unknowns' of the City, many of which are just a short walk away.
Directions: There are many entrances into this city. Crossing the canal at Dampoort, the Lange Rei leads, via Genthof, into Spiegelrei. It is recommended that travellers from Ostend or Paris take the ring road to Dampoort. There is a hotel carpark and another nearby. Price guide: Single Bf3950–Bf5500Bf; double/twin Bf4750–Bf6000; suite Bf7000–Bf7500.

In association with MasterCard

BELGIUM (Bruges)

ROMANTIK PANDHOTEL

PANDREITJE 16, 8000 BRUGES, BELGIUM
TEL: 32 50 34 06 66 FAX: 32 50 34 05 56

Once an 18th century mansion, the Pandhotel has been thoughtfully restored and transformed into an elegant small hotel. It stands in a leafy square, within sight and sound of the famous Belfry. Many charming features of the original house remain, and the original carriage house is now the Reception Hall. The suites and bedrooms are delightful, lovely antiques vying with fabrics that harmonise with the wallhangings. The two sitting rooms reflect the care with which the renovation has been carried out, and guests enjoy relaxing in front of the old chimney piece, in comfortable chairs and sofas surrounded by fresh flowers. A delicious breakfast is served, and although there is no dining room, the hotel has good relationships with the best restaurants in the area. A speciality are themed visits – options one and two include wonderful dinners, boat trips on the canals, sightseeing in a horse-drawn carriage and demonstrations of lace making. Other packages include golf, cycling, the fields of Flanders and the Summer and Winter exhibitions. These are arranged by Mrs Vanhaecke-Dewaele, who owns the Pandhotel, and is herself an Official Guide of Bruges. **Directions:** The hotel supplies a map with detailed instructions, and will recommend car-parking nearby. Price guide: Single Bf3890–Bf5290; double/twin Bf4690–Bf6290; suites Bf7290.

BELGIUM (De Panne)

In association with MasterCard

HOSTELLERIE SPARRENHOF

KONINGINNELAAN 26, B-8660 DE PANNE, BELGIUM
TEL: 32 58 41 13 28 FAX: 32 58 42 08 19

This is a sophisticated modern hotel, family run, in a quiet seaside town on the Belgian coast, just 30 miles of new motorway from Le Shuttle in France. Lovely gardens and tall trees create a sanctuary yet the villa and annexe buildings are only 200 yards from the beach. The bedroom classifications are luxury or super luxury, with long lists of the amenities provided – the latter have balconies, a safe and refrigerator. Other facilities include room service, private car parking, night reception, guards, and shops in the reception area. Guests enjoy the piano bar in the evenings or relax in the drawingroom before savouring the gastronomic delights of the smart 'La Bourgogne' restaurant, specialising in fish with live lobsters swimming in a tank awaiting 15 different recipes! The menu varies seasonally and is accompanied by a very fine wine list. In the morning a Royal Buffet Breakfast is provided. The outdoor pool (a warm 26°), only for hotel residents, is well supplied with comfortable chairs and garden service bringing drinks or snacks to sunbathers. Saunas, solariums and tennis are alternative pleasures within the grounds, or excellent golf at nearby Dunkirk. **Directions:** Entering the town from Ostend on Nieuwpoortlaan, fork left into Koninginnelaan at the east end of De Panne. Price guide: Single Bf2400; double/twin Bf3500–Bf4000; suite Bf4500–Bf5000.

In association with MasterCard

BELGIUM (Genval)

CHÂTEAU DU LAC
AVENUE DU LAC, B-1332 GENVAL, BELGIUM
TEL: 32 26 55 71 11 FAX: 32 26 55 74 44

Although built this century, the Château du Lac is a fairytale castle, its graceful white walls topped with colourful international flags and the traditional turret all reflected in the clear waters of Lake Genval with its spectacular fountain. Beyond it are the peaceful woodlands which make the Brabant Wallon an exceptionally beautiful part of Belgium. When entering the lobby with wide archways and tropical plants, guests are aware that this unique hotel has been carefully planned to provide 17 salons of different sizes, after which delegates relax in the spacious, smart 'Kingfisher' bar. The bedrooms are delightful, uncluttered and comfortably furnished in harmonious colours, with superb views from the large windows. The Château Du Lac is particularly proud of the new 1000sq.m. Argentine Room, equipped with state-of-the-art equipment for conferences, star-lit ceiling and a dramatic cascade. The elegant Le Trefle à 4 Restaurant has two Michelin stars and the extensive wine list is superb. John Harris' cardio-fitness centre has a Romanesque pool, sauna, Jacuzzi, haman and health bar. Strolling in the grounds or playing golf nearby are both relaxing. **Directions:** From Brussels Autoroute E411, then Exit 3 N253 following signs to Genval Lac. Price guide: Single Bf4600–Bf8750; double/twin Bf4600–Bf9900.

BELGIUM (Habay-la-Neuve)

In association with MasterCard

LES ARDILLIÈRES DU PONT D'OYE HOTEL

RUE DU PONT D'OYE 6, 6720 HABAY-LA-NEUVE, BELGIUM
TEL: 32 63 42 22 43 FAX: 32 63 42 28 52

This small hotel is a peaceful oasis set in a small park off the main route between Brussels and Luxembourg. A building, with tall windows, built this century, it is reached by a rose-lined driveway. It is owned by the Thiry family, who have designed Les Ardillieres to encourage their guests to relax and forget the stresses of life outside Habay-la-Neuve. The bedrooms are in restful colours and lead onto a sunny balcony, an ideal spot for breakfast from the efficent room service. The salon, with contemporary furnishings and filled with fresh flowers, looks out onto the delightful gardens, as does the English bar where guests enjoy apéritifs while reading the ever-changing menus of Les Forges du Pont d'Oye Restaurant overlooking the lake, which serves both lunch and dinner. A second restaurant specialises in organic foods. The excellent wine list will suit all pockets. Candle-light adds romance to the evening meal. An important facility is the leisure centre with a Jacuzzi, sauna, solarium and small gymnasium. Outside in the grounds are a man-sized chess board and gardens with fountains, a small river making tiny waterfalls and shady trees. **Directions:** Driving towards Luxembourg from Neufchateau, leave E25/E411 at Exit 29. The hotel is the other side of Habay-le-Neuve. Price guide: Single Bf3200–Bf5000; double/twin Bf3700–Bf5500; suites Bf12,000

In association with MasterCard

BELGIUM (Malmédy)

Hostellerie Trôs Marets

ROUTE DES TRÔS MARETS, B-4960 MALMEDY, BELGIUM
TEL: 32 80 33 79 17 FAX: 32 80 33 79 10

This delightful hotel, surrounded by forest, atop a small mountain, is close to Germany, Luxembourg and Holland. In winter the snow-clad terrain attracts skiers and in summer visitors enjoy the sunshine and fine air. The Trôs Marets has modern comfort and style. The lounge and dining room have spectacular views. The furnishings are elegant while creating a relaxing ambience, and the same theme has been applied in the bedrooms, well-equipped for today's traveller. The annex houses four superb suites, with balconies off the drawing rooms and luxurious bedrooms – the bathrooms have sunbeds! There is a small conference room. The pretty indoor swimming pool is in this part of the hotel and opens onto the garden in fine weather. There is an attractive terrace for alfresco meals, but serious eating is in the outstanding restaurant where succulent meals are served, including many fish dishes. Perfectly cooked vegetables, immaculate service and wine served at the correct temperature complete a memorable occasion. Nearby are the Ardennes and Bastogne, where the Americans victoriously battled in 1944. Energetic guests explore the forest but others unwind in the tranquil atmosphere. **Directions:** From Liege follow the E40 over the scenic viaduct to the Malmedy exit, then follow the N68 uphill for 5 kilometres. Price guide: Double/twin Bf3500–Bf7500; suite Bf8000–Bf18,000.

BELGIUM (Marche-en-Famenne)

CHÂTEAU D'HASSONVILLE
MARCHE-EN-FAMENNE, 6900, BELGIUM
TEL: 32 84 31 10 25 FAX: 32 84 31 60 27

This is a fairy-tale 17th century château, with turrets, spires and pinnacles and peacocks strutting on the lawns. It is owned by the Rodrigues family, delightfully described as the chatelains, hoteliers and their family! The interior is sumptuous and the decoration very grand – brilliant chandeliers, swagged silk curtains in jewel colours and exquisite antiques. The bedrooms facing the park have wonderful views, furnished for a sybaritic lifestyle, the huge bathrooms contemporary and luxuriously appointed. Guests start their day taking breakfast in the graceful conservatory, filled with exotic plants. Later in the day, after relaxing with apéritifs in the bar, they feast in the elegant restaurant amidst candles, sparkling crystal and gleaming silver. The menu is sophisticated, and the award winning sommelier advises on the choice of wine. There are museums and caves nearby or residents explore the countryside on the house bicycles or in hot air balloons. Others fish, take boats out on the river, play snooker, try clay pigeon shooting and watch falconry displays, while golfers use the hotel's practice ground before playing the three local courses. **Directions:** From Brussels take the outway No: 18 (Marche) on the E 411 Bruxelles–Namur. On the N4 go out on Km 98 (Aye) and follow 6Km the castle indications. Price guide: Single Bf4500; double/twin Bf4800–Bf6800.

LONDON

London, city of ceremony, overwhelms the visitor with history.

Home of Monarchy, of Parliament, of Theatre, a world famous Abbey and acclaimed art galleries. Much of London's rich inheritance of pageantry centres on Royalty.

London's best shopping areas range from the high elegance and high prices of Knightsbridge to the colourful markets and colourful language of Brick Lane and Portobello Road. The city is fertile ground for specialist shops: antique shops, antiquarian booksellers and art galleries. For the clothes shopper, London also offers an inexhaustible range of styles, price levels, quality and areas in which to browse.

Since medieval times London has secured large expanses of green. Some of these, such as Hampstead Heath, were originally common land, where smallholders could graze their animals. Others, such as Richmond Park and Holland Park, were royal hunting grounds or the gardens of large houses, several still have formal features dating from those times. Today you cross much of central London by walking from St James's Park in the east to Kensington Gardens in the west. Purpose built parks, like Battersea and the Royal Botanic Gardens at Kew.

Spring in London carries an almost tangible air of a city wakening up to longer days and outdoor pursuits. The cheerful yellow of daffodils studs the parks, and less-hardy Londoners turn out for their first jog of the year to find themselves puffing in the wake of serious runners in training for the Marathon. As spring turns into summer, the royal parks reach their full glory, and in Kensington Gardens nannies chat under venerable chestnut trees. As autumn takes hold, those same trees are ablaze with red and gold and Londoners' thoughts turn to afternoons in museums and art galleries, followed by tea in a café or pint at the local pub. The year draws to a close with one of London's favourite pastimes – shopping in the West End.

The weather during the spring months may be raw. Druids celebrate the Spring Equinox in a subdued ceremony on Tower Hill. Painters compete to have their works accepted by the Royal Academy. Footballers close their season with the FA Cup Final at Wembley, while cricketers don their sweaters to begin theirs. Oxford and Cambridge Universities row their annual boat race along the Thames, and Marathon runners pound the streets.

London's summer season is packed full of indoor and outdoor events. The selection includes many traditional events, such as the Wimbledon Tennis Championships and the Cricket Test Matches at Lord's and the Oval. The Queen holds garden parties for favoured subjects in the splendid grounds of Buckingham Palace. Summer public holidays are studded with funfairs in most of London's parks.

There is a sense of purpose about London in autumn. The build-up to the busiest shopping season, the start of the academic year, and the new parliamentary session, opened by the Queen.

Memories of a more turbulent opening of Parliament are revived on 5 November, when there are bonfires and fireworks to commemorate the failure of a conspiracy led by Guy Fawkes to blow up the Palace of Westminster in 1605. Later in the month, the dead of two World Wars are commemorated at a ceremony held in Whitehall.

Some of the most striking images of London are drawn from winter: paintings of frost fairs in the 17th and 18th centuries, when the River Thames froze over completely, and Claude Monet's views of the river and its bridges.

Christmas trees and lights wink at you from every window – from the West End shopping streets to construction sites. The scent of roasting chestnuts tickles the palate as street peddlers sell them from mobile braziers.

Seasonal menus feature roast turkey, mince pies and rich, dark Christmas pudding. Traditional fare in theatres includes colourful family pantomimes, where the customary cross dressing

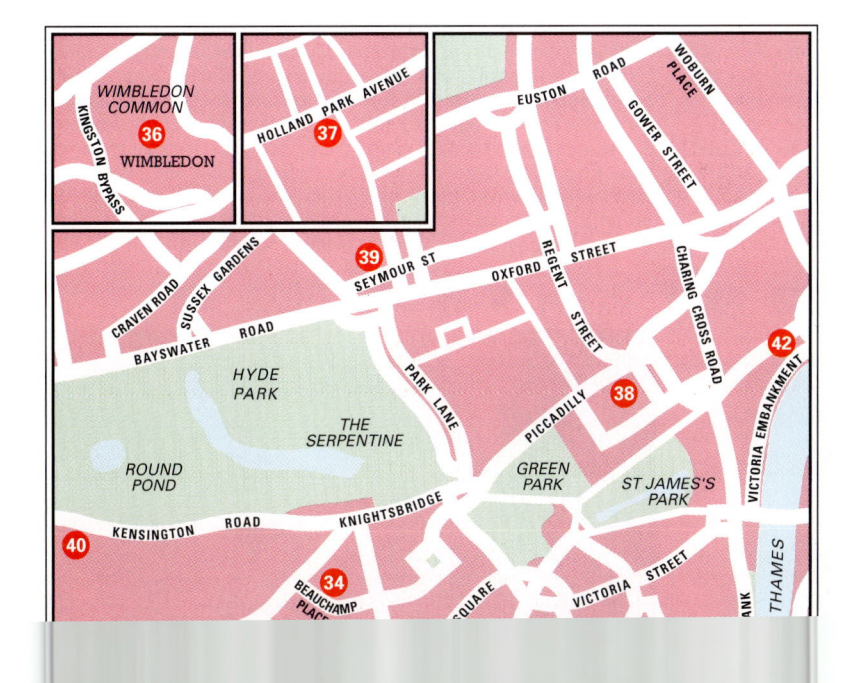

BRITISH ISLES (London)

In association with MasterCard

THE BEAUFORT

33 BEAUFORT GARDENS, KNIGHTSBRIDGE, LONDON SW3 1PP
TEL: 44 171 584 5252 FAX: 44 171 589 2834

The Beaufort offers the sophisticated traveller all the style and comfort of home – combining warm contempory colourings with the highest possible personal attention. The owner Diana Wallis (pictured below) believes that much of the success of the hotel is due to the charming, attentive staff – a feeling happily endorsed by guests. The Beaufort is situated in a quiet tree-lined square only 100 yards from Harrods and as guests arrive they are all greeted at the front door and given their own door key to come and go as they please. The closed front door gives added security and completes that feeling of home. All the bedrooms are individually decorated, with air conditioning and a great many extras such as shortbread, Swiss chocolates and brandy. The hotel owns a video and cassette library and is home to a magnificent collection of original English floral watercolours. Breakfast is brought to the bedroom – hot rolls and croissants, freshly squeezed orange juice and home-made preserves, tea and coffee. In the drawing room there is a 24-hour honour bar and between 4-5pm every day a free cream tea is served with champagne, scones, clotted cream and jam. The hotel is proud of its no tipping policy and is open all year. **Directions:** From the Harrods exit at Knightsbridge underground station take the third turning on the left. Price guide: Single £110; double/twin from £150; suites £240.

In association with MasterCard

BRITISH ISLES (London)

BLAKES HOTEL

33 ROLAND GARDENS, LONDON SW7 3PF
TEL: 44 171 370 6701 FAX: 44 171 373 0442 TELEX: 8813500 – FROM USA CALL FREE: 1 800 926 3173

Anouska Hempel, the celebrated London hotelier and fashion designer, created Blakes to offer style and elegance to the travelled connoisseur – and convenience and efficiency to the international business man or woman. *Architectural Digest* described Blakes as 'bedrooms and suites, each a fantasy created with antiques, paintings, rare silks and velvets'. Blakes is just a five minute walk through the leafy streets of South Kensington to London's new centre of smart shops in Brompton Cross and a five minute taxi ride from Harrods. Its restaurant is one of the finest in London, open until midnight and providing 24-hour room service. If you are travelling on business, you can have a fax in your room, full secretarial facilities, courier service, CNN news and other satellite television stations. *Architectural Digest* called Blakes 'Anouska Hempel's celebrated London refuge'. It is much more than that. It is a delight for all six senses. **Directions:** Roland Gardens is a turning off Old Brompton Road. South Kensington Underground is five minutes' walk. Price guide: Single £130; double/twin £155–£240; directors double £305; suite £495–£600.

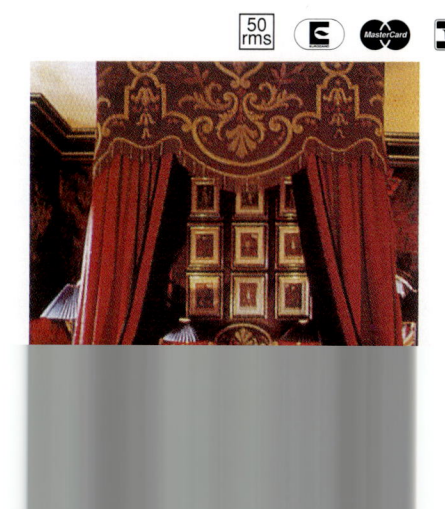

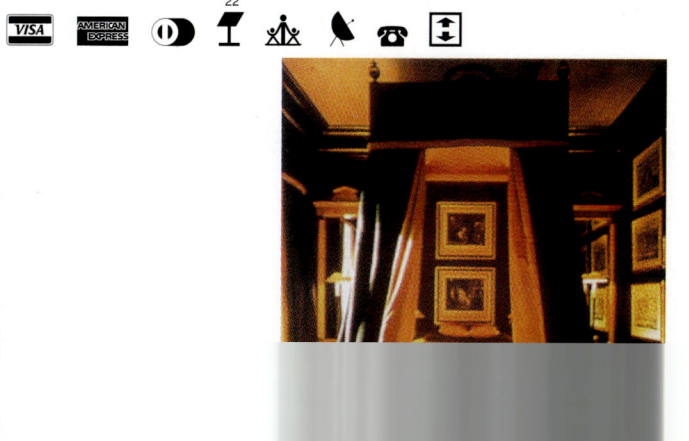

BRITISH ISLES (London)

In association with MasterCard

CANNIZARO HOUSE

WEST SIDE, WIMBLEDON COMMON, LONDON SW19 4UE
TEL: 44 181 879 1464 FAX: 44 181 879 7338

Cannizaro House, an elegant Georgian Country House, occupies a unique position on the edge of Wimbledon Common and is within an easy walk of Wimbledon Village. Despite the hotel's tranquil location, it is only 20 minutes by train from central London. Cannizaro House, built in 1705, has throughout its long and rich history welcomed royalty and celebrities such as George III, Oscar Wilde and William Pitt, and it is now restored as a hotel which offers the very highest standards of hospitality. The aura of the 18th century age is reflected in the ornate fireplaces and plaster mouldings, gilded mirrors and many antiques in the hotel. All of the hotel's 46 bedrooms are individually designed, with many overlooking beautiful Cannizaro Park. Several intimate rooms are available for meetings and private dining, with larger reception rooms for conferences and weddings. Ray Slade, General Manager of Cannizaro House for many years, ensures the high standards of excellence for which the hotel is renowned, are consistently met. The kitchen is run by award-winning chef Stephen Wilson, who with his brigade produces the finest of modern and classical cuisine, complemented by an impressive list of fine wines. **Directions:** The nearest tube and British Rail station is Wimbledon. Price guide: Single £115–£140; double/twin £135–£190; suite £250–£350. Special weekend rates available.

In association with MasterCard

BRITISH ISLES (London)

THE HALCYON

81 HOLLAND PARK, LONDON W11 3RZ
TEL: 44 171 727 7288 FAX: 44 171 229 8516 – FROM USA CALL FREE: 1 800 457 4000

This small, exclusive hotel in Holland Park offers an exceptional standard of accommodation and service. Essentially a large Town House, its architecture has been meticulously restored to the splendour of the Belle Epoque to take its place amongst the many imposing residences in the area. The generous proprotions of the rooms, along with the striking individuality of their furnishings, creates the atmosphere of a fine country house. Each of the bedrooms and suites has been beautifully furnished and has every modern amenity. All have marble bathrooms and several boast a Jacuzzi. A splendid restaurant, opening onto a ornamental garden and patio, serves distinctive international cuisine complemented by a well chosen wine list. The adjoining bar provides a relaxing environment to enjoy a cocktail and meet with friends. The Halcyon prides itself on offering a superb service and ensuring guests absolute comfort, privacy and security. Secretarial, telex and fax facilities are all available. London's most fashionable shopping areas, restaurants and West End theatres are all easily accessible from The Halcyon. **Directions:** From Holland Park tube station, turn right. The Halcyon is on the left after the second set of traffic lights. Price guide: Single from £165; double/twin from £235; suite from £275.

BRITISH ISLES (London)

In association with MasterCard

22 JERMYN STREET

22 JERMYN STREET, LONDON, ENGLAND SW1Y 6HL
TEL: 44 171 734 2353 FAX: 44 171 734 0750

The winner of many Hotel of the Year awards, 22 Jermyn Street has been in the same family ownership since 1915 and its tradition of providing luxurious accommodation and superb service continues into a third generation with Henry Togna. An ideal choice for guests who appreciate style and comfort, while preferring the personal feel of a smaller hotel to the anonymity of larger establishments. Each room and suite has been designed in complimentary yet different styles, expertly combining antique and contemporary furniture. Among the many services offered are concierge, valet, 24-hour room service, room bars and access to a nearby luxury health club with Nautilus gym, swimming pool and squash courts. There are many excellent restaurants within walking distance, with the hotel's proprietor strongly recommending Le Caprice, Quaglino's, The Square, The Greenhouse and Bistrot Bruno. A host of information covering everything from the arts to shopping, is provided in a room directory. 22 Jermyn Street is located in the heart of London's West End, close to the City, Bond Street's elegant shopping, the main auction houses, fine galleries, the Royal Parks and many of the best theatres and restaurants. **Directions:** Piccadilly Circus tube station is just 50 yards from the hotel. Price guide: Double/twin £199; suites £258.50.

In association with MasterCard

BRITISH ISLES (London)

THE LEONARD

15 SEYMOUR STREET, LONDON, ENGLAND W1H 5AA
TEL: 44 171 935 2010 FAX: 44 171 935 6700

Four late 18th century Georgian town houses set the character of this exciting new property due to open in December 1995. There was a hotel at this address in 1926. Now extensive reconstruction has created five rooms and twenty suites decorated individually to a very high standard. Wall coverings present striking colours, complemented by exquisite French furnishing fabrics creating a warm luxurious atmosphere. All rooms are fully air-conditioned and include a private safe, mini-bar, hi-fi system and provision for a PC/fax. Bathrooms are finished in marble and some of the larger suites have a butler's pantry or fully-equipped kitchen. For physical fitness and stress reductions there is an up-to-date exercise room. Experienced staff have been appointed to ensure that guests can enjoy the highest level of attention and service. Breakfast is available in the morning room and light meals are served throughout the day. 24-hour room service is also available. There are, of course, many good restaurants nearby. The Wallace Collection is just a short walk away and one of London's premier department stores, Selfridges, is round the corner in Oxford Street. **Directions:** The Leonard is on the south side of Seymour Street which is just north of Marble Arch and runs west off Portman Square. Car parking in Bryanston Street. Price guide: Double £140–£180; suites £200–£320.

BRITISH ISLES (London)

In association with MasterCard

THE MILESTONE

1–2 KENSINGTON COURT, LONDON W8 5DL
TEL: 44 171 917 1000 FAX: 44 171 917 1010 FROM USA TOLL FREE 1 800 854 7092

The new and luxurious Milestone Hotel is situated opposite Kensington Palace. It enjoys uninterrupted views over Kensington Gardens and a remarkable vista of the royal parklands. A Victorian showpiece, this unique mansion has been meticulously restored to its original splendour while incorporating every modern facility. The 45 rooms and 12 suites are unusual in design, with antiques, elegant furnishings and private balconies. Guests may relax in the comfortable, panelled Park Lounge, which offers a 24-hour lounge service and menu. Cheneston's, the hotel's exceptional restaurant, has an elaborate carved ceiling, original fireplace, ornate windows, panelling and an oratory, which can be used for private dining. The exciting and innovative menu presents the latest in modern international cuisine. Stables Bar, fashioned after a traditional gentlemen's club, makes a convivial meeting place. The health and fitness centre offers guests the use of a solarium, spa bath, sauna and gymnasium. Some of London's finest shops and monuments are within walking distance. **Directions:** At the end of Kensington High Street, at the junction with Princes Gate. Price guide: Single from £200; double/twin £245; suites from £275.

40

In association with MasterCard

BRITISH ISLES (London)

NUMBER SIXTEEN

16 SUMNER PLACE, LONDON, ENGLAND SW7 3EG
TEL: 44 171 589 5232 FAX: 44 171 584 8615

A passer-by may wonder what lies behind the immaculate pillared façade of Number Sixteen. Upon entering the hotel visitors will find themselves in an atmosphere of seclusion and comfort which has remained virtually unaltered in style since its early Victorian origins. The staff are friendly and attentive, regarding each visitor as a guest in a private home. The relaxed atmosphere of the lounge is the perfect place to pour a drink from the bar and meet friends or business associates. A fire blazing in the drawing room in cooler months creates an inviting warmth, whilst the conservatory opens on to a beautiful secluded walled garden which once again has won many accolades and awards for its floral displays. Each spacious bedroom is decorated with a discreet combination of antiques and traditional furnishings. The rooms are fully appointed with every facility that the discerning traveller would expect. A light breakfast is served in the privacy of guests' rooms and a tea and coffee service is available throughout the day. Although there is no dining room at Number Sixteen, some of London's finest restaurants are just round the corner. The hotel is close to the West End, Knightsbridge, Chelsea and Hyde Park. **Directions:** Sumner Place is off Old Brompton Road near Onslow Square. South Kensington Underground Station is 2 minutes' walk away. Price guide: Single £78–£99; double/twin £130–£155.

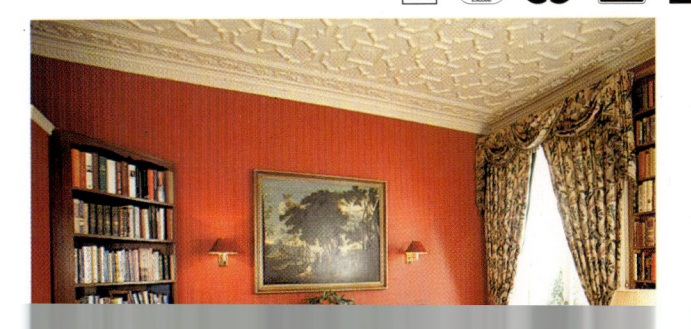

BRITISH ISLES (London)

In association with MasterCard

THE SAVOY

THE STRAND, LONDON WC2R 0EU
TEL: 44 171 836 4343 FAX: 44 171 240 6040 TELEX: 24234

Built on the site of the medieval Palace of Savoy, the hotel was created in 1889 by Richard D'Oyly Carte, the legendary impresario, as a result of the success of his Gilbert and Sullivan operas. The Savoy has a very English tradition of service and individuality. Bedrooms are decorated and furnished in a variety of styles – traditional, art deco and contemporary – and all share a standard of unrivalled comfort. In the restaurant, with its stunning views of the Thames, classic dishes by the legendary chef Escoffier are recreated, while the Savoy Grill is the meeting place for leading lights in the arts, media and the City. The Savoy Fitness Gallery boasts a roof-top swimming pool and state-of-the-art fitness facilities. Together with its sister hotels in The Savoy Group – The Berkeley in Knightsbridge and Claridge's in Mayfair – The Savoy offers a variety of short-break arrangements, some including dinner, others leaving one free to enjoy London at leisure – call 44 171-872 8080 for details.
Directions: The Savoy is on The Strand, to the west of Lancaster Place and Waterloo Bridge, in the heart of London's theatre district. Price guide: Single £180–£200; double/twin £205–£295, excluding VAT.

CYPRUS

The pleasures of Cyprus derive from its apparent simplicity – the straightforward physical charm of the island and the natural warmth of the people.

In the plains of the interior, villages nestle among olive groves and citrus orchards. Goats and sheep weave among ruins of ancient Greek temples and Roman markets. Vineyards climb the sunny hillsides and – higher up – cypress trees frame a lone abbey or the skeleton of an abandoned fortress.

Its origins are reflected in its three main regions – the Troodos Mountains in the West, the Central Mesaoria Plain and the Northern Chain of the Kyrenia Mountains. The Kyrenia Plain in the North, and the hills of the Coastal Plain in the South, complete the geographic structure of the island.

The boundry separating northern Turkish occupied Cyprus from the Greek Cypriot Republic since 1974 is rarely seen by visitors. A wall and barbed wire divides north and south Nicosia while visitors driving up from Agia Napa in the islands south east corner may glimpse an observation post for troops of the United Nations on the outskirts of the old port town of Famagusta.

It is complicated but not impossible for visitors from the south to cross into northern Cyprus. The only way across is through Nicosia. The border crossing opens at 8am. Be there early. Before crossing with passport, you must check in with the Greek Cypriot duty officer. You cannot drive over but Turkish Cypriot taxis – individual and shared service – are waiting on the other side. At the Turkish control point, you buy a visa for one Greek Cypriot pound. You can change money into Turkish Cypriot lire for museums and meals but Greek Cypriot money is accepted too. You can take photographs, but only of non-military or non-sensitive subjects about which your Turkish Cypriot taxi driver will advise you.

People in Cyprus eat well and plenty. Their island has the cuisine of its geography and history – conquerors and refugees alike have left their mark – Turkish, Greek, Syrian, Lebanese and Armenian. And the modern Republic of Cyprus has the prosperity to make the combination distinctive – good fresh vegetables, spicy meat dishes, fish and seafood – savoury but undisguised by dubious sauces. Best of all is the table breaking procession of meze where you have the delightful problem the French call embarras de choix – too much from which to choose.

Every town and village in Cyprus seems to jump at any excuse to celebrate. Holy days are celebrated with gusto and colour by every community – no matter how small or poor.

In January – on Epiphany, bishops bless the waters in all seaside towns, throwing their holy crosses into the sea. Boys dive for them, winning a small prize when they surface with one.

In February, large amounts of vegetables, olives and wine are consumed on 'Clean Monday' – the Monday before Lent. There is also a ten day carnival in Limassol featuring fancy dress balls and a spate of parades which – though not on the scale of Rio or New Orleans – do have just as much oomph behind the presentation.

In March, Orthodox solemn masses take place all over Cyprus, with a procession of the Holy Sepulchre in main streets and squares. Easter is also a time when midnight service takes place and people light their candles from the priests, moving around the church and chanting the litany in a kind of sound and light atmosphere which is wonderful to watch.

During May and June, there are mass parties, games, colourful parades, competitions held to celebrate the two day holiday of Pentecost. There's music, dancing and lots and lots of food.

In September, Nicosia holds its annual arts festival. This two week long event features everything from art exhibitions and folk dancing to avant garde ballet and rock concerts. Most of the events take place in the Famagusta Gate Cultural Centre. Limassol boasts a wine festival, while Agia Napa is

CYPRUS (Paphos)

THE ANNABELLE

P.O. BOX 401, PAPHOS, CYPRUS
TEL: 357 62 38 333 FAX: 357 62 45 502

Paphos, the birthplace of Aphrodite who rose from the sea, is a fitting setting for this luxurious hotel with elaborate tropical gardens stretching right down to the water's edge. Almost every room in the hotel overlooks the sea. The bedrooms and suites all have roomy balconies and the private bungalows have large terraces and lawns. They are beautifully decorated in cool colours and extremely comfortable, provided with every amenity demanded by today's 'five-star' travellers. A sybaritic lifestyle is offered, with a wide choice of bars, the Grotto, the Lobby, the Pool Bar and the Byzantine Bar which has live music and dancing into the night. In addition there are four restaurants from the sophisticated Fontana Amorosa through to the Cypriot Taverna serving local dishes, especially seafood. The Andromeda Health & Beauty Centre pampers guests who are not taking advantage of the tennis courts and swimming pools, attending the diving school or out fishing with the locals. Paphos Village, full of mythology with several archeological sites and a fishing harbour dating back to 1600BC is only minutes walk away.
Directions: Ten minutes by taxi from Paphos airport. The hotel is in the resort of Paphos right on the beach. Price guide: Single CY£69.50–CY£88.50; double/twin CY£108–CY£148; suites CY£156–CY£480.

CZECH REPUBLIC

When you think of the Czech Republic you automatically think of its beautiful capital Prague – as if the country had nothing else to offer the visitor other than this beautiful and cultural city. Yet the Bohemian countryside is a restful world of gentle hills and thick woods, especially colourful in autumn and spring. In this setting, you will fing Bohemian Spas which people from all over the world visit for health and recreation.

During the 19th and early 20th centuries, royalty and aristocrats of Europe came to ease their over indulged bodies – or indulge them even more – and today everyone is able to soothe their tired bones in the thermal springs of Karlovy Vary and Mariánské Lázné.

But it is Prague, that most visitors make for first.

Prague is a city of unexpected and rare delights – boasting an amazing number of baroque and renaissance palaces and fine gardens, ornate churches and synagogues and museums spanning centuries. From the wonderful Renaissance buildings of the 16th century Schwarzenberg Palace, the oldest Palace in Prague, the Royal Palace at Prague Castle dating back to 1135 to gardens such as the Wallenstein Ledebour Garden and the Kolowrat Cernin Garden laid out on a steep hill side – the visitor will not be short of places to visit and greenery in which to walk.

As Prague sees its first rays of spring sunshine, the city comes alive. A mass of colours, blooms and cultural events makes this one of the most exciting times of the year to visit. The city's blossoming parks throw open their gates again, after the colder months of winter. During April the temperatures rise and an entertainment programme begins – dominated by the Prague Spring Music Festival.

Summer arrives with high temperatures, frequent, sometimes heavy, showers and thousands of visitors. This is a beautiful, if busy, time to visit. Every weekend, Czechs set out for the country to go hiking in the surrounding hills or stay in country cottages. Those remaining in Prague visit the reservoirs and lakes just outside the city to try to escape the heat. There is a wealth of entertainment on offer as culture moves into the open air taking over the squares, streets and gardens. Street performers, buskers and classical orchestras all help to keep visitors entertained. Many cafés have tables outside allowing you to quench your thirst while watching the fun.

When the gardens below Prague Castle take on the shades of red and gold, and visitors start to leave, the city gets ready for the cold winter months. This is also the traditional mushroom gathering season when you encounter people with baskets full of freshly picked mushrooms. Market places are flooded with fruit and vegetables. The tree-lined slopes above the Vltava take on the beautiful colours of autumn. September and October still have a fair number of warm, sunny days, although November often sees the first snowfalls. Football fans fill the stadiums and the popular steeplechase course at Pardubice reverberates to the cheers of fans.

Czech cooking is very similar to Austrian – lots of meat – usually pork or beef – served with dumplings, potatoes or rice, in a sauce. Meat, poultry, fish, cabbage and potatoes are all prepared simply and without strong spices. Meats tend to be fried, roasted or oven baked in stock. On special occasions, game is usually the main course – venison, boar or quail.

In contrast, Czech beers are some of the best in the world. The Czechs take their beer – pivo – seriously and it is a great source of national pride. Pilsner and its various relations originate in Bohemia. It is generally agreed that the best Pilsners are produced close to the original source – and all the top producers are not far from Prague. Beers can be bought in cans, in bottles, and best of all, on draught. Canned beer is made mostly for export, and no connoisseur would ever drink it.

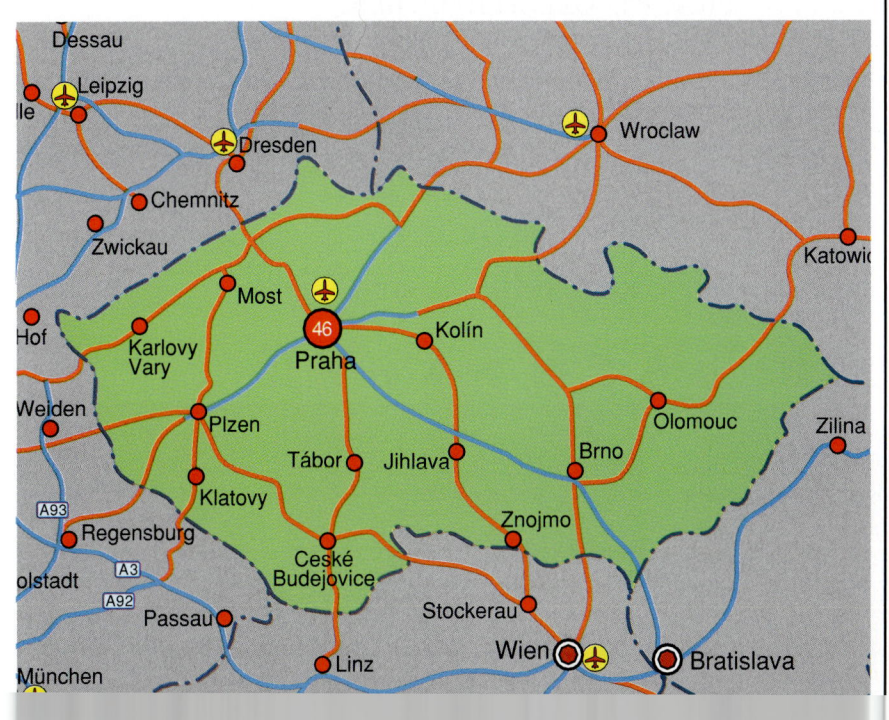

CZECH REPUBLIC (Prague)

In association with MasterCard

HOTEL PALACE PRAHA

PANSKÁ 12, 11121 PRAGUE, CZECH REBUBLIC
TEL: 42 2 24 09 31 11 FAX: 42 2 24 22 140

Superbly located at the centre of Prague, the Hotel Palace lies within blocks of Charles bridge, Old Town, and Wenceslas Square, in the cities business and shopping district. The Art Noveau-style building was built in 1906 and renovated in 1989. Hotel palace offers 124 luxury rooms and special suites with Italian marble bathrooms, complimentary breakfast and minibar, safes, comfort control, direct dial telephones, colour TV with satellite programmes and video movies. Gourmet Club Restaurant features the first class cuisine in the English club atmosphere complemented by the live piano music. Café restaurant, fine dining in in an informal Art Noveau setting. Piano Bar offers its guests their favourite drinks in an unusual blend of Art Noveau and modern styles. Business centre fully equipped with the latest technology is at the guest's disposal 24 hours. The four meeting rooms of varying sizes and capacities are ready to accommodate the groups up to 100 persons. The hotel will arrange tickets for the theatre, concerts and sight seeing tours. **Directions:** Near the Mustek Metro-station, the hotel is at the crossroads of Panská and Jindriská off Vaclavske namestri and has car-parking. Price guide: Single 340Dm–420Dm; double/twin 400Dm–500Dm; suites 500Dm–1170Dm.

46

DENMARK

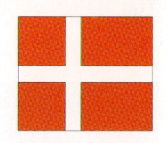

Denmark may be one of Europe's smaller countries, but it has a surprising amount to offer. Neither too foreign nor too remote, it has universal appeal, with its magnificent beaches, unspoilt islands, historic towns and lively culture.

Apart from the peninsula of Jutland, Denmark comprises over 400 islands, about 60 of them inhabited and four easily accessible with a car. Some of the islands are now linked by elegant and inspiring bridges. The coastline is extensive and mostly sandy, providing a perfect family holiday destination, while those who prefer to escape from the crowds will find a huge range of houses for rent on quiet islands, including traditional wooden summer houses.

It's a misconception that Denmark is totally flat, although its highest point is only 567 feet. The inland scenery is a diverse mix of rolling hills, heather-clad moors and fertile farmland, dotted with windmills, white-washed churches, thatched farmhouses and sleepy villages. And the sea is rarely out of sight. The towns are compact and easy to explore – many have an historic centre which has been lovingly restored, and probably a museum proudly displaying local antiquities. Copenhagen and the bigger cities boast excellent museums and galleries which compare favourably with any in Western Europe, and many towns have summer music festivals.

One hallmark of all things Danish is the uniformly high quality, and this applies equally to food and accommodation. Only the freshest ingredients, especially fish, are used to produce attractive and appetising dishes, cleanliness and comfort are assured wherever you choose to stay.

The Danes themselves are friendly and helpful and their gift for languages goes a long way toward making visitors feel at home in this charming country.

Denmark today is a small peaceful country welcoming visitors to its shores. Yet a thousand years ago its Viking people had a fearsome reputation throughout much of northwest Europe. The fact that Greenland and the Faroes are still within the kingdom of Denmark, although they now have Home Rule Government, demonstrates a long and complex history.

Denmark is a sophisticated country, and this is evident in its approach to culture. Civic pride also plays its part in attracting visitors, with well maintained buildings and gardens, statues of local worthies or modern sculptures and fountains placed at strategic points. There is keen competition between local museums for the most lively presentation of their town's history, which often goes far back to prehistoric times.

Throughout Denmark old buildings are being carefully restored, and there are a number of reconstructed villages. Much importance is placed on modern art, and numerous galleries, often privately owned, are open to the public.

The Danes love music and classical concerts are performed in museums, manor houses and churches as well as in large city concert halls.

Alborg, Århus and Odense have their own symphony orchestras. Live jazz is very popular everywhere, and all over Denmark there are open air concerts and music festivals in summer. Odense has an International Jazzhus. Street musicians swarm around pedestrianised streets, live bands play nightly in cafés and discos can be heard full blast in bars throughout the city.

Copenhagen has the most to offer – opera, ballet and theatre – although opera and ballet also flourish in Århus and Odense. Several towns have theatres, but most plays are performed in Danish. The capital also has the most varied night-life, from expensive night-clubs, through live jazz to discos and gay bars as well as the famous Tivoli Gardens.

Danes are a cheerful and relaxed people who like socialising and going to parties. Food and drink are taken seriously and at meals, often candle-lit, certain formalities should be observed. It is for example more polite to take several small helpings rather than one large one.

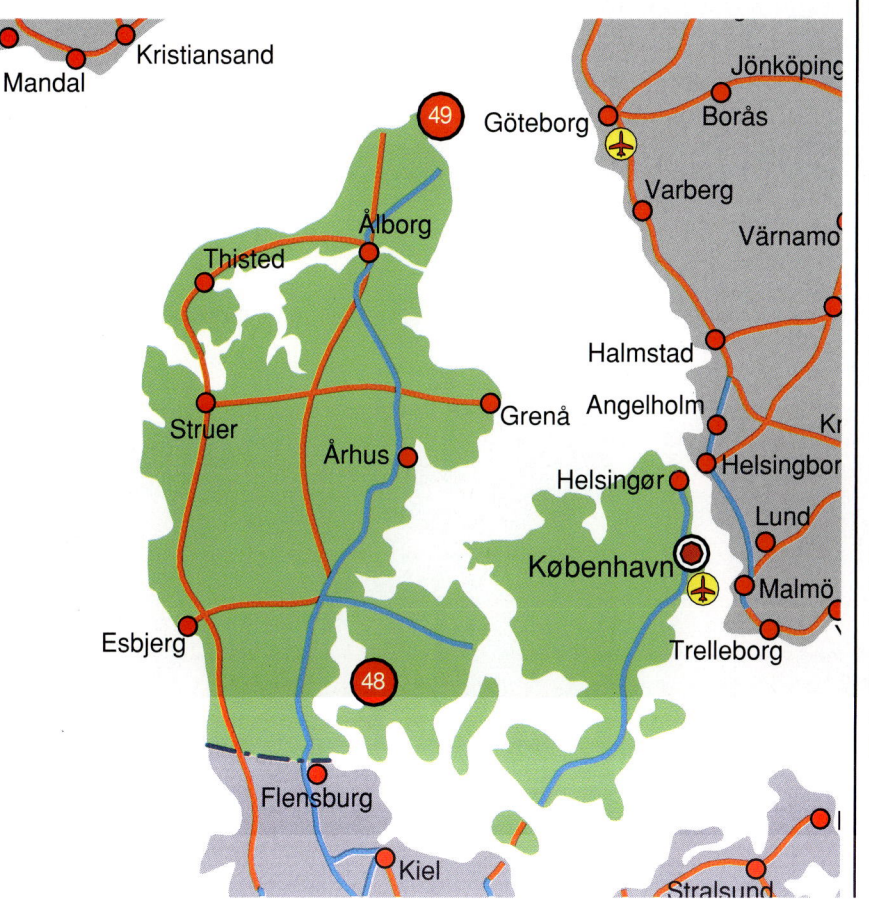

47

DENMARK (Faaborg)

In association with MasterCard

STEENSGAARD HERREGÅRDSPENSION

MILLINGE, STEENSGAARD, 5600 FAABORG, DENMARK
TEL: 45 62 61 94 90 FAX: 45 62 61 78 61

This hotel stands on the delightful island of Fyn, in 24 acres of parkland with its own game reserve. A 14th century manor house, it has been carefully restored to provide modern amenities without diminishing its historic appeal. Guests arriving find an attractive low stone and brick building, with marvellous old chimneys and oak beams, surrounding a cobbled courtyard. Inside are superbly panelled rooms with handsome oil paintings, lovely antiques, chandeliers and comfortable sofas in harmonious colours. A grand mahogany staircase leads to the bedrooms, decorated in peaceful colours, looking out over the estate. They have period furniture and up-to-date bathrooms. The library is a venue for pre-dinner drinks before entering the dining room with its tiled floor, family crests above the fireplace, ornately carved chairs and tables gleaming with silver. The menu offers traditional Danish fare; the wines are international. It is essential for guests to make reservations as it has a fine reputation in the neighbourhood. Guests can use the tennis court or stroll in the well-tended gardens, row on the moat or go for a walk in the Funen Alps or along the beaches. Golf is at Faaborg, riding is 2km away. Directions: By ferry from Middelfart, Fyns or Gelting. The nearest major airport is Billund. Three hours drive from Copenhagen. Price guide: Single 700kr; double/twin 880kr–1000kr.

DENMARK (Gl. Skagen)

STRANDHOTELLET

**JECKELSVEJ 2, GL. SKAGEN, DENMARK 9990
TEL: 45 98 44 34 99 FAX: 45 98 44 59 19**

Strandhotellet was built in 1912 and is a house of unmistakeable character with its white, sunlit walls and many chestnut dormer windows and verandahs. On the ground floor there is a cosy café where guests can enjoy their morning meal. There is also a sitting room with an open fire and a TV room where hot and cold drinks and a light lunch are served. Throughout Skagen there is a variety of notable restaurants, many with well earned reputations for their impressive culinary skills. The hotel's first floor bedrooms are all individually furnished and many have a view overlooking the sea. Guests have a choice of four suites, two junior suites, two double rooms and a single room. At a discreet distance from Strandhotellet lies Strandhuset, a house with six exclusive, two-storey flats. Each has two bedrooms, two bathrooms, a living room, a kitchen and its own terrace and balcony. Swimming and walking are popular pastimes for visitors to this area and Strandhotellet offers its guests an unforgettable angling trip aboard its cutter, "Oke". The skipper knows exactly where the old wrecks lie and that's where big cod, coalfish, hake and mackerel are to be found. Out of season it is possible to rent the whole hotel for company conferences, family gatherings or other purposes where peaceful surroundings are desirable. Price guide: Single: 450kr–550kr; double/twin 745kr–915kr; suites 840kr–1350kr.

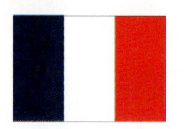

FRANCE

The French themselves are the best advocates for visiting France – convinced that their way of life is superlative, and that their country is the most civilised on earth. Their food, wine and joie de vivre are celebrated in style, with style.

France's landscapes range from high mountain plateaux to lush farmland, traditional villages to chic boulevards. This country belongs to both northern and southern Europe, encompassing Brittany with its Celtic maritime heritage, the Mediterranean sunbelt, Germanic Alsace-Lorraine, and the rugged mountain regions of the Auvergne and the Pyrenees. Paris remains the hub, with its abrupt citizens and intense pace of life. Other cities range from the huge industrial conglomeration of Lille in the north, to Marseilles, the biggest port in the Mediterranean.

Artists have always been inspired by France, especially since landscape became a legitimate subject for art in the 19th century. Art and tourism have been closely linked for over a century, when the establishment of artists' colonies in the forest of Fontainebleau, Brittany and the South of France did much to make these areas attractive to visitors. Today, one of the pleasures of touring the countryside is the recognition of landscapes made famous in paintings by artists such as Monet, Van Gogh and Cézanne.

'Douceur de vivre' – 'life in the country' – conjures up images of long tables set in the sun, ready for the flow of fine wine and good conversation, and perhaps a game of boules with friends. The picture is as seductive for locals as it is for visitors. Yet the rural way of life has changed considerably during the past decade. In 1945 one person in three worked in farming, today it is only one in sixteen.

The French are still firmly committed to their roots, and most retain a place in the country where they return for holidays or retirement. On average, more French have second homes than any other nationality, and in many areas such as Provence, the dying villages find a new life as chic summer residences for Parisians and foreigners.

The French still refuse to stagger their summer holidays, concentrating on the peak period of late July and August, when they take to the roads and coastal resorts. Modernity brings major changes to daily life. For example, France boasts Europe's largest hyper markets – steadily ousting the local grocery or corner shop. Though American in inspiration, these remain French in what they sell: a long delicatessen counter reveals a wonderful display of hundreds of French cheeses and charcuterie while the huge range of fresh vegetables, fruits and herbs is a tribute to their role in French cuisine.

Again, under modern pressure, eating habits have also polarised in a curious way. The French used to eat well every day as a matter of course. Today they are in a hurry, and for most meals of the week they will eat simply – either a quick fried steak or pasta dish at home, or a snack in town. But meals still remain an important part of French lifestyle – not just for the food and wines themselves but for the pleasure of lengthy, unhurried meals and good conversation around a table, among family or friends.

And then there is the wine.

Nowhere in the world is a country more synonymous with wine than France. Each of the principal wine producing regions reveals its own identity, based on grape varieties, climate and local culture. Winemaking in France dates back to Roman times, although it was the Romans who spread the culture of the vine and the practice of winemaking throughout the country. The range, quality and reputation of the fine wines of Bordeaux, Burgundy, the Rhône and Champagne in particular make them role models to the world.

The French with their farming roots, are deeply aware of the changing seasons, and the mild climate means they celebrate outdoors most of the year. History and tradition are honoured with fêtes, such as Bastille Day (14th July). For culture lovers, thousands of arts festivals are held in venues ranging from the huge Avignon Theatre Festival down to small village events. Large national sports events, such as the Tour de France cycle race, are a key feature in the calendar.

In spring, France's outdoor life resumes, terrace cafés fill in the sunshine. Easter is a time of Catholic processions, and concerts of sacred music. The Cannes Film Festival in May is the best known of the season's many conventions and trade fairs.

In summer, the holiday season begins in mid July, with the return to work and school (la rentree) in early September. Beaches, marinas and campsites are all full. Every village has its fête and there are countless festivals and sporting events, including the French Tennis Open in Paris, Le Mans 24 hour race in June and the Tour de France in July.

In autumn, the grape harvest is an occasion for much merry-making and every wine village has its wine festival. When the new wine is ready in November there are yet more festivities. The hunting season also begins – everywhere there is game shooting. In the south-west small migrating birds are trapped in nets, often to the fury of ecologists.

At Christmas, traditional nativity plays are held in churches and there are fairs and markets throughout France. In the Alps and the Pyrenees, and even the Vosges and Massif Central, the ski-slopes are crowded. In Flanders and Nice, carnivals take place before Lent.

One of the largest countries in Europe, France boasts airline connections with most cities in the world. Paris has two international airports, others include Bordeaux, Lille, Lyon, Nice and Toulouse. There are good, high speed TGV rail links with the rest of Europe including England via Eurotunnel, and a cobweb of efficient and toll-heavy motorways which are ideal for long distances. Smaller roads provide a far more interesting way to discover this country's varied landscape.

FRANCE
Dunkerque
Calais
Boulogne
Lille
Béthune
Abbeville
Dieppe
Arras
Cambrai
Amiens
Cherbourg
Le Havre
Bayeux
St Quentin
Rouen
Charleville Mézières
Beauvais
Caen
Lisieux
Granville
Louviers
Reims
Brest
Morlaix
St Malo
Verdun
Evreux
Paris
Argentan
St Brieuc
Chalons-sur-Marne
Metz
Quimper
Mayenne
Chartres
Alençon
Nancy
Rennes
Laval
Lorient
Strasbourg
Troyes
Vannes
Châteaubriant
Redon
Chaumont
Vittel
Le Mans
Epinal
Orleans
Mulhouse
Angers
Auxerre
St Nazaire
Nantes
Langres
Tours
La Roche-sur-Yon
Vierzon
Cholet
Loche
Avallon
Dijon
Bourges
Besançon
Châtellerault
Poitiers
La Rochelle
Bourg-en-Bresse
Mâcon
Rochefort
Saintes
Limoges
Clermont-Ferrand
Angoulême
Lyon
Périgueux
St Ettiene
Bordeaux
Brive-la-Gaillarde
Brioude
Grenoble
Marmand
Montélimar
Gap
Agen
Rodez
Biarritz
Bayonne
Mont-de-Marsan
Montauban
Millau
Digne
Avignon
Nîmes
Pau
Tarbes
Toulouse
Montpellier
Aix-en-Provence
Monte Carlo
Arles
Lourdes
Beziers
Nice
Carcassonne
Narbonne
Marseille
Cannes
Toulon
St.Tropez
Perpignan
N1
A26
A25
A2
N28
A1
A13
A4
A26
A11
A6
A31
A5
A10
A71
A31
A36
A38
A6
A40
A41
A72
A41
A75
A7
A62
A9
A51
A64
A64
A8
A9
91
77
67
63
76
68
74
60
62
71
61
58
59
64
65
66
93
73
53
54
70
55
96
97
95
92
94
69
52
98
56
75
57

FRANCE Arles (Le Sambuc-Arles)

In association with MasterCard

LE MAS DE PEINT

LE SAMBUC, 13200 ARLES, FRANCE
TEL: 33 90 97 20 62 FAX: 33 90 97 22 20

To be in the Camargue is to commune with nature, and Le Mas de Peint, dating back to the 17th century, stands in its own extensive manade (estate) in one of the most verdant areas of France. It is still a working farm, quite remote, and therefore this small, intimate hotel could almost be designated 'chambre d'hôte' as guests live in the proprietor's home. The salons are elegant and relaxing, with antique furniture from the region, low beams and stone floors. The bedrooms are charming, the bathrooms are modern. Meals are taken in a delightful Provençal room, once the kitchen. Dinner, a set menu including the wine, is superb. Recipes handed down by the Grandmère and now beautifully prepared in refined Provençal style – feature with delicious local specialities. Breakfast and lunch can be taken on the terrace or by the pool, which has its own poolhouse to change in. Monsieur Bon takes guests out in his four-wheel drive to see the famous wild horses and his magnificent Camargue bulls. Nearby are a nature reserve, museum, bird park and walkers can follow the river running down to the coast. **Directions:** Leave Arles on D570 towards Saintes-Maries-de-la-Mer. Take D36 to Salin-de-Giraud, finding Le Mas de Peint soon after Le Sambuc. Price guide: Single Ff980–Ff1500; double/twin Ff980–Ff1500; suites Ff1700–Ff1900.

In association with MasterCard

FRANCE (Avignon–Le Pontet)

AUBERGE DE CASSAGNE

450 AUE DE CASSAGNE, 84130 LE PONTET, AVIGNON, FRANCE
TEL: 33 90 31 04 18 FAX: 33 90 32 25 09

The enchanting Auberge de Cassagne, built in 1850, is typically Provençal, with a splendid courtyard surrounded by fine old trees and colourful plants. It is not far from Avignon, in the peaceful rural area known as Le Pontet. The spacious salon has a warm ambience, with its tiled floor, beamed ceiling and graceful furniture, big bowls of fresh flowers and wide archways. The bedrooms are charming with Provençal furniture and fabrics, colour co-ordinated with well-equipped bathrooms. Most have terraces, an ideal place for breakfast. Some are in the attractive annex by the pool. The restaurant is very special, in the expert hands of chef Philippe Boucher and sommelier André Trestour, who unite to make every meal memorable, be it lunch in the courtyard or dining in the handsome restaurant with its red and gold colour scheme, fine oak beams and splendid paintings. Relaxing by the pool, using the tennis court or playing golf just 2km away are favourite pastimes. Avignon has its famous bridge and Pope's Palace; the market at Isle-sur-Sorgue is great fun. The hotel arranges cruises on the Rhône. **Directions:** Cassagne is off the RN7 from Avignon, or leave Autoroute 7 at the Péage Avignon Nord exit. Price guide: Single Ff490 – Ff1180; double/twin Ff790 – Ff1180; suites Ff1380 – Ff1780.

53

FRANCE Avignon (Noves)

In association with MasterCard

AUBERGE DE NOVES

13550 NOVES, FRANCE
TEL: 33 90 94 19 21 FAX: 33 90 94 47 76

Home to the Lalleman family for three generations, this magnificent example of a 19th century manor house stands high up in a peaceful park filled with fragrant flowers, pools with water-lillies, shady terraces and tall pine trees. The salons are very elegant, furnished with superb antiques, fascinating memorabilia and fine paintings. The views across the valleys are wonderful. The charming bedrooms have cool, tiled bathrooms – many with separate showers and three with Jacuzzis! A few are in the original chapel, attached to the main house, others have been designed for those with mobility problems and two are designated non-smoking. There is a grand dining-room, but most memorable will be dining under the stars by candlelight, appreciating the aromatic Provençal dishes and mellow wines, perhaps having a lively discussion with Monsieur Lalleman on his cellar holding 65,000 bottles. Many guests just relax in the grounds, strolling in the park, playing a little tennis or using the swimming pool. Others go further afield for golf, or to visit the museums, galleries and, of course, Le Palais des Papes in Avignon. Additional facilities include a well-equipped conference area. **Directions:** Leave A7 at Avignon Sud and drive towards Chateaurenard, by-passing Noves. Hotel is marked. Price guide: Double/twin Ff1150–Ff1500; suites Ff1800.

In association with MasterCard

FRANCE (Biarritz)

HÔTEL DU PALAIS
64200 BIARRITZ, AVENUE DE L'IMPÉRATRICE, FRANCE
TEL: 33 59 41 64 00 FAX: 33 59 41 67 99

This is a true palace, having been the summer haunt of royalty since 1855 – balls, receptions, charades, picnics and fireworks were the programme then (as they are now!). It became a hotel in the fabulous Belle Epoque, the 1880s, when the guest list included Queen Victoria. In 1950 a famous decorator undertook the complete renovation of the Palais, maintaining its grand style and today it is a sumptuous residence overlooking the waterfront. The richly furnished foyer has marble pillars, glistening chandeliers, superb antiques and a dramatic staircase. The bedrooms are luxurious, many with balconies facing the sea, and access is easy for those with mobility problems. Sophisticated bars, cool in the hotel or on the terraces, are appreciated by guests before feasting in the elegant Michelin star restaurant, with a spectacular view across the sea. Lighter meals in an informal ambience are also served, including a buffet beside the pool. Families use the private beach huts between the pool and the sand. Sporting guests enjoy tennis, squash, 10 golf-courses, scuba-diving, riding or watching pelota, the Basque national game. Others explore the countryside, right up into the Pyrenees. At night the casino is a great attraction. **Directions:** Biarritz is signed from the A63 and N10. Price guide: Single Ff1150–Ff2000; double/twin Ff1450–Ff 2750; suites Ff 2000–Ff6250.

55

FRANCE (Cannes)

HÔTEL L'HORSET SAVOY

5 RUE FRANÇOIS EINESY, 06400 CANNES, FRANCE
TEL: 33 92 99 72 00 FAX: 33 93 68 25 59

This modern hotel with elegant balconies and terraces, is just off the famous Boulevard de la Croisette, easily accessible to the beach and to the town centre. Bedrooms provide modern comfort for the business or pleasure guest. The barman mixes cocktails in the intimate bar before guests enter La Roseraie, terraced restaurant in front of the hotel with its own waterfall. The menu offers good choices from the region including goats' cheese ravioli with rosemary and rouget with basil. A more modest menu reflects the best local market produce. Many of the wines listed are from the region. The Blue Beach on the 6th floor has a wonderful terrace alongside the swimming pool, serving drinks and buffet lunches to sun-worshippers. A private beach is ready for those who prefer sea and sand. Not far from the Palais des Congrès, L'Horset Savoy has its own well equipped conference suites, ideal for receptions and banquets. Exploring old Cannes and the modern shops is fascinating, as is the delightful countryside behind the coast. Tennis and watersports are available, and golf is not far away. **Directions:** 24km from the Nice Airport, driving take the N7 or leave the A8 motorway at the Cannes exit. There is parking under the hotel. Price guide: Single Ff575–Ff1315; double/twin Ff660–Ff1420; suites Ff2000–Ff4000.

In association with MasterCard

FRANCE (Cannes)

HÔTEL MAJESTIC

LA CROISETTE, BP163, CANNES CEDEX, FRANCE
TEL: 33 92 98 77 00 FAX: 33 93 38 97 90

Built in the grand Art Deco style of the 1930s, this distinguished hotel with its background of the exotic Casino gardens, in the midst of the legendary La Croisette with the Palais des Festivals, is extremely smart. Recent renovation has enhanced the exclusive ambience. The spacious salons, with tall pillars, marble floors and decorative Louis XV furniture are cool and welcoming. The glamorous, newly renovated bedrooms of which 23 are suites, all sound-proofed and air-conditioned, have terraces overlooking the sea. The Egyptian-style dining room is chic, with a big open terrace, perfect for indulging in classical French dishes accompanied by superb wines. Informal meals and drinks are served at the Beach Bar. There are extensive facilities for meetings and private functions, including receptions for 600 people. The outdoor pool is heated all the year, and the Majestic has its own private beach. Tennis and water-skiing can be arranged. Golf is played at the élite Mandelieu course. Night-time sport is at the Casino and Le Jimmy'z Discotheque. Watching glass-blowing at Biot, exploring St Paul-de-Vence and visiting the Lerins Islands are pleasant ways to spend the day. **Directions:** A6 from Paris, A8 from Nice. There is hotel parking. By boat, moor at Porto – Canto and Vieux Port marinas. Helicopter transfer from Nice. Price guide: Single Ff800–Ff2990; double/twin Ff1000–Ff3400; suites Ff2000–Ff13,000

FRANCE (Chambolle-Musigny)

Château Hôtel André Ziltener
F-21220 CHAMBOLLE-MUSIGNY, CÔTE D'OR, FRANCE
TEL: 33 80 62 41 62 FAX: 33 80 62 83 75

Chambolle-Musigny is a distinguished name on the 'Route des Grand Crus' and Château André Ziltener, given privacy by the stone walls surrounding the estate, is now a legendary hotel where wine connoisseurs gather. Guests are impressed by its classical architecture and delighted by the elegant salons, with high ceilings, antiques and immaculate decorations. The bedrooms are spacious, with enchanting chinz covers and reproduction Louis XVI furniture. Some have private sitting rooms and all have lavish marble bathrooms. There are many fine restaurants in the area, but none in the château although catering can be organised for private parties. Cold Burgundian dishes are provided in the informal wine-bar where a mural of 'Les Amoureuses' is the focal point. Splendid buffet breakfasts are served in the dining room, guests sitting at a big oval table. Wines from the property, labelled with the distinctive blue coat of arms, are tasted in the cellar. A fascinating wine museum includes an antique map of Burgundy and models of the Cistercian monks whose abbey stood on the site of the Château. Bicycles and hot-air balloons are suggested ways to explore the vineyards. Dijon is full of interest, especially Le Musée des Beaux Arts. **Directions:** Chambolle-Musigny is just off the RN74, between Dijon and Beaune. Price guide: Double/twin Ff900; suites Ff1200.

In association with MasterCard

FRANCE (Chamonix)

HÔTEL ALBERT 1ᴱᴿ

119, IMPASSE DU MONTENVERS, 74402 CHAMONIX – MONT BLANC
TEL: 33 50 53 05 09 FAX: 33 50 55 95 48

This small hotel in Chamonix has been owned by the same family since it was built in 1903, then called the Pension du Chemin de Fer. It stands against a background of snowclad mountains, not least of which is Mont Blanc. The second generation of the Carrier family changed the name of the hotel because the Belgian King Albert often visited the resort. The hotel has been discreetly modernised by Marcel and Andrée Carrier, whose clever use of wood, local stone and terracotta tiles has created a warm ambience. The bedrooms and suites are delightful, beautifully decorated and comfortable with views over the mountains, the parkland or flower-filled gardens. The bar and lounge are perfect for relaxation. The restaurant has always had a superb reputation, and Marcel's inspired regional dishes, cooked with love, have been recognised with a Michelin star. Excellent French wines are offered. The hotel has a pool, gymnasium and sauna for guests returning from exhilarating days skiing and skating in winter. In summer mountaineering, glacier skiing, tennis, golf, and paragliding are among the sports available. Chamonix has a lively night-life. **Directions:** Follow the Route Blanche past the station and over the railway, finding Impasse du Montenvers on the right. There is car parking. Price guide: Double/standard Ff660–Ff730; double/deluxe Ff1100–Ff1410.

FRANCE (Champigné)

In association with MasterCard

CHÂTEAU DES BRIOTTIÈRES
49330 CHAMPIGNÉ, FRANCE
TEL: 33 41 42 00 02 FAX: 33 41 42 01 55

This enchanting château, surrounded by well-kept lawns and 360 acres of parkland 'à l'anglaise', has been in the same family for over 200 years. Indeed this is not a hotel, but a stately home in which guests are graciously received. It is in Anjou, an unspoilt corner of France. The interior is lovely, filled with Louis XV antiques and memorabilia, family portraits and a pervading air of serenity. The once derelict stables have been transformed into a beautiful reception area. The bedrooms have windows looking out over the estate, letting in the fragrant perfumes of herbs and flowers. It is a joy to awake here in the mornings. Breakfast may be taken in the bedrooms or at separate tables downstairs. Lunch is not available and everyone meets again for apéritifs with the owner of the property, François de Valbray, before a convivial dinner (served at 8.30pm) in the impressive dining room – traditional family recipes accompanied by delicious Anjou wines. Cycling is the best way to explore the countryside. The château offers swimming in summer, fishing in the lake and billiards in the evenings; golf and riding are nearby. A little further away are the Loire châteaux, the Anjou wine trail and fascinating Brittany fishing ports. **Directions:** Leave the A11 at Angers and follow N162 toward Laval. At Le Lion turn right on D770. Price guide: Double/twin Ff450–Ff750; suites Ff600–Ff900.

In association with MasterCard

FRANCE (Chênehutte-Les-Tuffeaux)

LE PRIEURÉ

49350 CHÊNEHUTTE-LES-TUFFEAUX, SAUMUR, FRANCE
TEL: 33 41 67 90 14 FAX: 33 41 67 92 24

This magnificent Renaissance manor house stands on history – firstly the site was an important Roman camp and, in the 12th century, a famous abbey here overlooked the Loire. 15th and 16th century architecture brought turrets and cherubs to enhance this slate-roofed palace – inside, the spiral staircase has a vaulted ceiling with medieval gargoyles. The salons are regal, with tall fireplaces and Louis XV furniture, chandeliers and wonderful paintings. The bedrooms are spacious, beautifully decorated, many having canopy beds. Consideration has been given to visitors with mobility problems. Those on a budget might prefer one of the cottages among the trees. Apéritifs on the terrace, watching the sunset over the river is the perfect start to the evening. Guests dine by candle-light in the baronial restaurant, enjoying superb dishes reflecting the chef's generous use of local wines, fresh herbs, fruit and vegetables. All the Anjou vineyards are represented in the cellar. Active guests appreciate the pool, tennis courts and jogging trail, others relax in the well tended gardens. Fishing and golf are nearby. The area abounds with vineyards and châteaux to visit. Watching the famous Cadre Noir training their horses is fascinating. **Directions:** From Paris A10. N152 over the Loire. Pass through Saumur towards Gennes on the D751. Price guide: Ff500–Ff1500.

FRANCE (Colmar)

ROMANTIK HOSTELLERIE LE MARÉCHAL

4-6 PLACE DES SIX MONTAGNES NOIRES, 68000 COLMAR, FRANCE
TEL: 33 89 41 60 32 FAX: 33 89 23 73 61

This enchanting hotel in Colmar is in the old part of the town, known as 'Little Venice', as the half-timbered houses and terraces are close to the edge of the River Lauch. It is a fine example of 16th century architecture in Alsace. The ivyclad walls, striped blinds and window boxes are reflected in the clear water. The suites are regal, with grand drapery over the enormous beds and furnished with magnificent brocades and antiques. Other bedrooms have original beamed ceilings and pretty upholstery. The bathrooms are 20th century. All the rooms are named after famous musicians. The reception rooms are delightful, elegantly furnished to harmonise with the history of the house. Dinner is by candlelight, the river is floodlit and classical music plays in the background as guests feast on regional dishes. Wine from the local vineyards features on the comprehensive list. The dining room is non-smoking, as are three of the bedrooms. Colmar is a fascinating town to explore – there are the famous Unterlinden Museum and local vineyards to visit, sometimes a music festival to enjoy. Boats can be taken out on the river. Golf is 8km away.
Directions: From Strasbourg take the N83 towards Colmar and from Beaune the A.36m exit Cernay-Colmar. Find 'La Petite Venise', and carparking is in front of the hotel. Price guide: Single Ff450–Ff500; double/twin Ff900–Ff1200; suites Ff1400–Ff1500.

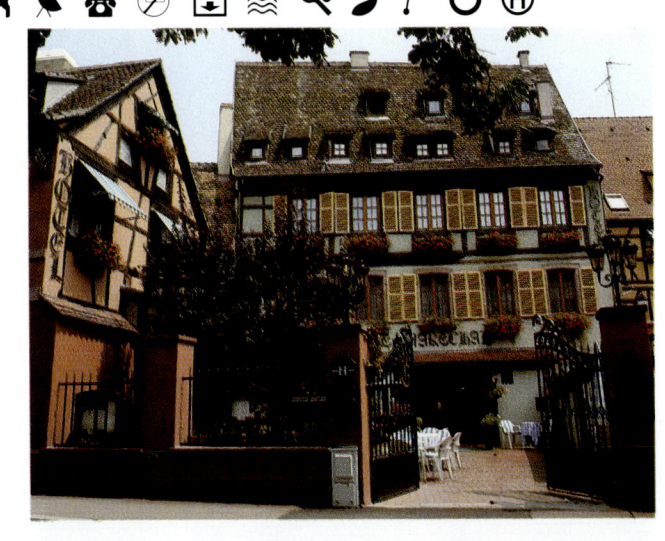

In association with MasterCard

FRANCE (Connelles)

LE MOULIN DE CONNELLES
40 ROUTE D'AMFREVILLE-SOUS-LES-MONTS, 27430 CONNELLES, FRANCE
TEL: 33 32 59 53 33 FAX: 33 32 59 21 83

On an island of its own in a by-water of the Seine a few miles above Rouen stands Le Moulin de Connelles, a fabulously beautiful old manor house and water mill. This is the part of the river that appealed to Monet and his fellow impressionists. There are six luxurious suites and seven luxurious bedrooms. Antiques and fine décor perpetuate the ambience of charming seclusion – the latest modern equipment provides, if audio-visual required, immediate contacts with the outer world. Comfort is similarly assured by the up-to-date amenities. The manor's lounge and bar welcome guests with furnishings that induce that sense of well-being that can be heightened only by a glass of calvados. The restaurant poised above the water is famed for the skill of its young chef. As early guide books might have said: Le Moulin is worth more than a détour. The manor's swimming pool, pool house and tennis courts, nearby international golf courses, riding school and sailing or water skiing on the lake are the breathtaking choice of sporting pursuits. **Directions:** 110Km from Paris motorway A13 exit 18; 28Km from Rouen motorway A13 exit 19; 15Km from Louviers. Price guide: Single Ff550–Ff700; double/twin Ff650–Ff800; suites Ff800–Ff950.

63

FRANCE (Courchevel)

In association with MasterCard

HÔTEL ANNAPURNA

73120 COURCHEVEL (1850), FRANCE
TEL: 33 79 08 04 60 FAX: 33 79 08 15 31

Hotel Annapurna is a sophisticated hotel in the midst of the Alps. Built this century, it has recognised the needs of its sporting guests when they leave the pistes. The interior is spacious and elegant, reflecting the designer's savoir-faire. There are relaxing lounges, with comfortable modern furnishings. The bedrooms are luxurious, with panelled walls and ceilings, all with a south-facing balcony. The piano bar is an ideal après-ski rendezvous, perhaps after taking advantage of the leisure centre. This has a magnificent pool, looking out to the snowfields, a Jacuzzi, sauna, gymnasium. masseur, table-tennis and billiards. After an exotic cocktail or two, studying the menu of the handsome restaurant, with its spectacular view of the mountains, the superb French food, beautifully served, is greatly appreciated, especially when accompanied by connoisseur wines. An orchestra plays on Thursday evenings. The Annapurna has become a popular location for seminars and conferences, and all appropriate facilities are available. Every form of winter sports is possible in Courchevel, wonderful runs, Langlauf, skating, curling and tobogganing. At night there are discothèques, cinemas, clubs. **Directions:** A41 to Montmelian, then A43 to Albertville, then N90 to Moutiers, after which Courchevel is signed. Price guide per person: Single Ff1000–Ff1900; double/twin Ff850–Ff1490; suites Ff2430–Ff2930.

In association with MasterCard

FRANCE (Courchevel)

L'HÔTEL DES NEIGES
RUE DE BELLECOTE, BP 96, 73121 COURCHEVEL 1850 CEDEX, FRANCE
TEL: 33 79 08 03 77 FAX: 33 79 08 18 70

This magnificent hotel in a skier's paradise is only open in the winter months. Set against a stunning backdrop of the snow-clad Alps, L'Hotel des Neiges is at the top of the village, just minutes from the lively Centre Croisette. Purpose-built for winter conditions, it has a long list of guests re-appearing year after year. The bedrooms are gorgeous, with pretty hand-painted traditional furniture, many having balconies looking out over the snow. The large bathrooms are well-appointed and have towelling robes for those wishing to visit the sauna. The large terrace is the perfect spot for lunch and for non-skiers to breathe the pure mountain air. There is a delightful cocktail lounge for aprés-ski pre-dinner relaxation. The restaurant menu is filled with enticing gourmet dishes and the wine list includes many illustrious Bordeaux chateaux. In the mornings a special hearty 'skier's breakfast' can be ordered for those planning a day on the slopes. The Courchevel Ski School is famous, and the hotel arranges everything for guests – lessons and ski-lift passes. Muscles are revived in the sauna, or by massage and hydrotherapy. The solarium tans those not attacking the elements. The town has two cinemas, a bridge club and concerts. **Directions:** Courchevel is signed from the N90 and D90. Snow-chains are advisable. The hotel has car-parking. Price guide: Single Ff935–Ff1385; double/twin Ff915–Ff1945; suites Ff1685–Ff2435.

FRANCE (Courchevel)

In association with MasterCard

HÔTEL DES TROIS VALLÉES

BP 22, F-73122 COURCHEVEL CEDEX, FRANCE
TEL: 33 79 08 00 12 FAX: 33 79 08 17 98

This hotel is the ultimate skiers' paradise, at Courchevel, the Olympic sports complex high in the Savoie mountains, located on the slopes (in and out skiing) close to the ski-lifts. Only open in the winter months, it promises marvellous snow conditions. After the rigours of the day, skiers appreciate the luxury of this elegant chalet-style residence just a two minute walk from the centre of town. The ambience of a sybaritic lifestyle is created by music, silk curtains, luxurious, classical modern furnishings, gleaming crystal and attentive staff. Those wanting total peace retreat to the contemporary and extremely comfortable bedrooms, with opulent bathrooms. The piano bar has large leather armchairs in which guests relax, enjoying a drink while listening to the music. The menu in the delightful and spacious restaurant concentrates on haute cuisine supported by a wine list of the highest calibre. Fine days bring a barbecue on the terrace. Après-ski activities include benefiting from hydromassage, saunas, Turkish baths, the solarium, gymnasium and beauty salon. **Directions:** Daily direct flights from Paris in the Twin Otter and at weekends faster journeys in the Dash Seven; alternatively the TGV Paris–Moutiers where the hotel will meet you. Driving from Lyon, A43, A430 and N90. Price guide: double/twin Ff900–Ff1400; suites Ff1500–Ff2400. Per person per day half board

In association with MasterCard

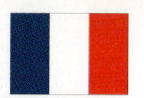

FRANCE (Deauville)

HÔTEL ROYAL

BOULEVARD CORNUCHÉ, 14800 DEAUVILLE, CALVADOS, FRANCE
TEL: 33 31 98 66 33 FAX: 33 31 98 66 34

A 20th century grand hotel, right on the waterfront in Deauville, the Royal has maintained its traditions of impeccable service in magnificent surroundings. It is part of the Lucien Barrier Group, who also own the nearby Hôtel Normandy, the famous casino, the thalasso-therapy centre in the town and the delightful Hôtel du Golf, built on the edge of the course at Mont Canisy. Special packages enable guests to take advantage of all these facilities. The spacious salons are very impressive, with huge sofas and magnificent flower displays. The bedrooms are enormous and beautifully appointed to meet the needs of the most demanding guests. Those with mobility problems will appreciate specially adapted accommodation. The hotel has two restaurants, one for gourmets for which extravagant dishes are prepared and the dining room where lighter meals are served. The cellar is extensive. The Bayeux Tapestries are of great interest to tourists, and Deauville itself is fascinating to explore. Excellent golf, with a choice of courses in the vicinity, is popular. The hotel has a splendid fitness centre, and outside in the grounds are tennis courts and swimming pool with a terrace bar. **Directions:** Following the coast road, the hotel is a landmark midway along the seafront. Price guide: Single/double/twin from Ff1250–Ff2200; suites Ff2200–Ff10,000.

67

FRANCE (Épernay)

In association with MasterCard

HOSTELLERIE LA BRIQUETERIE

4 ROUTE DE SÉZANNE, VINAY 51530, ÉPERNAY, FRANCE
TEL: 33 26 59 99 99 FAX: 33 26 59 92 10

La Briqueterie, standing at the foot of the Côte des Blancs, is surrounded by beautiful flower-filled grounds in the heart of the champagne country. It is owned by the Trouillard family, whose interest in vintage cars is evident from the unusual works of art in the informal reception area. The salons are elegant, and the quiet countryside even pervades the enchanting bedrooms and suites, identified by floral panel on the doors, the colours of which are echoed in the decor inside. The bathrooms are large and luxurious. The family have their own Champagne House, and their vintages are among the prestigious champagnes imbibed in the attractive conservatory bar in the garden summerhouse. A wonderful buffet is served in the Breakfast Room, overlooking the pool. At night, in the handsome beamed restaurant diners have a choice of Regional and Dégustation menus or they select succulent dishes from the à la carte suggestions. The wines are superb. A splendid private dining room and conference facilities are also available. Visitors explore Reims Cathedral, tour champagne cellars or cruise on the Marne. Others relax at the hotel, in the gorgeous pool or the gymnasium. **Directions:** Drive 6km along the Route de Sézanne, signposted from the centre of Épernay, or land on the helipad. Price guide: Single Ff600–Ff730; double/twin Ff710–Ff845; suites Ff1100.

In association with MasterCard

FRANCE (Eze Village)

CHÂTEAU EZA

RUE DE LA PISE, 06360 EZE-VILLAGE, FRANCE
TEL: 33 93 41 12 24 FAX: 33 93 41 16 64

Eze village is medieval, a total contrast to the sophisticated towns along the Côte d'Azur. The Château Eza is 1300 feet high on the great rock above the Mediterranean and was the residence of Prince William of Sweden from 1927 to 1957. Several 13th century houses have been transformed into this élite hotel, with its incredible view over the coast. The original stone walls and ancient oak beams are still evident in the graceful salons and magnificent suites. Log fires, unexpected alcoves, tapestries, superb rugs on tiled floors and fine antiques are part of the unique ambience of this historic hotel. Guests approach the château along a cobbled path, and once unloaded, hotel staff take cars to a parking area at the foot of the village. Lunch and dinner is served on the elegant terrace, with its fantastic outlook over the sea to the horizon, is a charming place for guests to watch a brilliant sunset, then at dusk the scenery becomes a mass of flickering lights. Dinner is also served in the lovely Chateau Eza restaurant appropriately named 'Restaurant Gastronomique' for the superb dishes created by the Chef de Cuisine and Chef Pâtissier. dinner is served on the terrace wheather permitting. 700 great wines are listed. Guests explore Eze-Village, visit perfume houses and wine caves, or tour the exotic Riviera with its beaches and casinos. **Directions:** Eza village is on the Moyenne Corniche between Nice and Monaco. Price guide: Ff1440–Ff2400; double/twin Ff1800–Ff3000; suites Ff2250–Ff3500.

FRANCE (Joucas)

In association with MasterCard

HOSTELLERIE LE PHÉBUS

JOUCAS, 84220 GORDES, FRANCE
TEL: 33 90 05 78 83 FAX: 33 90 05 73 61

A lovely stone, Provençal house, parts dating back to the 12th century, Hostellerie Le Phébus stands on top of a hill overlooking the Luberon, in a ten acre park scented with thyme and rosemary. A brilliant mélange of sophistication and simplicity, the exterior in local dry stone and the plain white interior walls provide the perfect background for gorgeous Soleido fabrics that blend harmoniously with antique furniture from the region. The simple elegance of the bedrooms complement marble state-of-the-art bathrooms while some of the stylish suites have private swimming pools. The owners, the Matthieu family, describe their kitchen as a temple of gastronomy. Al fresco eating is on the splendid, flower-filled terrace overlooking the pool, otherwise guests are seated in the handsome and spacious restaurant, with tapestries hung on the walls, looking across the Luberon Valley, perhaps to the vineyards that produced the fine wines on their table. Tourists visit medieval Gordes, The Vasarely Museum, the Fountain of Vaucluse and the museum at Apt. Others enjoy the hotel tennis courts, explore the country side on bicycles or laze by the large heated swimming pool. Good golf and riding are nearby.
Directions: The hotel is 20km from the Cavaillon exit of the A7, being 30 km from Avignon airport. Price guide: Double/twin Ff665–Ff1080; suites Ff1395–Ff1810.

In association with MasterCard

FRANCE (La Baule)

LE CASTEL MARIE-LOUISE

1 AVENUE ANDRIEU, 44500 LA BAULE, FRANCE
TEL: 33 40 11 48 38 FAX: 33 40 11 48 35

This delightful example of a Belle Époque manor house, set in lovely gardens stsretching down to the Atlantic Ocean, has been transformed into a magical hotel. The Castel Marie-Louise has been designed to encourage relaxation with its big windows looking down to the sea, charming wallpapers and pretty draped curtains, comfortable period furniture and fresh flowers everywhere. The bedrooms are romantic, beautifully decorated, and many lead on to balconies with colourful window boxes, the perfect spot to have a delicious breakfast. Many guests choose to have their apéritifs and meals alfresco on the green lawns, watching the yachts go by. Informal meals are available in the friendly bar-restaurant, and magnificent gourmet meals, with local sea-food a speciality, accompanied by wines from the Loire and Bordeaux, are enjoyed in the elegant restaurant with views of the ocean. Sports facilities in La Baule are excellent, the Castel guests having use of the Hotel Hermitage heated pool. Sailing and other watersports, tennis at the country club, riding and golf are all in the locality as well as the pampering seaweed treatment centre – Thalgo-La-Baule. At night the casino is a great attraction. **Directions:** From Nantes, N165 towards La Baule, via St-Nazaire. The hotel is on the coast, near the casino. Price guide: Single Ff890–Ff1550; double/twin Ff990–Ff2100.

FRANCE (Lyon)

LA TOUR ROSE
22 RUE DE BOEUF, 69005 LYON, FRANCE
TEL: 33 78 37 25 90 FAX: 33 78 42 26 02

Lyon is famous for its silks and for its gastronomy, the latter a legacy from the talented chefs who cooked for the famous banking and silk houses. Philippe Chavent has created a Tuscan garden with terraces, waterfalls and ornamental pools as the setting for La Tour Rose. Each of the twelve suites has been named after and decorated by a different Lyon manufacturer, often using the silks quite unexpectedly so that a variety of eras and styles is evident. La Tour Rose is, in fact, three Renaissance buildings. Guests walk through their courtyards perhaps to the Jeu de Paume bar and or relax in the sunlit gardens. Silk aficianados move from the restoration rooms to the textile designer's salons where magnificent exhibitions are staged. The restaurant is unique, a former chapel leading onto a terrace. Philippe Chavent's avant-garde talents transform classic dishes into nouvelle cuisine. Close by he has opened Le Comptoir du Bœuf where guests can taste vintage wine selected from the 35,000 bottles in his cellar. Lyon deserves exploring, with its musuems and historical buildings. Guests can attend the cookery school above the hotel kitchen, and enjoy jazz concerts in the evening. **Directions:** Old Lyon. Detailed directions and a map will be sent following reservations. Price guide: Single Ff950–Ff1650; double/twin Ff950–Ff1650; suites Ff1650–Ff2800.

In association with MasterCard

FRANCE (Monestier)

CHÂTEAU DES VIGIERS

24240 MONESTIER, FRANCE
TEL: 33 05 53 61 50 00 FAX: 33 05 53 61 50 20

A "Petit Versailles" offering golf and its own fine wines is near to Paradise for its guests! This beautiful 400 year old château on a 425 acre estate with its own vineyards, in the heart of the Bordeaux country, recently opened its doors as a luxurious hotel. Dagand, highly skilled in the renovation of old buildings, has been responsible for the renovation work, preserving much of its fine architecture while converting it into a prestigious golf and country club. Donald Steel has added Château des Vigiers to the list of élite courses which he has designed or improved, including St Andrews. Michel Roux, created the fantastic kitchen and gourmet restaurant. The bridge and tea salons, the library and billiard room are regal, with handsome antiques, rich rugs and fine paintings. The guest rooms are equally impressive, with French country house furniture. Perigordian suites in the adjacent Dépendences have their own terraces. Additionally excellent conference facilities are available. At night a sophisticated restaurant, Les Fresques, serves Perigord specialities such as home made foie gras with wines from the estate. At lunchtime Snack meals are served in the Club House. The estate also offers swimming, golf, tennis, cycling and fishing. **Directions:** From Bordeaux N89 to Libourne, D936 towards Bergerac, at Sainte-Foy-la-Grande D18 towards Eymet. Price guide: Single Ff600–Ff1100; double/twin Ff600–Ff860; suites Ff800–Ff1100.

FRANCE (Nancy)

In association with MasterCard

GRAND HÔTEL DE LA REINE

**2 PLACE STANISLAS, 54000 NANCY, FRANCE
TEL: 33 83 35 03 01 FAX: 33 83 32 86 04 TELEX: 960 367**

Nancy is particularly elegant – an early example of brilliant town planning which took place in the 18th century at the request of Stanislas I, King of Poland, Sovereign of Lorraine. The architect's masterpiece was the Place Stanislas, listed today in UNESCO's World Heritage. The Grand Hotel de la Reine, built in 1755, takes up one side of this square and owes its name to an early guest, Queen Marie Antoinette. Today, after dedicated restoration, it offers prestigious accommodation. The magnificent Louis XV salons can be transformed into meeting rooms and are a delightful setting for receptions. The charming bedrooms and suites are designed to satisfy the demands both of modern business travellers and of those enjoying this lovely town. The 'Le Stan' American bar is very smart and the menu of the handsome 'Le Stanislas' restaurant, which has a splendid terrace overlooking Place Stanislas, includes local specialities such as Meuse truffles and pike from the Moselle. Many of the wines are regional. The famous National Ballet and Opera are five minutes away, museums and the Baccarat crystalware factories are nearby. Golf, tennis, a heated pool, riding, shooting and archery are found within a few kilometres. **Directions:** Autoroute A4. Reaching Nancy, follow signs to Place Stanislas. Parking is 30m from the hotel. Price guide: Ff600–Ff2000, either single or double, breakfast not included.

In association with MasterCard

FRANCE (Nice)

HÔTEL LA PÉROUSE
11 QUAI RAUBA-CAPEU, 06300 NICE, FRANCE
TEL: 33 93 62 34 63 FAX: 33 93 62 59 41

Built at the foot of a rocky hill below the château, this 30's style hotel, with its fabulous outlook over the Baie des Anges, is named after the famous 18th century navigator, La Pérouse. It is in a quiet part of Nice, at the end of the Promenade des Anglais, very convenient for delegates attending the Palais des Congrès. All the air-conditioned bedrooms and suites have balconies, some with a view of the sea, others facing the gardens. Simply furnished, the bedrooms provide basic amenities in cool comfort. The bathrooms are modern, just a few only having showers. The swimming pool and enclosed terrace are surrounded by shady lemon trees, where guests can enjoy apéritifs and the simple, reasonably priced, menu which has a limited wine list that includes several Provençal rosés. In winter room service will supply the same selection. For summer, there is a panoramic solarium on the roof with Jacuzzi. La Pérouse is close to the flower market in old Nice, and just five minutes from the town centre with its theatre, opera and art museums. Eze and Saint-Paul-de-Vence are ideal for day excursions and active visitors can find tennis, water sports and golf in easy reach. **Directions:** The hotel is 6km from Nice Airport. The Promenade des Anglais runs along the waterfront, ending at the Quai Rauba Capeu. Price guide: Single Ff395–Ff1300; double/twin Ff650–Ff1300.

FRANCE (Normandy)

In association with MasterCard

CHÂTEAU DU TERTRE
SAINT MARTIN DE MIEUX, 14700 FALAISE, NORMANDY, FRANCE
TEL: 33 31 90 01 04 FAX: 33 31 90 33 16

Just a few minutes from William the Conqueror's castle and Swiss Normandy, in the midst of 160 acres of parkland and forest, discover the charm of this elegant and welcoming 18th century hotel. The spacious bedrooms are delightful, with wonderful views over the countryside. They are decorated in soft colours, with period furniture. Big cast iron baths are a unique feature of the bathrooms! The salons are filled with fine antiques, handsome oil paintings and big bowls of flowers. A unique feature is the Cavathèque, probably the largest collection of Calvados for public tastings in the world. Guests gather for apéritifs before adjourning to the graceful panelled dining room where Norman recipes inspire fine French dishes using produce from the chateau's own walled-garden and from the local markets , and the excellent wines are French. After dinner, a glass of Calvados, of course. Strolling in the park – or jogging – riding and hunting, croquet on the lawns and fishing (own rods needed) are ideal activities, golf is only 20 minutes away. Further away, see the Bayeux Tapestries. **Directions:** On arriving at first roundabout on four lane motorway from Caen to Falaise, continue on by-pass direction Argentan to next roundabout exit,signed Fourneaux-le-Val on D44 Le Tertre can be seen on the right skyline. Price guide: Double/twin Ff490–Ff880 suites Ff880–Ff1300.

In association with MasterCard

FRANCE (Paimpol)

RELAIS BRENNER

KERGRIST, ROUTE DE SAINT-JULIEN, PONT DE LEZARDRIEUX, 22500 PAIMPOL, FRANCE
TEL: 33 96 20 11 05 FAX: 33 96 22 16 27

The picturesque way to approach this stunning small hotel is by sail, heading for North Britanny, past the Ile de Bréhat and down the estuary to the hotel's private moorings just before Pont de Lezardrieux. This is a place for those who love the sea, sailing, fishing, small villages on the water's edge and a glass of wine while enjoying the spectacular scenary, relaxing in the gardens under the aromatic pinetrees. The hotel has its own style, uncluttered, modern art on the walls, some art deco pieces and ferns. The outlook from the big picture windows enhances the drawing room and sitting rooms. The bedrooms are charming and thoughtfully equipped, and there are also apartments. The friendly bar and enchanting restaurant both look down the estuary past the fishing village. The chef has Michelin star rating, and creates fabulous dishes, exquisitely presented, with fish as the main theme. This is the time to explore the interesting wine list. Fascinating art exhibitions, castles, mediaeval towns, islands and harbours are nearby. Active guests play golf at Orms, tennis nearby or swim from the beach. **Directions:** Non-mariners take the TGV to Saint-Brieuc or a ferry to Saint-Malo or Roscoff. By car, turn left before Paimpol to Treguier/Lannion. The hotel is on the right by the estuary. Price guide: Ff350–Ff700; double/twin Ff800–Ff1200; suites Ff1100–Ff2200.

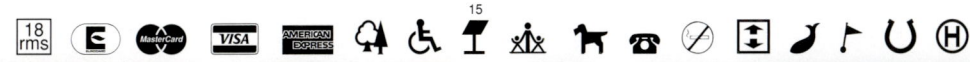

PARIS IN THREE HOURS
INCLUDING A TWO HOUR STOP FOR LUNCH

Eurostar to Paris or Brussels offers a very short travel time. And a very long lunchtime. A meal in First Class starts with a complimentary drink, just to get you into the spirit (or wine, or beer). Then your three course feast. Start, perhaps, with a plate groaning with smoked salmon. To follow? A roast fillet of beef smothered in goose liver pâté, or chargrilled cod steak with vegetables. To finish, and it probably will finish you, a summer fruit pudding. Dinner is on a similar scale. And we think we know where the producers of the Big Breakfast got their inspiration. For more information, call **0990 186 186**.

eurostar

LONDON TO THE CENTRE OF PARIS AND BRUSSELS. DIRECT.

Eurostar is a service provided together by the railways of Belgium, Britain and France.

PARIS

Paris is not France, but France would be unthinkable without Paris. Here, past and present cohabit, sometimes comfortably, sometimes uneasily. Paris is a city where, once you are known, shopkeepers greet you and proprietors shake your hand as you leave their restaurants.

There are thousands of places where one can get a cup of tea or coffee – or a glass of wine or beer – a convenience that is one of the finer attributes of French civilisation.

The French Government Tourist Office situated on the Champs Elysées near the Arc de Triomphè offers an extensive listing of Paris restaurants.

There are thousands of wine bars, bistros and cafés, where no reservations are required. If a table has no tablecloth, you can normally just sit down. Your best chance of getting a table, if you have not called ahead, is to go early, but not before 7.30 pm or you'll find the staff eating.

Nearly every building of note in Paris is either along the river bank or close to it. The apartments, magnificent town houses, world-renowned museums and striking monuments.

For centuries fleets of small boats used it, but motorised land traffic stifled this once-thriving scene. Today, the river is busy with commercial barges and massive bateaux-mouche pleasure boats carrying sightseers up and down the river.

The Right Bank is dominated by the modernistic Forum des Halles and Pompidou Centre in the Beaubourg. These are Paris's most thriving public areas, with tourists, shoppers and students flowing between them. Young people flock to Les Halles, shopping for the latest street fashions beneath the concrete and glass bubbles of the underground arcades. All roads from Les Halles appear to lead to the Pompidou Centre, an avant-garde assembly of pipes, ducts and cables housing the Musée National d'Art Moderne. The smaller streets around the centre are full of art galleries housed in crooked, gabled buildings.

On the Île de la Cité you'll find the impressive Notre Dame. No other building epitomises the history of Paris more than the awe inspiring Notre Dame. Built on the site of a Roman temple, the cathedral was commissioned by Bishop de Sully in 1159. The first stone was laid in 1163, marking the start of two centuries of toil by armies of Gothic architects and medieval craftsmen. Notre Dame has been witness to great events of French history ever since, including the coronations of Henry VI, King of England, who was crowned King of France in 1430 and Napoleon Bonaparte in 1804.

The Left Bank is associated with poets, philosophers, artists and radical thinkers. The area oozes bohemian street life and pavement cafés – although the smart set is gradually encroaching on the territory. The Latin Quarter is the ancient area lying between the Seine and Luxembourg Gardens, and is filled with book shops, art galleries and cafés. A maze of narrow cobbled-streets with ethnic shops and avant-garde theatre awaits the visitor.

Many of Paris's famous sights are slightly out of the city centre. Montmartre, long a mecca for artists and writers, still retains much of its Bohemian atmosphere, and Montparnasse is full of bustling cafes and theatre crowds. The celebrated Cimetière du Père Lachaise numbers Chopin, Yves Montand and Oscar Wilde among its dead – and along with the parks and gardens, provides a tranquil escape from sightseeing.

For many, Paris epitomises luxury and good living. Parisian shopping streets and markets are ideal for indulging the French custom of strolling for the express purpose of seeing and being seen. For up to the minute fashion, the rue Faubourg-St-Honoré is hard to beat, with names such as Lacroix, Laroche, Nina Ricci and Yves Saint Laurent selling their haute couture at astronomical prices.

There is an easy informality about attending Paris theatres. Many are small and intimate and one can normally get tickets at the last minute, except for hit shows, and prices are low. Whether your preference is for classical drama, avant-garde theatre, ballet, opera or jazz, cinema or dancing the night away, Paris has it all. There is plenty of free entertainment too, from the street performers outside the Pompidou Centre to musicians busking all over town and in the Métro.

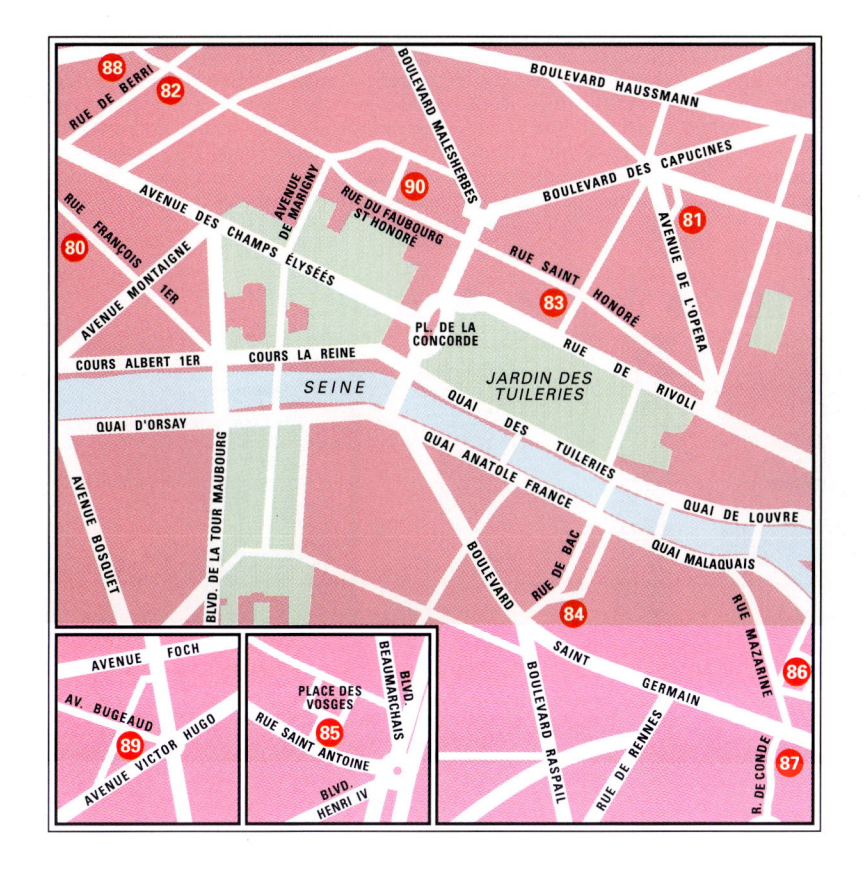

FRANCE (Paris)

In association with MasterCard

HÔTEL DU ROY
8 RUE FRANCOIS 1ER, 75008 PARIS, FRANCE
TEL: 331 42 89 59 59 FAX: 331 40 74 07 92

This hotel offers unique facilities in the very centre of Paris, with accommodation ideal for families or for those planning a long stay in the city. Full hotel services are available and yet the rooms and suites have the informality of apartments. The location is superb, close to the Seine, the Champs Elysées and the sophisticated Avenue Montaigne with its luxurious boutiques, ideal for public transport although some private parking is available. There is a bar on the ground floor where residents can meet friends with 24 hour reception/security. The efficient message and laundry service is useful. There is no restaurant but room service is available. The spacious bedrooms are comfortably furnished, air-conditioned and have minibars and a kitchenette, for which equipment will be supplied on request. A direct-dial telephone, satellite TV and safe complete the amenities. It is possible to rent a small meeting room for 10-20 people, with projectors and screens. A wide choice of restaurants, brasseries, bistros and créperies are available nearby and markets for those who choose to self-cater. **Directions:** Rue Francois is halfway down Avenue Montaigne between the Rond Point des Champs Elysees and Place de l'Alma on the Seine. Price guide: Single Ff1220; double/twin Ff1720; suites Ff2600.

In association with MasterCard

FRANCE (Paris)

HÔTEL L'HORSET OPÉRA

18 RUE D'ANTIN, 75002 PARIS, FRANCE
TEL: 331 44 71 89 00 FAX: 331 42 66 55 54

This is a delightful small hotel in the Opéra Garnier area, where many important events in the history of France have taken place. The surrounding streets are now a fascinating mélange of important monuments and sophisticated boutiques. On arrival guests first notice the elegant façade of L'Horset Opéra and once inside they are impressed by the spacious, attractive reception area and the efficient, friendly staff. The bedrooms are charming and comfortable. Downstairs in the bar, which has panelled walls and handsome furniture, the barman will mix wonderful cocktails and discuss the excellent wines listed. Breakfast is a superb buffet. This is a wonderful base for exploring Paris. The hotel will make reservations for a memorable night at the opera and recommend restaurants and bistros close by. Minutes away are the spectacular Place Vendôme, the Louvre, the Palais Royal, the Jardin des Tuileries and fascinating antique shops. Excellent department stores can be found in the Rue de la Paix, just round the corner. **Directions:** Rue d'Antin is off Avenue de l'Opéra. The hotel does not have car parking, but business people will appreciate its accessibility by Métro. Price guide: Single Ff1220; double/twin Ff1350.

FRANCE (Paris)

In association with MasterCard

HOTEL LANCASTER

7 RUE DE BERRI, CHAMPS ELYSÉES, PARIS, FRANCE 75008
TEL: 331 4076 4076 FAX: 331 4076 4000

The Hôtel Lancaster, just thirty seconds from the bustle of the Champs Elysées, is a revelation of civilised living. Originally a family home and built in 1899, its 58 rooms and suites are filled with treasures of the 18th century – antique furniture, clocks, tapestries and important works of art. There are no more than 10 rooms on each floor and every one is individually decorated to satisfy a variety of tastes. Great attention is given to detail, with large baths, soap from the finest parfumiers and huge, fluffy bathrobes. The restaurant opens onto a romantic courtyard garden, where honeysuckle, columbine and fuchsias provide a touch of the countryside in the heart of Paris. The bar, with its colourful murals and rich wood furnishings, is the perfect rendezvous and to complement the pervasive air of seclusion, the hotel has two air conditioned private rooms, ideal for small luncheons, dinners or top-level meetings for between 10 and 20 people. Nearby are some of France's leading fashion houses and stores, art galleries, banks and embassies, and all the famous sights are within easy reach, making The Lancaster the ideal base from which to enjoy Paris. Price guide: Single Ffr1850–Ffr1950; double/twin Ffr2350–Ffr2650; suites from Ffr3850.

In association with MasterCard

FRANCE (Paris)

HÔTEL ROYAL SAINT-HONORÉ

221 RUE SAINT-HONORÉ, 75001 PARIS, FRANCE
TEL: 331 42 60 32 79 FAX: 331 42 60 47 44

This delightful small hotel is perfectly situated for those wishing to stay in the very heart of Paris, the original residence dating back to before the Revolution, during which time it was occupied by various Republican committees. It first became a hotel in 1924 and, having changed hands several times, was completely renovated by its current owners, Hotels and Residences du Roy, officially re-opening in June 1993, with a new entrance right on Rue Saint-Honoré. Being central, an important feature of the charming bedrooms, with Louis XVI style furnishings, is that they are sound-proofed and air-conditioned. The bathrooms are in marble. There is no dining room, but room service is available and refreshments are served in the foyer and bar. Guests often prefer to explore the many restaurants and bistros nearby. There is, however, a formal salon where special functions can be arranged. The hotel is just minutes from the Jardin des Tuileries, Place Vendome, L'Opera and the sophisticated shops in Rue Saint-Honoré, so close to the Louvre and its carousel, and the rest of Paris to explore, Notre Dame, the Eiffel Tower and paintings to buy on the Left Bank. **Directions:** The hotel does not offer private car-parking, but is close to the Place de la Concorde. Price guide: Single Ff1250; double/twin Ff1550; suites Ff2350.

FRANCE (Paris)

In association with MasterCard

MONTALEMBERT

3 RUE DE MONTALEMBERT, 75007 PARIS, FRANCE
TEL: 331 45 49 68 68 FAX: 331 45 49 69 49

A unique and lovely hotel on the Left Bank, a 1926 town-house with many original and contemporary features blending with its classical architecture. Many of these – the wrought iron bannisters, cast bronze door handles and unusual lamps have been specially designed for the Montalembert. Clear lines, authentic panelling, handcrafted leather and superb fabrics all combine to create its Rive Gauche ambience. The bedrooms are in two styles, the Louis Philippe rooms having period marquetry furniture in harmony with modern striped duvets, while dramatic dark sycamore is used in others. The bathrooms are unexpected, in 20th century chrome and Cascais marble. Guests can retreat to a book-lined corner off the bar, make use of the garden patio or enjoy watching passers-by from the sidewalk café by the hotel entrance. The hotel restaurant, in the same light wood as the bar, hung with brilliant black and white photographs provides imaginative dishes that have made it a popular rendezvous. The Montalembert is surrounded by famous historic buildings and artists' ateliers, close to the Seine, near fascinating cafés, clubs and élite boutiques. **Directions:** Follow Boulevard Saint-Germain, turn left to Rue du Bac and then the second street on your right: Rue de Montalembert. Nearest Metro station: Rue de Bac. Price guide: Double/twin Ff1625–Ff2080; suites Ff2750–Ff3600.

In association with MasterCard

FRANCE (Paris)

Pavillon de la Reine

28 PLACE DES VOSGES 75003, PARIS, FRANCE
TEL: 331 42 77 96 40 FAX: 331 42 77 63 06

A 16th century palace, now a unique and exquisite hotel in a beautiful square in the centre of Paris. There is a delightful blend of the world of yesterday and today. Guests pass through an elaborate carved façade and enchanting courtyard to reach this idyllic mansion, with its tall windows and elegant wrought-iron balconies. Peace and tranquility are first impressions. The interior is baronial, with oil paintings, tapestries and big leather armchairs, a blazing fire in winter, a chess set waiting and the foyer lit by old street lamps. The bedrooms and suites are quiet, with delightful fabric-covered walls and double glazing to absorb any noise from the square, although many overlook the colourful gardens at the back of the Pavillon. Antique and period furniture are in harmony with modern amenities. Place des Vosges is in the historic Marais district, just across the Seine from Notre Dame, not far from the Louvre and close to the Picasso and Carnavalet museums. **Directions:** Consult your street map. Drivers reaching central Paris will appreciate the private parking facilities at the hotel. Price guide: Ff1500–Ff1700; double/twin Ff1900–Ff2100; suites Ff2700–Ff3200.

FRANCE (Paris)

In association with MasterCard

Hôtel Relais Christine

3 RUE CHRISTINE, 75006 PARIS, FRANCE
TEL: 331 43 26 71 80 FAX: 331 43 26 89 38

This is one of the charming small hotels we all dream of finding, in a little street near Notre Dame, close to the Seine, in a 16th century cloister where an Abbey once stood. The entrance is enchanting, big wrought iron gates leading into a verdant, paved courtyard with balconies at the front of the hotel festooned with hanging plants. A secluded flower-filled garden at the back of the hotel is another delight. The bedrooms and suites are all air-conditioned and have handsome, traditional furniture. Beautiful materials have been used to create harmonious wall-coverings and curtains. The panelled salon is magnificent, with fine paintings and superb antiques. Breakfast is served in one of the older parts of the hotel, with stone walls, vaulted archways and pillars. In summer guests may prefer to eat alfresco in the garden. There is no restaurant, but there is a wide choice of exciting places to eat nearby. The elegant St Germain des Prés is close to Relais Christine, as are many other fascinating aspects of the Left Bank, including the Latin Quarter. Visitors should cross the Seine and watch the artists at work in Montmartre, visit the museums and monuments and shop in the exclusive Faubourg St. Honoré. **Directions:** This hotel, in a one way system off Place Dauphine, has private car parking. Price guide: Single Ff1630; suites Ff2450.

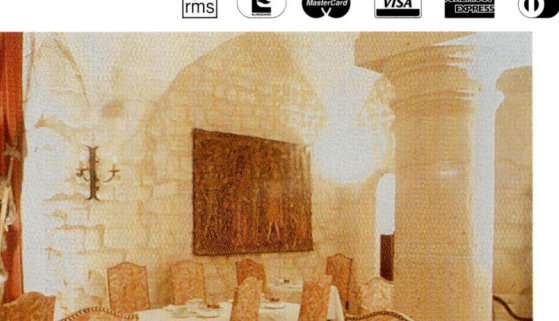

In association with MasterCard

FRANCE (Paris)

RELAIS ST GERMAIN
9 CARREFOUR DE L'ODÉON, 75006 PARIS, FRANCE
TEL: 331 43 29 12 05 FAX: 331 46 33 45 30

Le Relais Saint-Germain is an attractive small hotel in the heart of the Left Bank area, famous for its culture and association with the arts. Restoration has not detracted from the charm of this 17th century townhouse, where old and new have been carefully blended – warm tiled floors, handsome oil paintings and beautiful antiques unexpectedly harmonising easily with modern cupboards, mirrors and a fax machine. The character of this hotel is evident in that the bedrooms are named after famous French authors. They also have superb period furniture and enchanting chinz curtains and all still have their original beamed ceillings. They are peaceful and cool, being sound-proofed and air-conditioned. The bathrooms are luxurious, all in marble. A delicious breakfast is served and there is an efficient room service available. The hotel wine bar has an excellent selection of French wines. This lively part of Paris offers a choice of restaurants and cafés where they can mingle with artists, poets, musicians and the cognoscenti. They can enjoy Paris from a boat on the Seine, or cross the Pont Neuf to the Louvre and l'Opéra, the sophisticated boutiques and the Pompidou Centre. **Directions:** The hotel is just off Boulevard Saint Germain, close to Metro Odéon. Two public carparks are nearby. Price guide: Single Ff1260; double/twin Ff1500–Ff1650; suites Ff1900.

87

FRANCE (Paris)

In association with MasterCard

Royal Hôtel

33 AVENUE DE FRIEDLAND, 75008 PARIS, FRANCE
TEL: 331 43 59 08 14 FAX: 331 45 63 69 92

There has been a hotel on this site since 1905. It was purchased by Hôtels and Résidences du Roy in 1984. Extensive restoration in 1994 led to a grand re-opening in January 1995. The Royal Hôtel enjoys an excellent location so near the Arc de Triomphe and close to the delights of the Champs Elysées less than 100 metres away. The bedrooms are decorated with refinement, using quality fabrics and offer comforts expected by the modern traveller. All are air-conditioned and soundproofed, some designated non-smoking. The bathrooms, all in marble, are well appointed. A buffet breakfast is set in the morning to give a good start to the day. There is no restaurant but efficient room service provides good meals till late. Guests can sample the famous brasseries on the Champs Elysées and inviting restaurants in the side streets. A comfortable lounge has been added to the property with a delightful bar area, in which to relax after sightseeing or shopping. Choice will be difficult in the evening between the many shows and night clubs not far from the hotel. **Directions:** A car park with 500 spaces is located just beneath Avenue de Friedland with its own exit in front of the hotel. Métro and airport bus terminal two minutes away. Gare du Nord within easy reach for those coming on Eurostar. Price guide: Double/twin Ff1520–Ff1950. 30% discount offered to Johansens bookings.

In association with MasterCard

FRANCE (Paris)

SAINT JAMES - PARIS

43 AVENUE BUGEAUD, 75116 PARIS, FRANCE
TEL: 331 44 05 81 81 FAX: 331 44 05 81 82

This perfect château demonstrates the graceful proportions of 19th century architecture, and it has been transformed into an enchanting hotel in the very centre of Paris. It stands in a delightful walled garden and is approached by an impressive circular driveway. The suites and bedrooms are luxurious and so peaceful that guests forget they are in the heart of a major city. The art deco designs are most refreshing. The exclusivity of the hotel, originally the Saint James's Club, now privately owned by a French family, is evident in that only hotel residents and their guests have access to the traditional, panelled Library-Bar and Restaurant. The latter is famous for its brilliant cuisine and superb wines. The summer terrace provides opportunities for informal, occasionally alfresco meals and a magnificent venue for receptions, at which the hotel excels. The St James has a small gymnasium and leisure centre, but guests may prefer to exercise by strolling along the nearby Champs Élysées or in the Bois du Boulogne. Alternatives are wonderful art galleries, historic building and cruises down the Seine. **Directions:** The hotel is between Avenue Foch and Avenue Victor Hugo, close to the Arc de Triomphe. It has private parking. Price guide: Single Ff1500.

FRANCE (Paris)

In association with MasterCard

LES SUITES SAINT HONORÉ

13, RUE D'AGUESSEAU, 75008 PARIS, FRANCE
TEL: 331 44 51 16 35 FAX: 331 42 66 35 70

This extremely elegant establishment offers the best of both worlds – the privacy and freedom of an apartment while enjoying the full services of a hotel. It is perfectly situated, in the business area, yet only minutes away from the most prestigious shops and the Champs Elysées. The exterior is very graceful, with tall windows and elaborate wrought iron balconies. Once inside, there is a clever melange of old and new design creating a welcoming ambience for arrivals. The apartments all have living and dining rooms, fully equiped kitchens as well as one or two bedrooms, one or two bathrooms and some with studies and/or terraces. The apartments, which all have air conditioning, vary in size and can accomodate 1-5 people. All are beautifully decorated, with gorgeous fabrics and wonderful French period furniture. Crystal glasses, fine tableware. Businessmen can request facilities such as fax machines. There are impeccable staff awaiting residents' summons, whether to carry up delicious breakfasts or dinners. Theatre tickets can be arranged, plane tickets changed. A laundry service is available. Car parking is available for guests. **Directions:** The hotel will arrange a car/or limousine transfers on request. Price guide: Apartments from Ff2750 1/3 persons – Ff4620 1/5 persons.

In association with MasterCard

FRANCE (Port-en-Bessin)

LA CHENEVIÈRE

ESCURES-COMMES, 14520 PORT-EN-BESSIN, FRANCE
TEL: 33 31 21 47 96 FAX: 33 31 21 47 98 – SLH TOLL FREE: 0800 964470

A graceful Normandy château, with tall, shuttered windows, just 35km from the Port of Caen, La Chenevière is surrounded by extensive, well-manicured lawns where guests relax in the sun and mature trees provide shade in the heat of the day. The elegant salons, with polished floors, pale panelled walls and discreet lighting, are a perfect background for the period furniture. Looking across the gardens, the enchanting bedrooms have tranquil colour schemes with individual floral designs. The restaurant specialises in 'feasts of seafood' and regional dishes. The cellar is superb. Individual dining rooms are available for private entertaining. Many visitors enjoy La Chenevière Cookery Courses which extend from three to six days, and include visits to producers of Calvados and Camembert as well as the fish markets. A diploma and chef's hat are awarded on the final day! Sightseers visit the D-Day landing beaches, Bayeux tapestries and Mont St. Michael, or explore Deauville and Honfleur. More energetic guests play golf, tennis or squash or go to the many beaches. **Directions:** From Paris take the autoroute to Bayeux, drive eight kilometers on Départementale 6 towards Port-en-Bessin. The château is on the right, down a quiet lane. Price guide: Single Ff700; double/twin Ff700–Ff1100; suites Ff1300–Ff1500.

FRANCE (Roquebrune/Cap Martin)

In association with MasterCard

VISTA PALACE HOTEL
ROUTE DE LA GRANDE CORNICHE, F-06190 ROQUEBRUNE/CAP MARTIN, FRANCE
TEL: 33 92 10 40 00 FAX: 33 93 35 18 94

This ultra-modern hotel, having been built into the rocks high above Monaco, commands spectacular views of Monte Carlo, its harbour and Cap Martin. Exotic gardens and terraces are interspersed with blue swimming pools and colourful sunshades. Inside contemporary furnishings offer efficent, relaxed modern comfort. The well-equipped bedrooms all have sea views while four of the suites have private swimming pools. Most are in the main building, but a few are in the excellent conference complex which is interconnected to the hotel. The Presidential Suite is a true paradise, a quite superb penthouse high up in the sky! Breakfast and lunch are often taken on the terraces. At night guests enjoy cocktails in the spacious Lounge Icare which shares panoramic views of the lights of Monte Carlo and the waterfront with the fabulous Vistaero Restaurant and with La Corniche, famous for its Mediterranean specialities. The winelist is huge and includes a good selection of Provençal rosés. Historical tours of the Eze region can be arranged, while other visitors explore the town, or workout in the hotel's Fitness Centre. After dinner the Casino of Monte Carlo is the major attraction. **Directions:** Arrivals use the helipad or leave Motorway A8 at Exit 57 to Turbie, following signs to Roquebrune then the Vista Palace. Price guide: Single Ff1000–Ff2400; double/twin Ff1200–Ff2400; suites Ff1200–Ff5000.

In association with MasterCard

FRANCE (Saint-Émilion)

HÔTEL CHÂTEAU GRAND BARRAIL

ROUTE DE LIBOURNE, F-33330 SAINT-ÉMILION
TEL: 33 57 55 37 00 FAX: 33 57 55 37 49

A 19th century chateau, surrounded by the illustrious Château Figeac vineyard and recently transformed into a first-class hotel, providing superb accommodation both for those touring the St Émilion region and clients of the local winegrowers and businessmen. The graceful salons are handsomely furnished facing the landscaped lake and gardens. Collections of modern art hang in the Moresque Salon and Round Dining Room, renowned for their awesome stained glass windows. The capacious colour co-ordinated bedrooms and suites, many with balconies, are designed for modern life, with fax lines. The chef and sommelier work closely together so that diners, at the designated hour, assemble in the immaculate restaurant to appreciate the best regional dishes accompanied by appropriate fine local wines. Private wine-tastings can be arranged in the especially designed tasting room and tours to exclusive châteaux and vineyards. With this facility the château is an excellent venue for seminars and meetings. Guests relax on the sunny terrace or by the swimming pool. More energetic pastimes which can be arranged nearby include tennis, golf, riding, canoeing, cycling and hot-air ballooning. **Directions:** A10 from Paris to Bordeaux, exit St André de Cubzac. Bypass Libourne, then take the D243 towards St Émilion. Price guide: Single Ff750–Ff1400; double/twin Ff850–Ff1500; suites Ff1500–Ff2900.

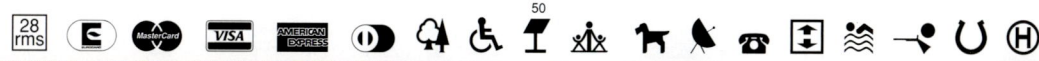

FRANCE (Saint-Paul-de-Vence)

In association with MasterCard

LE SAINT-PAUL

86 RUE GRANDE, 06570 SAINT-PAUL-DE-VENCE, FRANCE
TEL: 33 93 32 65 25 FAX: 33 93 32 52 94

Saint-Paul-de-Vence is a fascinating town protected by medieval battlements, and behind these walls, high up in the centre at the end of one of the many cobbled paths is this flawless 16th century townhouse, redolent of Provençal lavender. The ambience created by the hosts, is a sense of well-being. as guests absorb the beautiful antique and Provençal furniture, the colourful Souleïado fabrics, exquisite *objets d'art* and exciting paintings. The bedrooms are not large, but lovingly appointed with linen on the beds, sachets on the pillows, fresh water at the bedside and a bowl of fruit on arrival. One bedroom is designated nonsmoking. The bathrooms are small but well-designed with baths and hand-held showers. The suites are more spacious. In winter, dinner is served in the cellar restaurant with a vaulted ceiling, exposed beams and delightful murals, and in summer, enjoyed on the enchanting private terrace. The menus are a feast of Provençal specialities, accompanied by wines from Cassis, Bandol and Aix. The region has so much to offer – museums, art galleries, glass-blowing, the perfumeries at Grasse, the Côte d'Azur with its beaches, and excellent golf at Valbonne. **Directions:** A8 exit for Cagnes-sur-Mer, towards Vence then La Colle-sur-Loup. Publis parking is available 200m from the hotel. Price guide: Single Ff700–Ff1400; double/twin Ff700–Ff1400; suites Ff1250–Ff2100.

In association with MasterCard

FRANCE (St Paul)

MAS d'ARTIGNY
ROUTE DE LA COLLE, 06570 SAINT-PAUL, FRANCE
TEL: 33 93 32 84 54 FAX: 33 93 32 95 36

A unique hotel set in the hills high above Antibes with uninterrupted views of the Côte d'Azur, has 25 individual swimming pools and superb conference facilities. The striking white marble entrance immediately alerts arrivals that their stay at Mas d'Artigny will be memorable. The interior is sophisticated, spacious and uncluttered, with wide archways and graceful furniture, while the magnificent pool is the central focus point. The accommodation offered is superb, the bedrooms, all with luxurious bathrooms, have their own balconies, while the apartments lead onto private patios with their own pool. Additionally there are three villas, ideal for families, with their own pools and gardens. Six meeting rooms have state-of-the-art conference equipment. The fabulous dining room extends onto the Terrace, with a glorious outlook right across to the coastline. Guests linger here while studying the delicious regional and classical dishes that have won a Michelin star. Wines are from the reasonable to the sublime. Mas d'Artigny has its own golf practice ground and tennis courts and the beaches are not far away. **Directions:** Leave A8 at Cagnes-sur-Mer exit taking Route de Grasse, turning left after La Colle sur Loup, before reaching St-Paul-de-Vence on the right. There is a helipad. Price guide: Single Ff460–Ff1650; double/twin Ff635–Ff1830; suites Ff1585–Ff2680.

FRANCE (St-Rémy-de-Provence)

In association with MasterCard

Château Des Alpilles

ROUTE DÉPARTEMENTALE 31, ANCIENNE ROUTE DU GRÈS, 13210 ST-RÉMY-DE-PROVENCE, FRANCE
TEL: 33 90 92 03 33 FAX: 33 90 92 45 17

This very elegant 19th century château, just a short distance from St. Rémy, is wonderfully secluded. Rare old trees provide avenues, shade and add a touch of the exotic to the verdant surroundings. There are two other buildings, the original Mas, now known as 'la ferme', rebuilt to provide modern suites and apartments, and the original 'Chapelle', now available to guests as a lovely private villa. The salons in the château reflect its age-old grandeur, with moulded ceilings, mosaic floors, tapestries on the walls, enormous gilded mirrors, antique furniture and rich festooned curtains. Some of the bedrooms repeat this splendour, others are more contemporary with pretty Provençal fabrics. Some are air-conditioned. Rooms equipped for seminars are also available. Guests mingle in the intimate bar, and those not dining out can enjoy simple regional dishes in the dining area adjoining the reception lounge. Exploring the country side on foot or on the hotel bicycles is a popular pasttime, going down the Old Road to Les Baux. Others stay close to the Château, lazing in the cool gardens, playing tennis or sunbathing by the swimming pool. **Directions:** Leave St. Rémy on the D31 towards Tarascon. Price guide: Single Ff860; double/twin FF860–Ff1080; suites Ff1290–Ff1660.

In association with MasterCard

FRANCE (St Rémy)

DOMAINE DE VALMOURIANE

PETITE ROUTE DES BAUX, 13210 SAINT RÉMY DE PROVENCE, FRANCE
TEL: 33 90 92 44 62 FAX: 33 90 92 37 32

This delightful farmhouse in the hills known as La Chaîne des Alpilles, built in the attractive stone familiar to this area, is now an intimate and luxurious family-run hotel, which stands in flower filled grounds with a background of vineyards and olive trees, the air redolent of lavender and herbs. The salon is elegant, cool and comfortable and the spacious bedrooms are charming, decorated in traditional Provençal fabrics. The attractive terrace is where guests often gather for apéritifs before dinner and light informal meals are served. Memories of dining in the handsome restaurant will linger for a long time – the exquisite interpretation of regional dishes, fish from the Mediterranean, salads dressed in interesting oils, lamb cooked with herbs from the garden, gorgeous puddings and fine French wines, including local roses. Guests enjoy the swimming pool with its Jacuzzi or tennis on the hotel courts and strolling in the park, visiting local markets and antique shops, exploring the countryside, tasting wine, going to see Nimes or Avignon, or playing golf close by. At night a gentle game of billiards is very pleasant. **Directions:** Leave the A7 at Avignon South exit, taking D571. At the centre of Saint-Rémy-de-Provence, take the D99 towards Tarascon then the D27 signed Les Baux de Provence. Price guide: Double/twin Ff590–Ff1140; suite Ff1160–Ff1550.

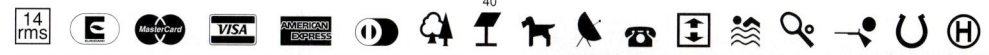

97

FRANCE (Saint Rémy-de-Provence)

Hostellerie Du Vallon De Valrugues
CHEMIN CANTO CIGALO, 13210 SAINT-RÉMY-DE-PROVENCE, FRANCE
TEL: 33 90 92 04 40 FAX: 33 90 92 44 01

A unique modern day Roman villa surrounded by the wonderful scented trees, shrubs and herbs of Provence, cicadas chirping in the background, is the setting for this prestigious hotel. The reception hall is in marble, immaculate staff wait to greet arrivals or assist guests with plans for the day. There is a very grand suite with its own swimming pool, 18 apartments with Jacuzzis and 31 bedrooms. All have been beautifully decorated and well equipped with luxurious bathrooms. Most have balconies or terraces overlooking the main pool or across the cousntryside. The cool salons are superb, spacious, in restful colours, with elegant furniture and delightful murals. Guests rendezvous in the smart, roomy bar for apéritifs while deciding whether to eat delicious Provençal dishes alfresco under the mulberry tree by the pool or adjourn to the handsome, light and airy restaurant to enjoy a gastronomic meal accompanied by their choice from 630 interesting wines, many of them from local vineyards. Delegates from the state-of-the-art conference room relax over 'billiard' or use the tennis courts. Golf is ten minutes away. Cruises on the Rhône, exploring Provence from a hot-air balloon and safaris in the Camargue can be arranged.
Directions: Saint-Rémy-de-Provence is signed from the autoroutes at Nimes and Cavaillon. Price guide: Single/double/twin Ff764–Ff1146; suites Ff1605–Ff4011.

Enjoy Europe in the most individual ways

Just like the independent and lovely hotels represented in this guide, Romantik Hotels & Restaurants International are a collection of unique individual experiences!

180 Romantik Hotels in 17 countries (including the US, Canada and The Caribbean) have distinct characteristics:

– All our hotels are historic
– They are privately owned and managed by their owners who provide gracious and personal service
– Excellent cuisine is a trademark. Many have Michelin stars or are renowned regionally for first-class dining 

We are waiting to welcome you and give you a wonderful experience of old world hospitality with today's comforts.

Pick up your FREE copy of the Romantik Guide '96 in any Romantik Hotel or order it by fax (please reference Johansens): +49 6188 6007

ROMANTIK HOTELS & RESTAURANTS INTERNATIONAL

Romantik Hotels & Restaurants International
Postfach 11 44, D-63786 Karlstein a Main, Germany

GERMANY

Germany, the homeland of Bach, Beethoven and Brahms is a country of diverse and contrasting landscapes and cultures, dialects and politics.

Northwest Germany includes the two great Hanseatic seaports of Hamburg and Bremen, as well as the whole of the Land of Schleswig-Holstein and nearly all Lower Saxony. The area lacks the scenic wonders of the south, but it has its own quiet beauties, such as the Luneburg Heath, and many historic and picturesque towns with buildings of mellow red brick, half timbers and stepped gables.

The westernmost part of Germany focuses on the mighty Rhine and its tributaries, some of them scenic rivers in their own right – the Mosel, the Lahn and Ahr – while others – the Saar and above all the Ruhr – have given their names to great industrial conurbations. The region's vineyards are the world's northernmost, with delightful wine-villages and cheerful cellars and taverns. Life is taken less seriously here than in other parts of Germany, particularly in the Catholic cities of Cologne and Mainz, where exuberance knows no bounds during the carnival period before Lent. This was the most Romanised part of Germany, with the Rhine forming the frontier of the Empire for centuries.

Then there is central Germany – which the Germans tend to keep to themselves. Only a handful of towns, such as Hamelin, with its Pied Piper fable and spectacular Weser Renaissance houses, are on the international tourist circuit. Although it has none of the drama of the Alps, it can be rewarding making your own discoveries in the numerous attractive small towns and rolling, forested uplands. Hesse, traversed by the River Main and with Frankfurt as its chief city, was founded by the Americans as an administrative centre after World War II, and it is very much the commercial centre of Germany.

Eastern Germany has great cultural and historical importance, reflected in many cities, castles and historic houses which have survived. The painter Albrecht Dürer and composers Bach and Handel were all born here. Modern literature had its beginnings in Wartburg Castle at Eisenach, where Martin Luther translated the Bible into German. And later in Weimar, Germany had a literary centre of world-wide importance, as home of Goethe, Schiller and Herder, then in the next century it was the one time capital of the ill fated republic that bore its name.

Northern Bavaria boasts some of the most fascinating historical cities, including Nürnberg, Regensburg and stretches of unspoiled countryside. The world famous Romantic Road or Romantische Strasse links medieval towns, while backwaters of the Bavarian Forest are reached from the Bayerische Ostmarkstrasse. National Parks offer unparalleled opportunities for exploring on foot by bike or by canoe along the rivers. Rural scenery ranges from the romantic Altmuhl valley to the mysterious depths of Europe' last remaining fragments of virgin forest in the Bayerischer Wald. The food of this region is particularly good. Try the spicy sausages from Nürnberg, complemented by famous beers – the world's oldest brewery is at Freising – or wines from Franconia, rivalling those of the Rhine and Mosel.

Southern Bavaria - with the notable exception of liberal Munich – is staunchly conservative, both politically and in outlook. You will see men wearing Bavarian hats and Lederhosen (leather trousers) and women with Dirndl (embroidered dresses); festivals are celebrated with great gusto, particularly May Day, when huge maypoles are erected and decorated. The tradition of painting murals on house exteriors is widespread. Food is hearty and traditional – quantities of pork, dumplings, potatoes and sauerkraut are de rigueur in country areas. The region is strongly Catholic and Gruss Gott (God's greeting) is the standard greeting and churches have a prosperous look. Much of the region is accessible within a day trip from Munich, but beware of crowds and traffic jams at peak times in the main sights and resorts.

The easy going cosmopolitan Bavarian capital of Munich lies on a fertile plain that extends southwards towards the snowy peaks of the Alps, Germany's highest and most dramatic mountains. In between are neat, clustered villages, pine forests, sparkling lakes and gently rolling pastures.

And then there is Berlin.

Since the Berlin Wall began to crumble on that night in November 1989, the city's two halves have slowly and painfully attempted to fuse. Berlin is now as fascinating for a visitor as it ever was in the midst of the Cold War. The minor thrill of crossing Checkpoint Charlie (and doubting if you would ever return has vanished), and you can now drive unhindered across the Glienicke Bridge where once only spies set foot, but Berlin remains a compelling city. As it struggles to regain its former status as the capital of a reunited Germany, Berlin is perhaps a litmus test for relations between East and West. Berlin has always been a place on the fringe, bursting with avant-garde ideas and sometimes subversive culture. Its reputation for decadence, even vice, is not unfounded – mostly a legacy from the Weimar years of the 1920s. It's a city of youth, and a cosmopolitan one.

And as for food and alcohol. Well, it's hard to generalise about German food – although standards are high and portions are large. Beer restaurants in Bavaria, Apfelwein taverns in Frankfurt, and Kneipen – the pubs on the corner in Berlin – nearly always offer best value and atmosphere. But throughout the country you'll find Gaststatten – local inns – where a welcome atmosphere and regional specialities are always available.

Germany is also a major wine producing country, and most restaurants will produce a good quality Moselle served in an earthenware pitcher as their house wine. If you want something more expensive – all wines are graded in one of three basic categories – Tafelwein (table wine), Qualitälswein (fine wines) and Qualitätswein mit Prädikat (top quality wines).

GERMANY
117
Flensburg
102
Kiel
Bergen
Stralsund
Cuxhaven
Neumünster
Rostock
Bremerhaven
Lübeck
Neubran-
denburg
Wilhelms-
haven
Hamburg
111
A27
A24
Schwerin
A28
Oldenburg
Lüneburg
Prenzlau
Bremen
A7
A1
Verden
Lingen
A27
Berlin
107
108
Stendal
Osnabrück
Braunschweig
A30
A30
Hannover
Brandenburg
104
A2
Münster
Magdeburg
Bielfeld
Cottbus
A7
A1
Dessau
Essen
112
Dortmund
Göttingen
A44
Leipzig
Düsseldorf
Kassel
Halle
Dresden
Köln
109
Aachen
A5
Chemnitz
Bonn
Erfurt
Giessen
Suhl
A3
Zwickau
Fulda
115
Koblenz
116
Frankfurt
113
Hof
Wiesbaden
Bamberg
Würzburg
Trier
Weiden
Darmstadt
114
Ludwigshaven
Heidelberg
Nürnburg
Saarbrücken
A5
A93
Landau
Karlsruhe
A6
Ansbach
Regensburg
103
A8
Stuttgart
A3
105
Baden
-Baden
Ingolstadt
A92
106
Heidenheim
Passau
A9
A5
A8
Ulm
Augsburg
München
Freiburg
Schwenningen
A7
Rosenheim
A81
A95
A8
Kempten
Lörrach
Ravensburg
Garmisch
110

GERMANY (Alt Duvenstedt, near Rendsburg)

HOTEL TÖPFERHAUS

AM BISTENSEE, D-24791 ALT DUVENSTEDT, GERMANY
TEL: 49 43 38 333 FAX: 49 43 38 551

The Hotel Töpferhaus is a charming country hotel close to Alt Duvenstedt in the heart of Schleswig Holstein. It is in a lovely verdant setting, overlooking the beautiful Bistensee in the Hüttener Berge National Park. The hotel was purpose-built this century, and it is very light and spacious, the Reception area leading into a cool tiled hall with elegant pine chairs and contemporary sofas. The bedrooms are charming, with comfortable modern furniture. Many have balconies, and not all are in the main building, some being in the attractive Landhaus. The rustic restaurant is enchanting, and has spectacular views over the lake. The menu contains traditional and regional dishes, all beautifully presented at candle-lit tables. Pike perch is the speciality of the house! Good wines are listed. There are also excellent facilities for meetings or private functions, regularly reserved for the Prime Minister of Schleswig Holstein. Relaxing in the gardens is a favourite pastime with guests. Alternatives are the sauna, solarium, tennis, swimming in the lake or exploring the neighbourhood on the hotel bicycles. Five golf courses are nearby.
Directions: From the South leave A1 at Rendsburg/Büdelsdorf exit, B203 towards R1 Eckernforde, after 2km turn left and watch for signs to the hotel. Price guide: Single 100Dm–185Dm; double/twin 195Dm–295Dm; suites 325Dm.

In association with MasterCard

GERMANY (Bad Herrenalb)

MÖNCHS POSTHOTEL

D-76328 BAD HERRENALB, GERMANY
TEL: 49 70 83 74 40 FAX: 49 70 83 74 41 22

Bad Herrenalb is an attractive small town in the Black Forest, and the Posthotel, with its traditional half-timbered façade enlivened by green and white shutters, has extensive shady parkland at the back, much appreciated by guests in hot weather. The interior is beautifully decorated in harmony with the wooden beams that remain from the original building, flowers and plants in every corner, fine paintings and lovely antiques completing the picture. The bedrooms and suites have delightful colour schemes, comfortable furniture and opulent bathrooms. The intimate piano bar is an elegant meeting place. The two restaurants are very different – the sophisticated Klosterschänke has fine panelled walls, a reputation for superb cooking and an extensive selection of Bordeaux and Italian wines. The Locanda specialises in Mediterranean dishes, including a variety of pastas. A smart meeting room, with full presentation equipment, is available for seminars. Guests enjoy strolling in the park and relaxing by the heated swimming pool. They can play tennis and golf, walk in the Black Forest and ski in winter. Baden Baden, half an hour away, is full of history. **Directions:** On the A5 from Basel exit at Rastatt, following signs to Gernsbach or from Frankfurt exit for Bad Herrenalb. Price guide: Single 195Dm–220Dm; double/twin 280Dm–350Dm; suites 490Dm–520Dm.

GERMANY (Bad Salzuflen)

HOTEL ARMINIUS

RITTERSTRASSE 2-8, D-32105 BAD SALZUFLEN, GERMANY
TEL: 49 52 22 53 070 FAX: 49 52 22 53 07 99

Hotel Arminius, in the spa town of Bad Salzuflen, is a restored townhouse dating back to the 15th century. It is in the heart of this small town where many of the buildings are clad in the intricate diagonal designs unique to this region. Old stone walls, shutters and beams are also much in evidence in the cobbled streets. Inside the hotel, however, time has not stood still and the bedrooms and suites are spacious and light, with elegant contemporary pine furniture. Because the Arminius is a conference hotel, there are some single rooms. The Wintergarden is a delightful room for informal meals. Dinner in the restaurant, with the original stone walls, is splendid, including regional specialities. The wine list is international. There are non smoking rooms designated. The hotel has a leisure centre which is appreciated by delegates making use of the excellent meeting rooms, with full presentation equipment available. Large private dinners and receptions can also be arranged. While benefiting from the thermal baths and the local 'waters' is a reason to visit Bad Salzuflen, it is also known for its culture, music and theatre, historical buildings and beautiful countryside. **Directions:** Leave the A2 at Herford, following signs for Bad Salzuflen. Car parking is available at the hotel. Price guide: Single 140Dm; double/twin 160Dm–200Dm; suites 300Dm.

GERMANY (Baden Baden)

DER KLEINE PRINZ
LICHTENTALERSTRASSE 36, D-76530 BADEN BADEN, GERMANY
TEL: 49 72 21 34 64 FAX: 49 72 21 38 264

This exclusive hotel's charming logo, a little fairytale prince against a background of stars and planets, is an indication that Der Kleine Prinz is a magical place to stay – a delightful 19th century town-house in the centre of Baden Baden. The graceful entrance, which is on Du Russell Strasse, leads guests into the welcoming Lobby Bar, a delightful rendezvous at anytime of the day. The charming bedrooms have special features, some with a balcony, others with a fireplace, the English room is decorated by Laura Ashley, Americans can sleep under a collage of Manhattan skyscrapers, while the Tower Room has its own well equipped babyroom. The Penthouse Suite has a glass roof which can be opened in fine weather. The dining room is enchanting with elegant furnishings and murals from Saint Exupery's famous book, The Little Prince. The à la carte and two table d'hôte menus, one with a gourmet selection, list delicious cosmopolitan dishes. Wines are French and German. Baden-Baden is a famous spa. Golf, swimming and tennis are within walking distance. The countryside offers ski-ing in winter and walks in summer. Concerts, theatre and the casino occupy the evenings. **Directions:** Lichtentalerstrasse is the main street, reached from the Autobahn A5 and the Michaelstunnel. Price guide: Single Dm275; double/twin Dm375; suites Dm495.

GERMANY (Baden Baden)

In association with MasterCard

SCHLOSSHOTEL BÜHLERHÖHE
SCHWARZWALDHOCHSTRASSE 1, D-77815 BÜHL/BADEN BADEN, GERMANY
TEL: 49 72 26 55-0 FAX: 49 72 26 55 777

The impressive Schlosshotel in the Northern Black Forest some 800m above and 15km away from Baden-Baden, was built in 1911, a baroque castle in its own enormous park. The entrance to the hotel is splendid and the drawing rooms lead onto terraces with spectacular views across the Rhine Valley. Archways, mosaic marble floors and tall windows combine to give a feeling of peace and space. The bedrooms are luxurious, the bathrooms opulent. The bar has panelled walls, while the Imperial Restaurant boasts fantastic murals. This gourmet restaurant is proud of its wine list. The Schlossrestaurant, with stunning views over the Black Forest, specialises in regional dishes. The outstanding conference complex, with several meeting rooms, has state-of-the-art presentation equipment and its own restaurant. The health and leisure centre has an exotic swimming pool, and a large cool beauty salon with a health-food bar and private treatment rooms. Active guests can enjoy the tennis courts and jogging trail, ski in winter and play golf on the nearby course. Others visit Baden-Baden, famous for its spas, casino and race course. **Directions:** There is a helicopter service from Baden-Baden. Autobahn A5 exit Buhl, or B500 from Baden-Baden (direction Schwarzwaldhochstrasse). Price guide: Single 300Dm–450Dm; double/twin 510Dm–690Dm; Alcove suites 750Dm–990Dm; suites 1150Dm–2500Dm.

GERMANY (Berlin)

HOTEL BRANDENBURGER HOF

EISLEBENER STRASSE 14, D-10789 BERLIN, GERMANY
TEL: 49 30 214050 FAX: 49 30 21405 100

This imposing hotel is in the very centre of Berlin, close to the famous Tiergarten Park and the Kurfürstendamm, an imaginative transformation of a 1900's mansion into a state-of-the art hotel, meeting the demands of the modern traveller. Many natural materials have been used to create the sophisicated interior achieved by master craftsmen – stone pillars, the pure lines of contemporary design, discreet colour schemes and light from the enormous windows surrounding the verdant courtyard that is the heart of the Brandenburger Hof. The fabulous conservatory, filled with plants and overlooking the Japanese garden, where guests can breakfast or relax over afternoon tea, is a favourite place in the hotel, it occasionally houses an art exhibition or concert. In the evening the Piano Bar provides background music for those enjoying cocktails while studying the gourmet dishes featured in the restaurant's menu. The fine wines listed are from Germany, France and Italy. The bedrooms, many with a small traditional balcony outside, reflect modern luxury. Berlin has a wonderful Zoo, beautiful parks, fascinating buildings and marvellous shopping. It is famous for its nightlife. **Directions:** Leave the Berlin Ring (A110) at exit Wilmersdorf; exit Kurfürstendamm then drive 4km along Kurfürstendamm, turn right at the Gedächtniskirche. Price guide: Single 275Dm–395Dm; double/twin 330Dm–445Dm.

GERMANY (Berlin)

In association with MasterCard

KEMPINSKI HOTEL BRISTOL

KURFÜRSTENDAMM 27, D-10719 BERLIN, GERMANY
TEL: 49 30 8 84 340   FAX: 49 30 8 83 60 75

A brilliant 20th century hotel on the main boulevard in Berlin, ideal for visitors attending conferences and exhibitions at the nearby Trade Fair Centre. The lobby is stunning, with marble floors and a great feeling of space. Multi-lingual, immaculate staff attend to guests' needs round the clock. Relaxing in the comfortable lounges is pleasant before meeting colleagues in the excitingly designed cocktail bar. The bedrooms have been carefully furnished and equipped to meet the exacting demands of today's business traveller. One floor is designated non-smoking. There is a choice of places to eat, the traditional Kempinski Eck offering regional specialities and the elegant Kempinski Restaurant with an international menu. The hotel has a fine cellar with wines from all round the world. Private dining rooms abound, from small salons to ballrooms seating 400 people. Conferences and seminars can be arranged. The leisure centre is excellent, with a pool, sauna, solarium and massage room. The concierge arranges golf and tennis, makes theatre reservations or recommends appropriate nightclubs. **Directions:** The hotel is 20 minutes from the airport, near the Zoo Railway station. From the Ring road (A110), the Wilmersdorf exit leads to the Kurfürstendamm. Price guide: Single 340Dm–480Dm; double/twin 390Dm–530Dm; suites 850Dm–4740Dm.

In association with MasterCard

GERMANY (Dresden)

BÜLOW RESIDENZ

RÄHNITZGASSE 19, 01097 DRESDEN, GERMANY
TEL: 49 35 14 40 33 FAX: 49 35 14 40 34 10

A magnificent baroque Saxon mansion, dating back to 1730, the Bülow Residenz has successfully brought together all the gracious attributes of its history and the luxury of today's prestigious hotel. The façade is a welcoming golden yellow and there is an enchanting inner courtyard, cool and green, where guests can relax over a long drink. The glamorous bedrooms have tall windows, hand crafted furniture and lavish bathrooms. The fourth floor is designated non-smoking. Once the coal cellar, the attractive vaulted Caroussel Bar is the perfect place to enjoy a cocktail at the end of the day before adjourning to the elegant Caroussel Restaurant with its team of talented chefs preparing modern interpretations of delicacies from Swabia (a duchy in South West Germany) and classical gourmet meals. Many fine châteaux are included in the extensive wine list. Guests enjoy exploring Dresden, which has a wonderful cathedral and museums dedicated to the famous fine china. There is an excellent theatre and opera house. Alternatively take a boat trip along the Elbe. **Directions:** The railway station and airport are both nearby. By car, cross the Elbe by the Augustbrücke and Rähnitzgasse is reached turning left from the Hauptstrasse. The hotel has a car park. Price guide: Single 290Dm; double/twin 340Dm–390Dm; suites 420Dm.

GERMANY

In association with MasterCard

POSTHOTEL GARMISCH PARTENKIRCHEN

LUDWIGSTRASSE 49, 82467 GARMISCH PARTENKIRCHEN, GERMANY
TEL: 49 88 21 51 067 FAX: 49 88 21 78 568

This is a truly romantic hotel in the famous mountain resort of Garmisch Partenkirchen. It is typically Bavarian, with colourful window boxes and elaborate wrought ironwork. A warm ambience prevails throughout, starting in the baroque reception area with its carved vaulted ceiling, tiled floors and lovely antiques. The bedrooms are enchanting, with crisp white linen, panelled walls and pretty painted furniture, those at the back having balconies looking across to the mountains. Guests have a wide choice when it comes to eating and drinking. The long Post-Taverna is popular with residents and the townspeople enjoying the small Italian dishes and assorted wine directly from the vineyard Informal meals, including many local specialities, are served in the rustic dining room or in the café. The restaurant is prestigious, having won the coveted Chaines des Rotisseurs for its inspired French cuisine. The hotel cellar is immense. Private dinners can be held in the handsome meeting room. The hotel faces the fascinating Ludwigstrasse and historic town centre. Winter-sports are the main activity when the snows come, with climbing and hiking as summer recreations. Fishing and golf are nearby. **Directions:** Take the A95 from Munich, watching for signs for Garmisch–Partenkirchen and then to Partenkirchen. The hotel has a car-park. Price guide: Single 100Dm–145Dm; double/twin 200Dm–250Dm; suites 270Dm–320Dm.

In association with MasterCard

GERMANY (Hamburg)

Kempinski Hotel Atlantic Hamburg
AN DER ALSTER 72-79, D-20099 HAMBURG, GERMANY
TEL: 49 40 28 880 FAX: 49 40 24 71 29

This grand hotel, beside the Alster, was built in 1909 to accommodate guests from the luxury liners arriving in Hamburg in the style to which they had become accustomed on board ship. Today, following discreet modernisation, it has the same immaculate standards. Multi-lingual staff await guests in the spectacular lobby with its sweeping staircase and marble pillars. This is an ideal meeting-point, with its own buffet serving refreshments and the convivial Atrium Bar close by. The bedrooms and suites are delightful, many overlooking the water. All are hospitably furnished and the bathrooms are lavishly equipped. Guests who enjoy regional dishes and draught beer appreciate the informal 'Mühle', with its rustic furniture while others prefer the regal Atlantic-Restaurant with its haute-cuisine menu and fine wine list. The Grand Ballroom is magnificent for functions and there are salons for meetings or private entertaining. Active visitors use the pool or jog round the Alster. The concierge will arrange golf, tennis or sailing on the lake. Shopping, boat trips and art galleries fill the day; later there is the theatre and opera or the famous Hamburg night-life. **Directions:** Parking: Hotel garage for 75 cars. Connections: Main railway station app 3 min with taxi, 5 min walk. Airport Fuhlsbüttel app 20 min with taxi Price guide: Single 370–440Dm; double/twin 420–490Dm; suites 700–1700Dm.

GERMANY (Kettwig)

SCHLOSSHOTEL HUGENPOET
AUGUST-THYSSEN-STRASSE 51, 45219 ESSEN-KETTWIG, GERMANY
TEL: 49 20 54 12 040 FAX: 49 20 54 12 04 50

This enchanting Renaissance castle close to the banks of the Ruhr, although halfway between Essen and Düsseldorf, is very secluded, being surrounded by moats, a bridge and extensive parkland. The regal reception area has a black and white marble floor, pillars and alcoves and a superb carved chimney piece. The salons are extremely elegant, filled with lovely antiques and works of art standing against beautiful traditional wall-hangings and curtains. The ceremonial halls are stately settings for special functions. The bedrooms are exquisite, some with ornate 16th century furniture, others reflecting later eras. The bathrooms are 20th century. The restaurant is vibrant, with golden walls and red and gold upholstery, a colour scheme echoed in the delightful private dining room. The sophisticated menu has a strong French influence. Lighter meals are served in the attractive terrace room. The wine list is enormous and includes exceptional dry white wines from the Rhine and Mosel regions. Musical evenings are held in spring and autumn. The area is known as 'Little Paris' because there are so many shops and sources of entertainment. There is tennis in the hotel grounds, but golf is five km away. **Directions:** At the Breitscheid interchange (A3/A52) take the Ratingen–Breitscheid exit to Mülheim and head for E-Kettwig. Price guide: Single 265Dm–355Dm; double/twin 295Dm–470Dm; suites 750Dm.

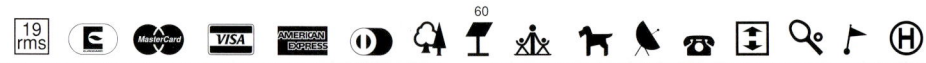

In association with MasterCard

GERMANY (Oberwesel/Rhein)

BURGHOTEL AUF SCHÖNBERG
D-55430 OBERWESEL/RHEIN, GERMANY
TEL: 49 67 44 93 930 FAX: 49 67 44 16 13

High up on the Schönburg, a hill overlooking the Rhine, close to where the Lorelei used to lure sailors onto the rocks, there is a romantic castle, built in the 10th century. Behind its ramparts and towers is an intimate and élite hotel. Many of the original features, the stone walls and pillars, archways and old beams have been carefully restored so that history and luxurious comfort are both in evidence. Outside, vineyards slope down to the river and ivy clings to the castle walls. The bedrooms are enchanting with fairytale drapery over the beds, lovely traditional furniture, and big bowls of fruit and flowers. The bathrooms are modern and quite opulent. In the evenings guests gather for a Bellini in the magnificent salon with stone walls, a handsome fireplace, crossed swords and shelves of leatherbound books before dining on specialities of the Middle Rhine Valley or indulging themselves with the gourmet menu. Dinner is served either in the knights' Dining Room or on the Rhine terrace with its spectacular view of the river. Prestigious wines are listed. This is a marvellous base for exploring this part of Germany. **Directions:** Take the Oberwesel exit off the A61. Once in the town take a right turn at the Schönberg sign and then follow hotel signs up the hill. Price guide: Single 105Dm–120Dm; double/twin 230Dm–310Dm; suites 340Dm–360Dm.

113

GERMANY (Pegnitz)

In association with MasterCard

PFLAUMS POSTHOTEL PEGNITZ
NÜRNBERGERSTRASSE 12-16, 91257 PEGNITZ, FRANKISCHE SCHWEIZ, GERMANY
TEL: 49 92 41 72 50 FAX: 49 92 41 80 404

Guests entering this lovely old posthouse may feel they have reached the millenium as the interior styles stretch from the 18th century through to today and beyond. Missoni is among the many famous contemporary designers who have played a part in this fascinating decor. The same family have owned the Posthaus for 11 generations and Napoleon left in 1804 without paying his bill! Now the celebrities coming to the hotel are from the music festivals in Bayreuth. All 25 bedrooms and 25 suites are different some traditional in the Bidermeier-style wing, others ultra-modern, such as the exciting 'Venus in Blue' suites with bathrooms from outer space! The reception rooms are elegant, possibly eccentric, and breakfast is theatrical, the sumptuous buffet prepared on five round tables. By contrast the bar is franconian. In the elegant panelled restaurant pipe and cigar smoking is forbidden. With a Michelin star, the menu is for gourmets, the wine for connoisseurs. Leisure facilities include a small indoor golf range, a 27 hole course, polo, fly fishing, a foaming swimming pool and high-tec gymnasium. Wonderful treatments take place in the healthclub. **Directions:** From Berlin, A9, exit Pegnitz, from Frankfurt A3, exit Hochstadt-Ost. Price guide: Single 140Dm–390Dm; double/twin 250Dm–845Dm; suites 450Dm–1800Dm.

GERMANY (Plauen)

HOTEL ALEXANDRA

BAHNHOFSTRASSE 17, 08523 PLAUEN, GERMANY
TEL: 49 37 41 22 14 14 FAX: 49 37 41 22 67 47

This hotel in the former East Germany contrasts with the opulent establishments on the Western side of the country. The building, a 19th century town-house, has been carefully renovated. Comfortable furniture, highly polished floors and vases of fresh flowers together create a pleasant, relaxing ambience in the hotel lobby and lounges. The bedrooms are equipped to match the criteria of modern travellers. Some are designated non-smoking, others are for those with mobility problems. Chefs prepare delicious traditional dishes which are served in the spacious restaurant, lit by crystal chandeliers and standard lamps. The wines listed are mostly French and German. The bar is convivial, and the adjacent informal café is delightful. The Alexandra also has two excellent conference rooms, with smart furnishings and full presentation equipment. There is a small leisure centre, a unique feature of which is a waterfall shower from cleverly simulated rocks. Golf is 18km distant, but tennis, fishing and riding are nearer. Plauen is an interesting city to explore, with its colourful historic buildings, fine ornamental clocks, and its museum showing early wool weavers' looms. The park is lovely and in the evenings there is the theatre and dancing. **Directions:** Plauen is signed from the A72, Dresden to Berlin – A9 Munich to Berlin. Price guide: Single 115Dm–140Dm; double/twin 150Dm–200Dm; suites 220Dm–360Dm.

GERMANY (Schlangenbad)

In association with MasterCard

PARKHOTEL SCHLANGENBAD
RHEINGAUER STRASSE 47, D-65388 SCHLANGENBAD, GERMANY
TEL: 49 61 29 420 FAX: 49 61 29 41 420

Schlangenbad is a village on the outskirts of the Rhine-Taunus Nature Park, and the Park Hotel stands in lovely, peaceful countryside. It is a haven for many guests needing revitalisation, and ideal for conferences. The entrance is spacious and impressive, with archways and marble columns. The elegant salon has a long white terrace and below is a large courtyard for alfresco living. The bedrooms are delightful, the curtains and covers in beautiful materials and many lead onto a balcony. In the sophisticated piano bar wonderful cocktails will be concocted by the barman, non-alchoholic drinks for those guests who prefer them. Menus in the glittering Les Therms restaurant are hedonistic yet health-conscious. Many German wines are listed and occasionally a wine seminar is held, followed by a feast. Conference facilities are magnificent, with a big theatre for presentation. State-of-the-art equipment is available in all rooms in this complex. The hotel has a big pool, a gymnasium where exercise classes are organised and a beauty salon. The energetic ride mountain bikes or follow the jogging trail. Golf, tennis, horse riding and shooting are other sports in the neighbourhood.
Directions: The B260 from Martinsthal leads to Schlangenbad.
Price guide: Single Dm170–Dm205; double/twin Dm250–Dm320; suites Dm340–Dm500.

116

In association with MasterCard

GERMANY (Westerland/Sylt)

Hotel Stadt Hamburg

STRANDSTRASSE 2, D-25980 WESTERLAND/SYLT, GERMANY
TEL: 49 46 51 85 80 FAX: 49 46 51 85 82 20

The gleaming white Hotel Stadt Hamburg, in the seaside resort of Westerland on the island of Sylt, has been cared for by the same family for three generations. It is a peaceful and elegant Shangri-la, richly decorated to complement its 19th century architecture. The crimson lounge, with its big fireplace, is filled with highly polished antiques and traditional comfortable furniture. Twenty magnificent grandfather and grandmother clocks, some highly ornamental, are scattered throughout the hotel, as are beautiful bowls of fresh flowers. The guest rooms, all different and some in the new wing, are enchanting, lovely fabrics being part of the harmonious colour schemes. Many have balconies overlooking the gardens. The sophisticated Bistro and restaurant "Stadt Hamburg" have a talented team of chefs preparing marvellous local specialities, which naturally include delicious fresh fish. The wine list is extensive with over 300 entries, mostly from France or Germany. Half-bottles and wine by the glass are also available. Walking on the dunes breathing the sea air is superb. Sports include swimming from the white beaches, golf, riding and fishing. The town has designer shops and an excellent spa. **Directions:** From Hamburg head for Flensburg on A7, then make for Niebüll on B199 before putting the car on the train to Sylt (45 mins). Price guide: Single 185Dm–258Dm; double (no twins) 320Dm–450Dm; suites 490Dm–540Dm.

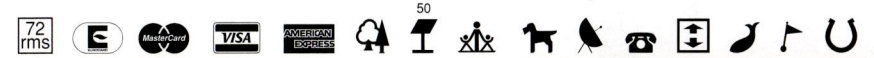

HUDSON'S
HISTORIC HOUSES AND GARDENS
including HISTORIC SITES OF INTEREST

The renowned Guide to over 1200 properties in Great Britain

Privately owned, National Trust, English Heritage, National Trust for Scotland and Historic Scotland properties and historic sites open to the public

Over 800 full-colour illustrations.

Descriptions, opening times, admission charges, telephone numbers and directions

Special Events Diary

Listing of Johansens recommended hotels by region

1996 edition on sale from February 1996 in all good bookshops or direct from the publishers.
ISBN: 0 9514157 7 8.   **Price UK: £6.95.**

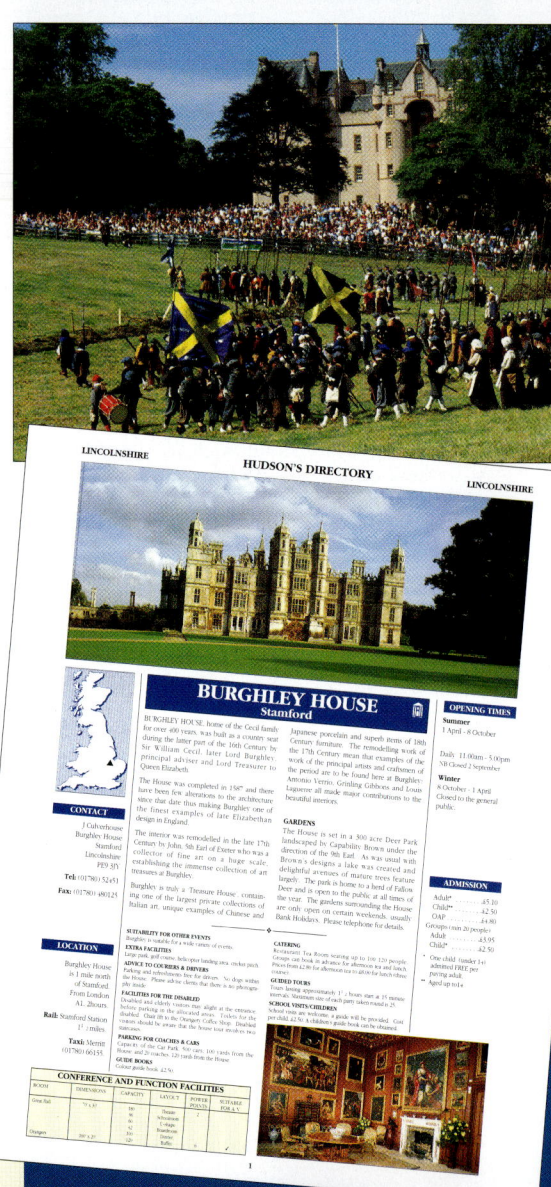

Hudson's Directory, PO Box 16, Banbury, Oxon OX17 1TF.   Tel: 01295 750750   Fax: 01295 750800

GIBRALTAR

Gibraltar is owned by the British. The Gibraltarians are proud of the fact. Although relatively close to the busy sea ports of Malaga and fashionable resort of Marbella – those who live on Gibraltar are proud to be under British governership – and do not regard The Rock as part of the Costa. The British influence is visible in architecture, the food and the street names.

True, there is also a Spanish influence and the weather is thankfully nothing like one finds in Britain. In general you'll find everyone speaks English and there are just as many pubs as there are tavernas and tapas bars.

The rock of Gibraltar acquired its name in 711 AD when it was captured by the Moorish chieftain Tarik at the start of the Arab invasion of Spain. It became known as Jebel Tarik – Rock of Tarik, later corrupted to Gibraltar. After successive periods of Moorish and Spanish domination, Gibraltar was captured by an Anglo Dutch fleet in 1704 and ceded to the British by the Treaty of Utrecht in 1713. This tiny British colony, whose impressive silhouette dominates the Strait between Spain and Morocco, is a rock just 3½ miles long, ½ mile wide and 1,369 feet high.

Europa Point, Gibraltar's most southerly tip gives a remarkable view, across the Strait to Morocco – 14 miles away. You stand on what in ancient times was called one of the two Pillars of Hercules. Across the water in Morocco, a mountain between the cities of Ceuta and Tangier formed the second pillar. The Europa Point lighthouse has stood above the meeting point of the Atlantic and the Mediterranean since 1941.

Travel down Old Queen's Road and you'll find the Apes' Den near the Wall of Charles V. The famous Barbary apes are a breed of cinnamon coloured, tail-less monkeys, natives of the Atlas Mountains in Morocco and you will want to take one home. Legend holds that as long as the apes remain, the British will continue to hold the Rock. Winston Churchill himself issued orders for the maintenance of the ape colony when its numbers began to dwindle during World War II. Today the apes are the responsibility of the British army, and a special officer in charge of apes is assigned to feed them twice daily at 8am and 4pm.

Take a cable car to the Rock's summit and ascend the Upper Galleries at the northern end of the Rock. These huge galleries were carved out during the Great Siege of 1779 – 83, and are worth the trek.

Willis Road leads steeply down to the colourful, congested town of Gibraltar, where the dignified regency architecture of Britain blends with the shutters, balconies and patios of southern Spain. Apart form the attractions of shops, restaurants, and pubs on Main Street, there is also the Governor's Residence – where the ceremonial Changing of the Guard takes place, the Law Courts, where the famous case of the Mary Celeste sailing ship was heard in 1972, and the Gibraltar Museum, whose exhibits recall the history of the Rock throughout the ages.

As well as being rich in history, Gibraltar is also on one of the main migration routes of the world, with millions of birds crossing from Africa to Europe between February and April to return south between late July and October.

They come in two distinct streams – by day, the soaring birds, including most of the storks, gain height on the thermal winds overland and cross the Strait on a long and gentle glide. The smaller birds, who must cross the water by muscle power, usually come in the relative safety of night and fly higher, so that often the only hint of their passing is their song drifting down from the darkness.

As for food, Gibraltar has no shortage of restaurants, bistros, pubs and bars catering for all tastes and budgets. Gibraltar's top restaurant is at the International Casino Club, the former casino by the Rock Hotel – it's also the top spot for nightlife.

Travelling in Gibraltar has its problems. As there are 1,000 people – not counting visitors – for every mile of road, travelling by car is a stressful experience. The options are to go by taxi, hire car, bus, on a cycle, or on foot – the last of which is probably the best and healthiest way to see the peninsula.

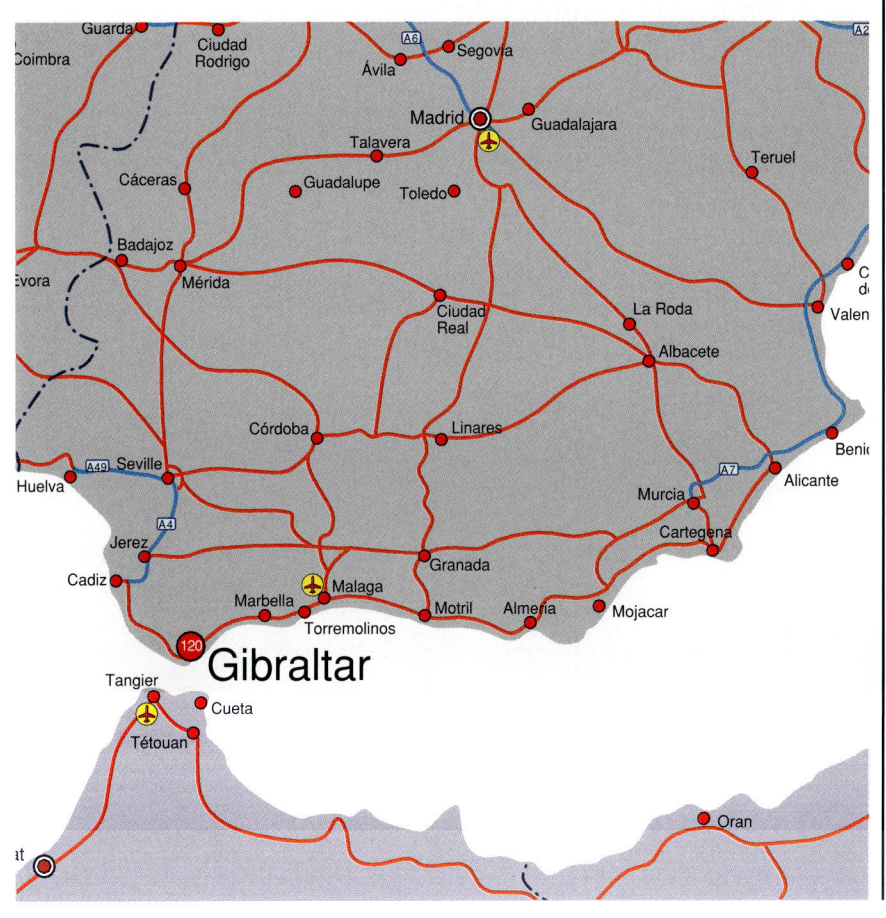

GIBRALTAR

In association with MasterCard

THE ROCK HOTEL

3 EUROPA ROAD, GIBRALTAR
TEL: 350 73 000 FAX: 350 73 513

Built over sixty years ago, The Rock has long been one of the grand hotels of Europe, and its high standards have been maintained, thoughtful modernisation having enhanced its colonial elegance. The setting is superb, high up above the city, with spectacular views over the Mediterranean, to Spain on one side, to North Africa on the other. It is surrounded by tropical gardens, which house an enchanting aviary and a splendid swimming pool. Impeccable service is provided by the staff and, significantly, the bedrooms are charmingly described in the brochure as guest rooms. The Barbary Bar is popular and the barman will mix imaginative drinks for every occasion. On hot days visitors prefer apéritifs on the cool Wisteria Terrace watching the brilliant sunsets. The menu of the Rib Room Restaurant has a strong English flavour and the winelist is excellent. A tour of the famous stalagmite and stalactite caves and the World War II tunnels will be memorable, and the famous apes still roam. Dolphin safaris and daytrips to North Africa can be arranged, sailing and tennis abound and golfers cross into Spain for the famous courses along the coast. **Directions:** Fly direct to the airport, ten minutes drive by taxi. Price guide: Single £60–£95; double/twin £80–£100; suites £150–£270.

120

Hungary

Because Hungary today is a small, agriculturally orientated country, visitors are often suprised by its grandeur and architectural splendour, especially in the capital Budapest, once known as "the Paris of the East", which positively buzzes with life.

Two important rivers nourish the country. The famous Danube flows from the west through Budapest on its way to the southern frontier, while the humbler Tisza, lacking any musical publicity from Strauss, flows less colourfully from the northeast across the Great Plain. What Hungary lacks in size, it makes up for in beauty and charm. Western Hungary is dominated by the largest lake in Central Europe, romantic Lake Balaton, which is 50 miles long and lined with Baroque villages, relaxing spas, magnificent vineyards, and shaded garden restaurants serving the catch of the day.

In Eastern Hungary, the Nagyalföld offers visitors a chance to explore the folklore and customs of the Magyars – the Hungarian name for themselves. It is an area of spicy food, strong wine, and proud horsemen. The unspoilt towns of the provincial areas are as rich in history and culture as the capital of Budapest.

Much of the pleasure of a visit to Budapest derives from the scenic views over the Danube and the Art Nouveau buildings. Although some 30,000 properties were destroyed during World War II and in 1956, the past lingers on in the architectural details of the antique structures that remain and in the memories and lifestyles of Budapest citizens.

The principal sights of the city fall roughly into three areas, each of which can be easily reached on foot. The Budapest hills are best explored by public transport. Note that street names have been changed over the last few years to purge reminders of the communist regime. No nation suffered more from being the wrong side of the Iron Curtain. Bullet-holes and the marks made by the tracks of Russian tanks are lasting mementos of enforced captivity.

The principal shopping district in Pest is the pedestrian zone on and around Vaci Utca between the Elisabeth and Chain bridges, but for a real taste of Hungarian shops try the vast flea markets situated on the outskirts of the city. Ecseri Piac, a colourful, chaotic market flocked to for decades, is an arsenal of second hand goods where you'll find everything from frayed Russian army fatigues to Herend and Zsolnay porcelain vases.

Hand made articles, such as embroidered tablecloths and painted plates, are sold all over the city by Transylvanian women wearing traditional scarves and colourful skirts. Recordings of Hungarian folk and gypsy music or classic pieces played by Hungarian artists are available increasingly on compact discs, though cassettes and records are much cheaper.

Eating out in Budapest should provide you with the best value for money of any European capital. Soups are always excellent.

Meats, rich sauces, and creamy desserts follow, but the more health conscious will also find salads, even out of season. There is a good selection of restaurants, from the grander establishments that echo the imperial past of the Habsburg era to the less expensive spots favoured by the locals.

Hungarians are known for their hospitality and love of talking to foreigners, although their strange language, which has no links to other European tongues exept Finnish, can be a problem. Today, however, everyone seems to be learning English, especially young people. But what all Hungarians share is a deep love of music, and the calendar is studded with music festivals, from BUDapest's famous opera, its annual Spring music festival, to the gypsy violinists who will serenade you during your evening meal as you enjoy your Tokay.

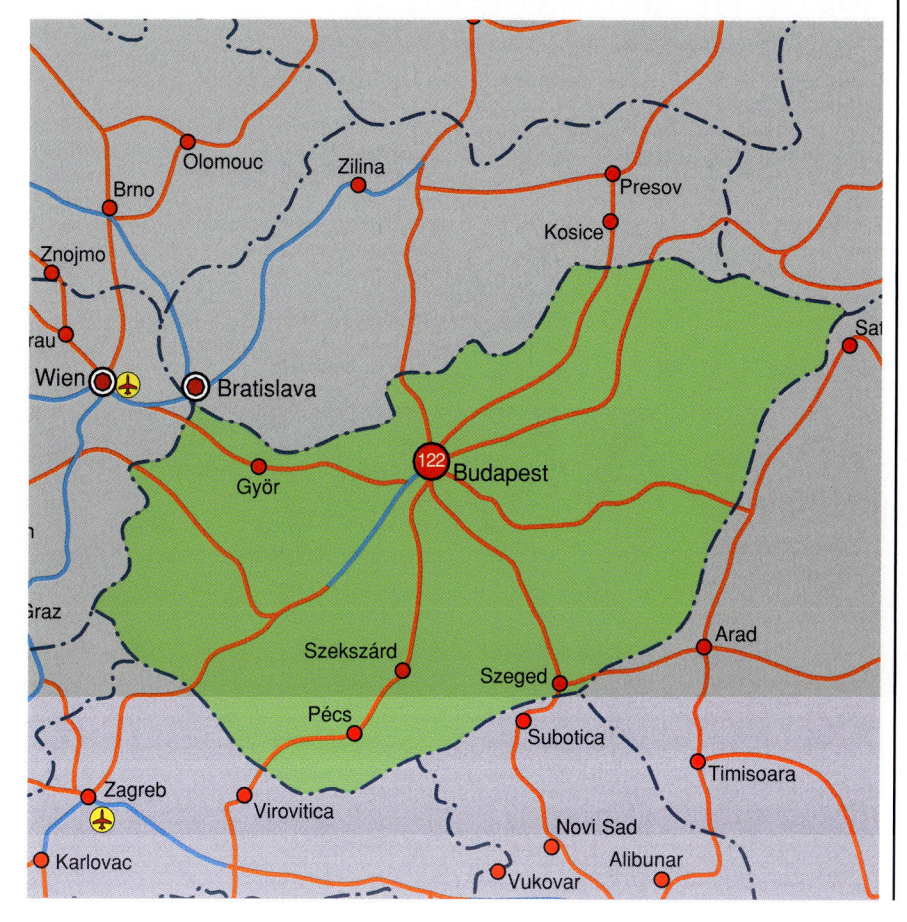

HUNGARY (Budapest)

In association with MasterCard

HOTEL GELLÉRT

GELLÉRT TÉR 1, H-1111 BUDAPEST, HUNGARY
TEL: 36 1 185 2200 FAX: 36 1 166 6631

Historically this is one of the 'grand' hotels of Europe and with many businessmen and travellers coming again to Budapest, it is ready to regain this accolade. The Gellért is in one of the most beautiful parts of the city, the central district in Buda, with the River Danube on one side and a green hill on the other. The style of the interior is art nouveau, with high glass domed ceilings and ornate ironwork. The furnishings are formal, of traditional Central European design. There are many single bedrooms in addition to double rooms and delightful suites, some overlooking the Danube, others Gellért Hill. The hotel has retained its gastronomic reputation, offering Hungarian specialities and international dishes, accompanied in the evening by gypsy music. The wines are mostly local led by the majestic Tokay, beloved by Louis XIV. The Coffee Shop is famous for its patisseries and ice-creams. The spa-baths cure many ailments. The 'sparkling' swimming pool, with its glass roof open in summer, and another pool with artifical waves are usually surrounded by sun worshippers. Budapest prides itself on its music, bridges, healing springs, monuments and pretty women! **Directions:** Take an expensive taxi or the inexpensive minibus from the airport, or the hydrofoil down the Danube from Vienna. Price guide: Single 138Dm–245Dm; double/twin 326Dm–378Dm; suites 466Dm–500Dm.

ITALY

Italy is perhaps the most sensual, and evocative of countries in Europe. It is the simplicity of the people and the place that returns you to the simplest human emotions – living among people for whom life's pleasures are celebrated rather than guiltily indulged. It is the heightened sense of romance evoked by the Mediterranean heat and the layers of history gradually unfolding – the serenity of Bellini's altar piece in San Zaccaria, the compassion of Michelangelo's Pietà in St Peter's, the symmetry of a Palladian villa rising from the earth of the Veneto. Whatever it is, to experience Italy one needs time – not necessarily measured in days but in solitude.

It is in the silent times that Italy will be revealed to you. Early morning, watching the light shine on the Pantheon, while strong Italian coffee wakens your senses. Dawn on the Grand Canal as dark green water is sprayed with gold and the only sound is a gondolier's oar breaking the silent surface. Midnight in the Forum, sunrise in Stelvio National Park, where swallows soar overhead and you find yourself knee deep in wildflowers. Drift into the dream and allow yourself to be charmed.

For the hedonist, the taste buds are awakened by the clear, true flavours of wine and food that taste faintly of the earth and sea from which they came. Buckwheat pasta in Bormio, served black with squid ink in Venice, creamy gelato at Gioliti in Rome or the comforting bowl of risotto in Siena, served by a family in their restaurant with no name.

Each region has its own speciality in food and wine – totally distinct from its neighbour. Restaurants in Venice and the Veneto, for example, serve specialities relying on the freshest of seasonal produce, meat and cheese from the mainland, and – unsurprisingly – a huge variety of fish and seafood. Pasta is eaten here, as all over Italy, but more typical is polenta.

In Rome, the traditional cucina romanesca relies on local markets full of fresh seasonal vegetables, fruit, cheese and meat from the nearby countryside plus seafood from the Mediterranean.

In contrast, Tuscan food has its roots in peasant cooking, relying on the basic staples of olive oil, for which the region is well known, tomatoes, beans, hams and salamis. Chewy saltless bread or thick vegetable soups such as ribolita often take the place of pasta, followed by grilled or roast meats – the great stand-bys of rustic cooking. Try Siena's nougat-like dense dark cake spiced with cloves and cinnamon – panforte, or the famous cantucci – sweet biscuits – accompanied by the dessert wine vin santo.

Tuscany produces the Italian red wines closest in form to the great red Bordeaux – Chianti Classico, while Umbria's most famous wine – the white Orvieto – is outshone by Lungarotti's Rubesco Torgiano Riserva – a rich, complex wine from near Perugia.

After all the poetry about the food and wine of Italy, there is need for a stroll through some of the regions themselves. From the Veneto to Tuscany and Umbria to Rome, the city to where all roads lead.

The Veneto lies in the northern most sector of Italy, and stretches from the Dolomite mountains in the north to the flatlands of the Venetian lagoon in the south. Venice is a romantic tourist city frozen in time – the Veneto a forward – thinking and cosmopolitan part of the new Europe.

Venice is small and most of the sights can be comfortably visited on foot. The heart of the city is the Piazza San Marco – overlooked by the great Basilica and the wonderfully gothic Doge's Palace. For many, these are attractions enough, but there are delights worth exploring beyond the Piazza, such as the gallery of the Accademia, Ca' Rezzonico and the imposing Frari church.

Venice is a city that can be enjoyed at all times of the year. Even winter's mists add to the city's romantic appeal, though clear blue skies and balmy weather make spring and autumn the best times to go. This is especially true if you combine a visit to Venice with a tour of the Veneto, where gardens and alpine meadows put on a colourful display from the beginning of April. Autumn sees the beech, the birch and chestnut trees of the region turn every shade of red and gold. In summer the waters of Lake Garda, fed by melted snow from the Alps, serve to moderate the heat. Winters are mild, allowing some of the crops typical of the southern Mediterranean, such as lemons and oranges, to grow.

Tuscany is at its prettiest in May when meadows and waysides are carpeted with the same bright flowers that Botticelli's Flora blithely scatters in Primavera, his celebration of Spring. Autumn is equally colourful, when the beech and chestnut woods turn a glorious blaze of seasonal red and gold. The best months for escaping the heat and the crowds are May, September and October. To see traditional festivities like the Palio in Siena or Arezzo's Joust of the Saracen, you will need to book well in advance, but there are many other local festivals to enjoy – such as the Pistoia Blues – an international festival of blues music lasting a week, and the Settimana Musicale Sienese in Siena, where chamber music is performed by members of the renowned Accademia Musicale Chigiana in splendid settings, such as the Palazzo Chigi-Saraceni.

Rome, the capital, is a city where antiquity is taken for granted, where you can have coffee in a square designed by Bernini and go home to a Renaissance palace. Normal life in Rome is carried on in the most extraordinary of settings.

The city is noisy, afflicted with hellish traffic, and exasperatingly inefficient. But the traffic problem is being tackled and sizeable areas of the city centre have been designated for pedestrians only.

The environs of Rome are overshadowed by the overwhelming attractions of the Eternal City. However, the surrounding region, known as Lazio, has plenty to offer – ancient art and archaeology, medieval hill towns and abbeys, Renaissance pleasure gardens, lake and mountain scenery, and an easy-going pace, not to mention great local wines and home made pasta. A breath of country air and a change of scenery enhance your enjoyment of Rome and offer a new perspective on many of its delights.

ITALY
SARDINIA
SICILY
Aosta
Como
Bergamo
Novara
Milano
Vercelli
Cremona
Turino
Piacenza
Alessandria
Genoa
Cúneo
Sàvona
Alássio
La Spézia
Parma
Réggio
Bologna
Verona
Pádova
Trento
Bolzano
Cortina
Belluno
Udine
Trieste
Treviso
Venezia
Ferrara
Ravenna
Forlì
Rimini
San Marino
Fano
Ancona
Firenze
Viaréggio
Pisa
Livorno
Siena
Piombino
Grosseto
Orbetello
Perugia
Assisi
Giulianova
Pescara
L'Aquila
Chieti
Roma
Avezzano
Ánzio
Cassino
Fóggia
Barletta
Bari
Benevento
Napoli
Sorrento
Salerno
Altamura
Bríndisi
Potenza
Táranto
Lecce
Ótranto
Gallípoli
Sala
Scanzano
Páola
Cosenza
Crotone
Nicastro
Catanzaro
Messina
Réggio di Calábria
Palermo
Trápani
Marsala
Caltanissetta
Catánia
Sciacca
Agrigento
Ragusa
Siracusa
Gela
Pachino
Calvi
Bastia
Porto
Ponte Leccia
Aléria
Propriano
Porto Vecchio
Bonifacio
Ólbia
Sássari
Siniscóla
Nuoro
Abbasanta
Arbatax
Oristano
Sanlurí
Muravera
Cágliari
S Antíoco
Pula
A5
A4
A21
A10
A1
A12
A15
A22
A13
A23
A14
A24
A3
A19
A20
A29
125
126
127
128
129
130
131
132
133
134
135
136
137
138

In association with MasterCard

ITALY (Ferrara)

RIPAGRANDE HOTEL
VIA RIPAGRANDE 21, 44100 FERRARA, ITALY
TEL: 39 53 27 65 250 FAX: 39 53 27 64 377 TELEX: 521169 RIP.HOT.

Ferrara is the perfect place to stay or to break a journey between Venice and Florence, for it's a lovely university town and the capital of the Dukes of Este. On the the banks of the Po in the old part of the town is this superbly restored XV century palace – the élite Ripagrande Hotel. The Renaissance interior is appropriate to the history of the hotel, and the entrance hall is spectacular with its marble staircase and pillars, wrought iron banisters and beamed ceiling. Cool, elegant salons and terraces encourage guests to relax while upstairs the spacious bedrooms are in excellent contemporary style, some having terraces cut into the slope of the tiled roofs. The furnishings are comfortable, in discreet colours. The attractive Riparestaurant serves many traditional Ferrarese specialities. Superb Italian wines are featured. Two enchanting courtyards make wonderful settings for banquets. The breakfast room offers an excellent buffet to start the day. perhaps before a seminar in the well-equipped meeting room. Bicycles are the popular way to explore this fascinating medieval town, with its castle, cathedral and the Diamond Palace. Sophisticated boutiques offer fine leather and high fashion. **Directions:** Ferrara is off the A13, 112 km from Venice and 150 km to Florence. Price guide: Single 230,000 lire; double/twin 300,000 lire; Junior suites 320,000 lire–360,000 lire.

125

ITALY (Florence)

In association with MasterCard

HOTEL ALBANI

**VIA FIUME, 12, 50123 FLORENCE, ITALY
TEL: 39 55 26 030 FAX: 39 55 21 10 45**

The elegant Hotel Albani is in the centre of Florence, close to the International Congress Centre, the Business Centre and the Exhibition Centre. It also has its own ever-expanding private conference facilities. The talents of Luigio Sturchio, the well-known architect and interior decorator, are evident in the exciting use of exclusive, colourful fabrics and the dramatic furnishings found throughout this carefully restored townhouse – a unique and successful blend of Renaissance and contemporary style. The reception area, has a ramp to assist those with mobility problems. At the back of the hotel is a pretty courtyard garden. Dedicated non-smoking areas respect guests' wishes. The handsome Florentine bedrooms have mahogany furniture, brass fittings and marble bedrooms. Those on the top floors have views over the city. Guests mingle in the American Bar and select Italian specialities from the international menu offered in the charming restaurant. The Albani has an extensive cellar, with wines form all parts of the globe. Florence has wonderful buildings, many art galleries and its famous Opera House to visit.
Directions: Driving is not recommended as parking is difficult. The hotel is a short walk from Central Station. Price guide: Single 240,000 lire–280,000 lire; double/twin 300,000 lire–380,000 lire; suites 700,000 lire.

In association with MasterCard

ITALY (Florence)

HOTEL REGENCY
PIAZZA MASSIMO D'AZEGLIO 3, FIRENZE, ITALY
TEL: 39 55 24 52 47 FAX: 39 55 23 46 735

This charming 18th century villa is in a peaceful, tree-lined residential area of Florence, away from the busy city life and yet only a few minutes' walk from the sophisticated boutiques. The interior is delightful, appropriate to the era when the hotel was built yet matching today's criteria for comfort. The bedrooms are quiet, light and spacious, thoughtfully furnished in harmonious colour schemes, some of them designated non-smoking. Bowls of flowers add the finishing and welcoming touch. Guests enjoy drinks on the lawn, in the intimate bar or elegant salon. Informal meals and breakfast are served in the dining room. Lunching or dining in the formal Relais Le Jardin restaurant is a memorable experience – a soft boiserie room with exquisite stained glass panels, superb dishes created by a master chef downed with delicious Italian wine. In warm weather the Jardin opens its verandah through to a romantic garden with candle-lit tables. There are wonderful museums, art galleries and historic buildings to visit, shopping is superb and exploring Tuscany is a pleasant day away from the city. Golf and fishing are not far away. **Directions:** From the motorway, follow Viali Circonvallazione-Centro to the Piazzale Donatello. The hotel has private car-parking. Price guide: Single from 300,000 lire; double/twin from 360,000 lire; suites from 550,000 lire.

ITALY (Marling/Meran)

In association with MasterCard

ROMANTIK HOTEL OBERWIRT

ST FELIXWEG 2, I-39020 MARLING/MERAN, ITALY
TEL: 39 473 22 20 20 FAX: 39 473 44 71 30

An inn offering hospitality since the 15th century, this hotel has been owned by the Waldner family since 1749. Part of it has an even longer history, the outdoor pool being a genuine Roman bath. The traditional architecture has not been marred by modernisation. Window-boxes and shutters enhance the original tower and white walls set against a background of the majestic Dolomites. There are now 44 bedrooms, luxuriously appointed, with views across the valley to the mountains. The Tyrolean bar is very convivial, although on fine days guests prefer their aperitifs on the flower-bedecked terrace, which is floodlit at night. The Waldners are proud of their elegant restaurant. The meals are exquisite and the carefully selected wines reasonably priced. When sunbathing by the Roman pool is not possible, guests appreciate the fitness centre, with its indoor heated pool, sauna, Jacuzzi and massage facilities. The hotel has a relationship with the Dolomite Golf Club reducing green fees for guests, also with the Riding Club of Meran. Five tennis courts, two indoor, with a coach available are 1km away. **Directions:** Leave the Innsbruck Verona road at Bozen Sud for Meran, then follow signs to Marling (3km). Price guide: Single 110,000 lire–130,000 lire; double/twin 110,000 lire–130,000 lire per person; suites 130,000 lire– 170,000 lire per person.

In association with MasterCard

ITALY (Naples)

ALBERGO MIRAMARE

VIA NAZARIO SAURO, 24 NAPLES, ITALY
TEL: 39 81 76 47 589 FAX: 39 81 76 40 775

This élite hotel, overlooking the Bay of Naples, was built at the turn of the century as a master's private dwelling, and the house has been carefully restored to meet modern criteria without destroying the charm of its Liberty era. The interior is delightfully art nouveau, reflected by the elegant furniture, frescoes on the walls, unusual fabrics, the appropriate lamps, large green plants and unique paintings. The bedrooms are in tranquil shades of blue and grey, some overlooking the waterfront. Quieter rooms are available at the back of the hotel. The mirrored American bar has great style, and it is here that guests mingle while deciding which local speciality to eat in the restaurant, which has a lovely terrace with a view across the Bay to Vesuvius and the sound of mandolins played in the street below. The wines are predominantly Italian. There is a beach opposite the hotel, and the fascinating port of Santa Lucia to explore. The Capodimonte Museum is close by. Excursions can easily be made to Pompeii, Capri and Ischia. Visits to Sorrento and Amalfi would take a little longer. **Directions:** Following the road along the Bay, the hotel is between Castel dell'Ovo, the port and Palazzo Reale, and the head porter will advise about car parking. Price guide: Single 200,000 lire–250,000 lire; double/twin 249,000 lire–335,000 lire; suites 386,000 lire.

ITALY (Porto Ercole)

In association with MasterCard

IL PELLICANO

HOTEL IN PORTO ERCOLE, 58018 PORTO ERCOLE (GR), ITALY
TEL: 39 564 833801 FAX: 39 564 833418

No hotel in Italy can compare with the spectacular setting of Il Pellicano. One of the most delightful, intimately-sized hotels in the world (Sunday Telegraph). A cluster of cottages, centred around the main ivy-clad villa, with traditional tiled roofs, ochre walls and flower patios intersperse with tall pine, cypress and olive trees overlooking the breathtaking Argentario Peninsula. The atmosphere of Il Pellicano is like a very private club (Harpers & Queen). The bedrooms and suites are individually furnished and enjoy spectacular views. Guests can choose between the mouth-watering barbecue buffets or romantic candelit dinners in the beautiful restaurant, providing the best in national and international food and wines. Enjoy sports like water-skiing, tennis, cycling, or just relax in the heated swimming pool or on the terraced private beach or in the beauty centre. If it's more activity you crave, then there's plenty going on in the nearby marina and waterfront. Play a game of golf or explore the Roman and Etruscan ruins, within driving distance in the hotel limousine if preferred. On a verdant hillside, overlooking a shimmering sea, you'll find Il Pellicano – a hotel in a class of its own. **Directions.** Take the A12 from Rome towards Civitavecchia, then the Orbetello exit towards Porto Ercole. Double 275,000 lire–840,000 lire; suites 680,000 lire–1,700,000 lire.

In association with MasterCard

ITALY (Rome)

Hotel Farnese

VIA ALESSANDRO FARNESE, 30 (ANGOLO VIALE GUILIO CESARE), 00192 ROME, ITALY
TEL: 39 6 321 25 53 FAX: 39 6 321 51 29

An aristocratic 19th century villa set in a quiet tree-lined residential area of Rome. You enter through a small, lovely fronted garden, up an impressive stone stairway to the reception desk. Graceful archways and elegant classical Italian furniture, chandeliers from Murano and decorative frescos, antiques and fine colourful rugs together make-up the charming reception areas of the ground floor of the original villa. Downstairs a buffet breakfast is the only meal served in the subterranean dining room – but drinks will be brought to the roof garden overlooking St.Peter's Square or the terrace off the reception lounge. Raphaël murals, parquet floors and period furniture make the bedrooms very attractive, and they have delightful marble bathrooms, equipped to meet the needs of modern travellers. Most conveniently situated among all the historical buildings to explore in this city, it is particularly close to the Castel St. Angelo, St. Peter's and the Vatican. Those visiting Rome on business appreciate the easy accessibility to the commercial districts. **Directions:** There is private parking space for residents' cars, alternatively the Lepanto Metro station is only 50 metres from the hotel. Price guide: Single 240,000 lire–280,000 lire; double/twin 330,000 lire–380,000 lire.

ITALY (Rome)

HOTEL LORD BYRON

VIA G. DE NOTARIS 5, 00197 ROME, ITALY
TEL: 39 6 32 20 404 FAX: 39 6 32 20 405

The palatial white villa is set in the exclusive tree-lined Parioli residential area just north of the centre of Rome. The ambience is that of a large private house, offering wonderful hospitality away from the crowds. Byron is said to be buried under the hotel. On arrival guests instantly appreciate the artistic reception rooms – harmonious colour schemes, graceful furniture, gleaming antiques, and lovely blooms in ceramic vases. Doors lead to 'secret' courtyard gardens. The bedrooms are colour-co-ordinated, using subtle wallpapers and fabrics. Careful attention has been given to the demands of modern travellers, especially in the bathrooms. The bar and restaurant are scenic with brilliant mirrors, marble columns, Roman murals and flower-covered chairs. A jazz pianist entertains visitors enjoying evening cocktails. A coveted Michelin Star has been awarded to the Relais le Jardin restaurant, recognising the creative talents of the master-chef who has introduced Roman specialities to the menu. The cellar is awesome, and has featured in international wine magazines. There is an art gallery nearby, and the Villa Borghese park. This hotel is a member of The Leading Hotels of the World. **Directions:** Head north of the Villa Borghese, near the Piazza Don Minzoni. The hotel has private car parking. Price guide: Single: from 310,000 lire; double/twin from 360,000 lire.

In association with MasterCard

ITALY (Rome)

HOTEL MAJESTIC ROMA

VIA VENETO 50, 00187 ROME, ITALY
TEL: 39 6 48 68 41 FAX: 39 6 48 80 984

A grand fin-de-siècle hotel, its imposing façade distinguished by graceful columns and tall windows, can be found on one of the most elegant streets in Rome. This is a golden establishment in every sense, reflected both in the many shades of gold featured in the lavish interior and in the high standards that prevail throughout the Majestic. The opulent foyer has a regiment of attentive staff waiting to assist new arrivals; the lift is art deco, the stairs are marble, the drapery and furniture are regal. The drawing rooms have rich festooned curtains, chandeliers, the main salon a magnificent painted ceiling, and the banqueting room beautiful 19th century frescoes. Gracious private sitting rooms are available for meetings. Bedrooms and suites, a few with balconies, are of similar splendour and exquisitely furnished with period furniture. The bathrooms are spacious and absolutely luxurious. The sophisticated American Bar, with its exciting terrace looking out over Rome and with a pianist playing at night, is where guests enjoy apéritif before adjourning to the soigné conservatory restaurant serving delicious dishes accompanied by fine Italian wines. There is all Rome to explore, ancient ruins, religious edifices, art galleries and very smart modern shops. **Directions:** It is in the centre of the city. Price guide: Single 380,000 lire; double/twin 520,000 lire; suites 800,000 –1,500,000 lire.

ITALY (Rome)

In association with MasterCard

HOTEL RAPHAËL

LARGO FEBO, 2 (PIAZZA NAVONA), 00186 ROME, ITALY
TEL: 39 6 68 28 31 FAX: 39 6 68 78 993

Approached across cobblestones, just a few metres from the spectacular Piazza Navona, almost hidden by a cascade of ivy, this small hotel is friendly, comfortable and a veritable art museum. A valuable collection of ceramics by Pablo Picasso is displayed in the lobby, which is also filled with many superb antiques and paintings. High up in the Bramante roof garden guests can overlook all ancient Rome – the Pantheon, St Peter's, St. Angels Castle and the Santa Maria della Pace. The Restaurant Café Picasso is cosmopolitan, Mediterranean specialities sharing the menu with international dishes. A comprehensive breakfast buffet is also served in the Café. The bedrooms are comfortable and the new deluxe rooms have been redesigned to a very high standard with all the latest amenities and exquisite hand–decoration by Venetian artists. There is a small fitness centre, for visitors not exhausted from sight-seeing and shopping and the staff will give advice on concerts and cultural events taking place at the Cloisters or in the hotel. There are also meeting facilities, a brand new fully-equipped conference room. A Summit International hotel. **Directions:** The hotel is in the very heart of ancient Rome, off the Piazza Navona. Price guide: Single 240,000 lire–333,000 lire; double/twin 370,000 lire–540,000 lire; suites 480,000 lire–611,000 lire. 10% VAT excluded.

In association with MasterCard

ITALY Sicily (Taormina)

ROMANTIK HOTEL VILLA DUCALE
VIA LEONARDO DA VINCI, 60, 98039 TAORMINA, SICILY
TEL: 39 94 22 81 53 FAX: 39 94 22 81 54

Once a coaching inn, then the summer villa of a nobleman – an ancestor of the present owner – on the edge of Taormina, this delightful small hotel with spectacular views of Naxos Bay and Mount Etna is in rural surroundings. The interior is charming, with a déjà-vu ambience, and guests can relax in the small lounge decorated with fine pieces of Sicilian pottery. The bedrooms, all different shapes and sizes, have individual colour schemes, fresh flowers, tiled floors and elegant period furniture. There is no formal restaurant but a leisurely breakfast, with a wide range of sweet and savoury dishes, is served until 11.30am on the terrace, where delicious hot snacks and wines are available all day. From the terrace on clear days you can see across Catania. There is a good choice of restaurants, pizzerias and cafés in the village round the corner. A cable car descends to a sandy beach at Mazzaro, and buses go to Etna and Agrigento. Golfers will enjoy the superb Il Picciolo Golf Course, some 30 minutes' drive away. **Directions:** Take the N114 from Catania to Taormina, then take the road to Castelmola. The hotel has a small car park. Price guide: Single 140,000 lire–190,000 lire; double/twin 220,000 lire–300,000 lire; suites 300,000 lire–320,000 lire.

ITALY Venice (Lido)

ALBERGO QUATTRO FONTANE
30126 LIDO DI VENEZIA, ITALY
TEL: 39 41 526 0227 FAX: 39 41 526 0726

A unique country house set in an idyllic garden on the Lido amongst orchards and productive vineyards on this long island, away from the hustle and bustle of Venice, the Albergo is only ten minutes by water-bus from San Marco square. The outside is more reminicent of a Swiss chalet, while the interior is more traditional, with tiled floors and big stone fireplaces. Signore Bevilacqua, whose family has owned Albergo Quattro Fontane for over forty years, has collected some very unusual antique furniture, art and artefacts from all over the world. African artefacts strike one when you enter the Barchessa, the attractive annexe adjacent to the Albergo, where the bedrooms maintain the simplistic charm of individually chosen antique furniture. Large windows look out over the extensive terraces, where there is an outdoor dining area for summer meals. The menu is based on Venetian specialities, with the emphasis on traditional country cooking. The wines are from local vineyards. Regular water-buses to Venice. The Lido has its own famous beach and a golf course by day, and the casino at night. **Directions:** Either a private water-taxi from the airport straight to the Albergo with its own canal or a public water-bus every hour from the airport to the Lido via San Marco, then five minutes taxi ride to the Albergo. Price guide: Single 240,000 lire; double/twin 330,000 lire.

In association with MasterCard

ITALY (Venice)

HOTEL CIPRIANI & PALAZZO VENDRAMIN

GIUDECCA 10, 30133 VENICE, ITALY
TEL: 39 41 520 77 44 FAX: 39 41 520 39 30

An exceptional hotel, built on the Island of Giudecca, just four minutes by private launch from its own jetty by St Mark's Square. The hotel is surrounded by three acres of verdant gardens, providing seclusion, and the low, sun-kissed pink buildings have tiled roofs and green shutters. The elegant interiors exploit Venetian style to create sophisticated settings. Bathrooooms are marble, and the bedrooms luxurious. Reached through a flowered courtyard, discreet suites and apartments in the 15th century Palazzo Vendramin have their own butler service. The service is immaculate, whether you are enjoying breakfast alongside the lagoon, an al fresco buffet lunch by the pool, Bellini cocktails in the piano bar, or dining in the graceful Venetian Restaurant or on the Terrace by the water's edge. The wines are superb, the menus designed for connoisseurs of gourmet Italian cooking although lighter repasts can be ordered. Sporting guests will appreciate the only swimming pool and tennis court in Venice. Golf is played on the Lido. Others will wish to absorb history and art on the mainland, or visit the famous Harry's Bar, a forerunner of the Cipriani. **Directions:** The hotel launch will collect guests on arrival at the private jetty at St Mark's Square. The Orient Express is an alternative to air travel. Price guide: Single 650,000 lire–850,000 lire; double/twin 850,000 lire–1,200,000 lire; suites: 1,850,000 lire–3,900,000 lire.

ITALY (Venice)

HOTEL LONDRA PALACE
RIVA DEGLI SCHIAVONI, 30122 VENICE, ITALY
TEL: 39 41 520 05 33 FAX: 39 41 522 50 32

Situated right on the Grand Canal, The Londra Palace is just a minute from St. Mark's Square. The impressive exterior is enhanced by an attractive terrace bar from which guests enjoy watching the marina. First impressions are of efficient and courteous staff and a lavish interior – wonderful wall-hangings, chandeliers, furniture by top Italian designers and tiled floors with colourful rugs. The handsome bedrooms and suites have harmonious colour schemes and brilliant bathrooms. A maid will attend to those guests wishing to sunbathe on the solarium terraces. Guido mixes exotic cocktails in the Piano Bar, overlooking the lagoon. Diners in the exclusive, mirrored restaurant can see the lights on the water as they enjoy a sophisticated interpretation of Venetian cooking and distinguished wines. Much thought has been given to guests' needs, including free entrance to the Casino. The hotel has prepared its own multi-lingual guidebook to little known Venice, to the artisan quarter, small restaurants and antique shops. There are rubber boots ready for high tides in winter! Those wishing to visit Murano to see glass-blowing travel in a private launch. The concierge will arrange golf, tennis and swimming on the Lido for sporting guests **Directions:** There are water-taxi links to the airport. Price guide: Single 260,000 lire–390,000 lire; double/twin 470,000 lire–610,000 lire; suites 1,000,000 lire.

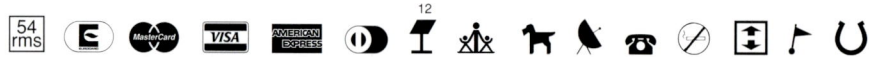

138

LUXEMBOURG

Luxembourg is a linguist's dream. Its citizens speak an essentially oral tongue called Letzeburgesch – Luxembourgish – descended from an ancient dialect of the Moselle Franks. Luxembourgers are educated in German while learning in French, eventually completing higher studies in French; the current generation also learns English. The language used for government documents is French, but many are translated into German. Within the tourist industry, most Luxembourgers you'll meet will speak some English with you, better French, and even better German, but they'll talk about you in Luxembourgish.

The Grand Duchy of Luxembourg, a small land-locked state, with a long and influential history, has been since World War II a leading exponent of European political and economic unity. After rebelling in 1830 against Dutch rule and gaining its full independence and national status in 1848, Luxembourg became in 1948 one of the three founding members of Benelux in partnership with its close neighbours Belgium and The Netherlands.

A Luxembourgish menu provides the quality of French cuisine and the quantity of German portions. Cuisine bourgeoise – veal with cream and mushrooms, beef entrecôte with peppercorn sauce is on most restaurant menus, but the more adventurous should try Luxembourg's own earthy cooking – such as smoked pork with fava beans and pink raw smoked ham served cold with pickled onions, or treipen – blood pudding and kuddlefleck paniert – plain breaded tripe. Yum, yum! A few restaurants still feature the local cooking for sentimental more than economic reasons and more upmarket additions to the national specialities such as crayfish and trout cooked with local wine may appeal more to the inexperienced palate. There are more star studded gastronomique restaurants per capita than in any other European country. Many restaurants – including some of these world class venues – offer an accessibly priced menu at lunch.

Luxembourg takes pride in its Moselle wines, grown in the hills that rear up from the riverside and take maximum advantage of the region's faint sunlight. Their bottles – slim and tapered – and some of their names suggest Alsatian and German wines, and they do share a certain fruitiness with these white wines. But Luxembourg's versions are sharper and lighter and when poured from an iced bottle into a green stemmed glass, they're an ideal companion to a cream sauce veal dish.

If you visit one place only in the Grand Duchy of Luxembourg, it will be Luxembourg Ville – Luxembourg City – a city of 79,000 people in a nation of 400,000. Explore the old cobbled streets, the parks, the cathedral, the museum – and after shopping, relax in a terrace café shaded by sycamores, listen to street musicians. The City can be 'done' in a day – but don't rush! Little Luxembourg is a romantic base for trips and it harbours a magical atmosphere during the summer evenings, with its illuminated monuments ancient walls and charming leafy squares. The city overlooks the river-valleys of the Alzette and the Pétrusse and there are fine views to be had from the Promenade de la Corniche and the Bock Casemates.

Out of the City, vast green hills and dense fir forests alternate in Luxembourg's northern highlands, the southeast corner of the rocky, woody Ardennes Plateau. Higher, harsher than the duchy's southern area, with bitter winters and unforgiving soil, this land remains isolated and inaccessible. The Luxembourg Ardennes has been the hunting ground of kings and emperors, Celts, Romans and Gauls. Shaggy deer and bristling wild boar still charge across a forest road. Castles punctuate its hills and valleys, rocky rivers and streams pour down its slopes.

Luxembourg is a northern country – parallel in latitude to Newfoundland in Canada – and it experiences extreme changes in day and night length from season to season. Late Spring, Summer and Autumn give long days of light until 10pm. In Winter, dusk descends before 4pm. There's rarely heavy snow, but winters are frequently grey and rainy. Summer is probably the best time to visit – although everyone else will be visiting at this time as well.

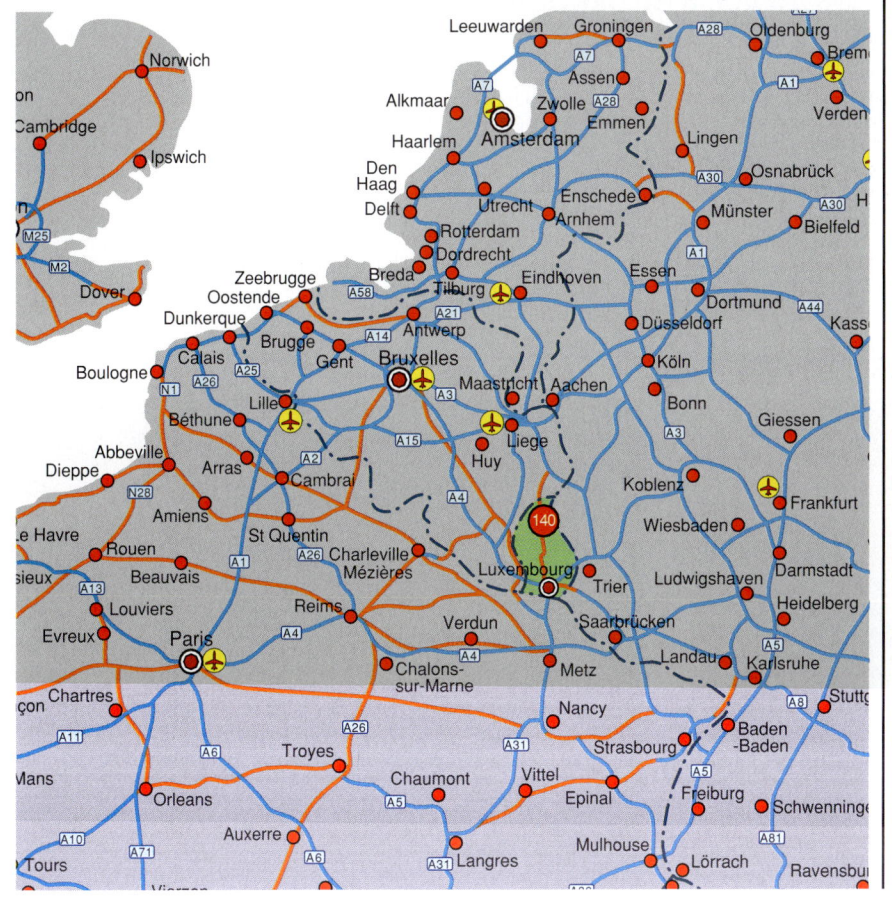

LUXEMBOURG (Berdorf)

In association with MasterCard

Parc Hotel

16 RUE DE GRUNDHOF, L-6550 BERDORF, LUXEMBOURG
TEL: 352 79195 FAX: 352 79223

This charming hotel on the outskirts of the village of Berdorf built on the forest edge was founded some sixty years ago. It is a peaceful retreat away from the commercial activity of Luxembourg, standing in its own parkland, the well tended gardens having romantic pools with bulrushes and waterlilies as well as rare, exotic trees. The bedrooms retain their original charm, but have been modernised to suit today's traveller. Many have balconies looking across the verdant countryside. The panelled salon is handsome, the ideal spot for a digestif after enjoying dinner in the spacious restuarant, with its unusual circular serving area in the centre of the room. The chefs are very creative, the menu cosmopolitan and the dishes beautifully presented. The wine list is extensive and reasonably priced. On fine days guests take their apéritifs and eat alfresco on the cool terrace, with green vines winding up the pillars and across the ceiling. Relaxing on comfortable garden chairs in the park is a popular pastime while more energetic guests walk in 'Little Switzerland' or use the hotel open-air pool. Tennis and mini-golf are nearby. **Directions:** Leave the E44 from Luxembourg City, taking the E29 to Echternach, following signs to Berdorf. There is parking at the hotel. Price guide: Single Bf2200–Bf3800; double/twin Bf3000–Bf4900.

MONACO

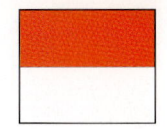

Monaco as a principality tends to be forgotten as visitors focus on its capital Monte Carlo. Made famous both in song and film, Monte Carlo is perceived as a place suited only to the glamorous, wealthy, pretty playboys and girls of the world who want to party, gamble, see and be seen. Streets full of designer shops, roads buzzing with Porsche and Ferrari, harbour sheltering yachts with telephone number price tags. Where it is easier to buy an original Chanel than a loaf of bread.

There is an element of truth is this – Monte Carlo is glamorous rather than beautiful. It is probably the most glamorous capital in all Europe. You are more likely to rub shoulders with famous names in Monte Carlo than in Hollywood.

But leave the centre and enter Monaco Ville where streets are narrow and cobbled, the buildings seem to topple over one another and prices in the cafés and bistros are designed for the local and not the tourist, where the views are spectacular and free, and the talk is of grandmère not Gaultier – and the area becomes resonant with beauty again.

If your destination is Monaco, fly to Nice and hire a car. Drive along the Moyenne Corniche, one of the most beautiful highways in the world, and marvel at the incomparably lush views of the Mediterranean coastline. Turn a corner and you'll arrive abruptly among the skyscrapers of Monaco. At first a Greek settlement, later taken by the Romans, it was bought from the Genoese in 1309 by the Grimaldis who, in spite of bitter family feuds and at least one political assassination, still rule as the world's longest established surviving royal family. It occupies an area smaller than that of New York's Central Park.

Since 1949, Monaco has been in the charge of its most effective ruler. Businesslike Prince Rainier III is descended from a Grimaldi who entered the Monaco fortress in 1297 disguised as a monk. Rainier's wife, former film star Grace Kelly, died tragically in 1982 and their son Albert, is heir to the throne although his sisters Caroline and Stephanie are usually the main focus of media attention.

Monaco owes its fame principally to its Grand Casino. Source of countless legends, it was instituted in 1856 by Charles III to save himself from bankruptcy.

Visitors come from all over the world for the Grand Prix de Monaco in May and the Monte Carlo Rally in January and many of the greatest singers perform during the Opera season. There are fireworks in July and August, and an international circus festival at the end of January as well as world class ballet and concerts. Facilities exist for every sort of leisure activity, and there is much else to enjoy without breaking the bank, including Fort Antoine and the Neo-Romanesque Cathédrale.

Monaco Town, the principality's old quarter, has many vaulted passage ways and an almost tangible medieval atmosphere. The magnificent Palais du Prince, a grandiose structure with a Moorish tower, was largely rebuilt in the last century. Here, since 1297, the Grimaldi dynasty has lived and ruled. The spectacle of the Changing of the Guard occurs each morning at 11.55am – while inside guided tours take visitors through state apartments and a wing containing the Palace Archives and Musée Napoléon.

The Moneghetti area is the setting for the Jardin Exotique – or Tropical Garden, where 600 varieties of cacti and succulents cling to the rock face, bewildering visitors.

Monaco's cathedral is also worth a visit. The cathedral is a late 19th century confection in which Philadelphia born Princess Grace lies in splendour, along with past members of the Grimaldi dynasty. The Musée Océanographic is internationally famous for its research – the well-known underwater explorer Jacques Cousteau is the present director. The aquarium is the undisputed highlight, where a collection of the world's fish and crustacea live out their lives in public, some colourful, some drab, some the stuff of which nightmares are made.

Like the French, the Monégasques consider eating well as an essential part of their birthright. Brasseries, bistros, world-famous restaurants, bars, fast food places are all to be found in this tiny and most exclusive of principalities.

MONACO (Monte Carlo)

In association with MasterCard

HOTEL MIRABEAU

1, AVENUE PRINCESS GRACE, MONTE CARLO, MC 98007, MONACO
TEL: 33 92 16 65 65 FAX: 33 93 50 84 85

This luxurious hotel offers the highest standards of accommodation, cuisine and service. Most of the newly decorated and spacious rooms, which include ten suites and four junior suites, overlook the swimming pool and sun terrace. All offer a full range of modern amenities to guarantee maximum comfort and convenience for guests. The restaurant which has one Michelin Star, La Coupole, boasts a Roman patio and is renowned for its inventive yet classical cooking. At cocktail time, the bar Le Fiacre offers a warm welcome and live music. The heated, sea water swimming pool on the upper floor is a favourite spot, with the Café Mirabeau serving provencal dishes – broche (roasted). On arrival at the hotel, guests are presented with the "Carte d'Or" Société des Bains de Mer entrance card. The SBM offers sport in some of the most privileged settings in the world – water sports at the Monte Carlo Beach Hotel with its Olympic swimming pool, tennis at the Monte Carlo Country Club and golf at the Monte Carlo Golf Club and the new thalassotherapy centre within five minutes walking distance. In Monte Carlo the season lasts all year, with a continuous programme of ballets, concerts and other festivities at the Monte Carlo Sporting Club, the Casino Cabaret, Jimmy'z night club and the Monte Carlo Opera House. Price guide: Single Ff1000–Ff1600; double/twin Ff1200–Ff2000; suites Ff200–Ff5800.

THE NETHERLANDS

The Netherlands is not a flat pancake of a country. Certainly low lying Zeeland lives with the sea and on the sea – its **oysters and mussels are world famous.** But this country is full of hidden surprises – all agreeable. In the north you'll discover sand dunes, bulb fields and melancholy seascapes, in the southern provinces you'll find a glorious nature reserve, glistening inland lakes, colourful lush valleys and rolling hills. The Netherlands has colour.

If you travel to the Netherlands expecting to find residents wearing wooden shoes, you're years too late. Sophisticated, modern Holland has more art treasures per square miles than any other country on earth, as well as a large number of ingenious, energetic people with a remarkable commitment to quality, style and innovation.

Like Belgium, the Netherlands is a good place to shop for diamonds. But you can also find Delft and Makkumware art, antiques, tulip bulbs (of course!) and cheese. Amsterdam has numerous department stores and boutiques that range in character from conservative to funky. Utrecht is the site of the largest enclosed shopping centre in the Netherlands. Maastricht before the 'Treaty' used to be known for its elegant shops and designer boutiques. Diamonds are found exclusively in Amsterdam, as is the best selection of antiques. The Hague is a centre of art.

As for food, the Dutch has a dining advantage over other Europeans in the quantity and quality of the fresh ingredients available to them. Their national green thumb and green houses produce the Continent's best and greatest varieties of vegetables and fruits, and their dairy farms supply a rich store of creams, cheeses and butter for sauces – the forests yield a wide range of game meats in the winter wild season, and the sea dykes are covered with rare herbs and other vegetation that offer a rich diet to their lambs and calves to produce exceptionally tasty, tender meat all year round.

Amsterdam, the capital, is a city with a split personality. It's a **gracious, formal, cultural centre built on the canals, and it's the most offbeat metropolis in the world.** Home to the Rijksmuseum and the Vincent Van Gogh Museum, it creaks under the weight of its historical heritage and oozes romance – each elegantly gabled house telling a tale as you walk the streets, and each museum worth a day's visit if your feet can stand the pace.

But there is also an innate seediness in Amsterdam, where soft drugs are legalised, houseboats are infested with stray cats and where prostitutes brazenly display themselves in windows facing the city's oldest church. Admittedly, by night this side of Amsterdam has a charm. In daylight, some areas are decidedly tacky.

The city is laid out in concentric rings of canals around the old centre, intertwined with a network of access roads and alleys connecting streets. You will easily be able to see the city on foot, although it can be dangerous as trams and cars seem to play Russian roulette along the narrow streets. Most of the art museums are clustered conveniently at the edge of the canal district.

Like bears to honey, the population of the Netherlands clusters in the arc of Amsterdam's attraction. More than 25% of the population live in and around 10 small to medium size cities that are within 50 miles of the capital. And that doesn't include the tulip growers, vegetable farmers, dairy farmers, and villagers who fill in what little open land remains in this area. The Dutch call the circle formed by the four cities of Amsterdam, The Hague, Rotterdam and Utrecht, the Randstad – Ridge City – because the cities lie along the same ridge. The Hague harbours the capital of international justice, while Rotterdam is the world's largest port. The Randstad is also a cultural mecca, playing host to top class music and dance festivals, and pop and rock extravaganzas.

As for night life, you'll find cafés in every town in the Netherlands, but most entertainment for all ages will be found in the large cities in the Randstad.

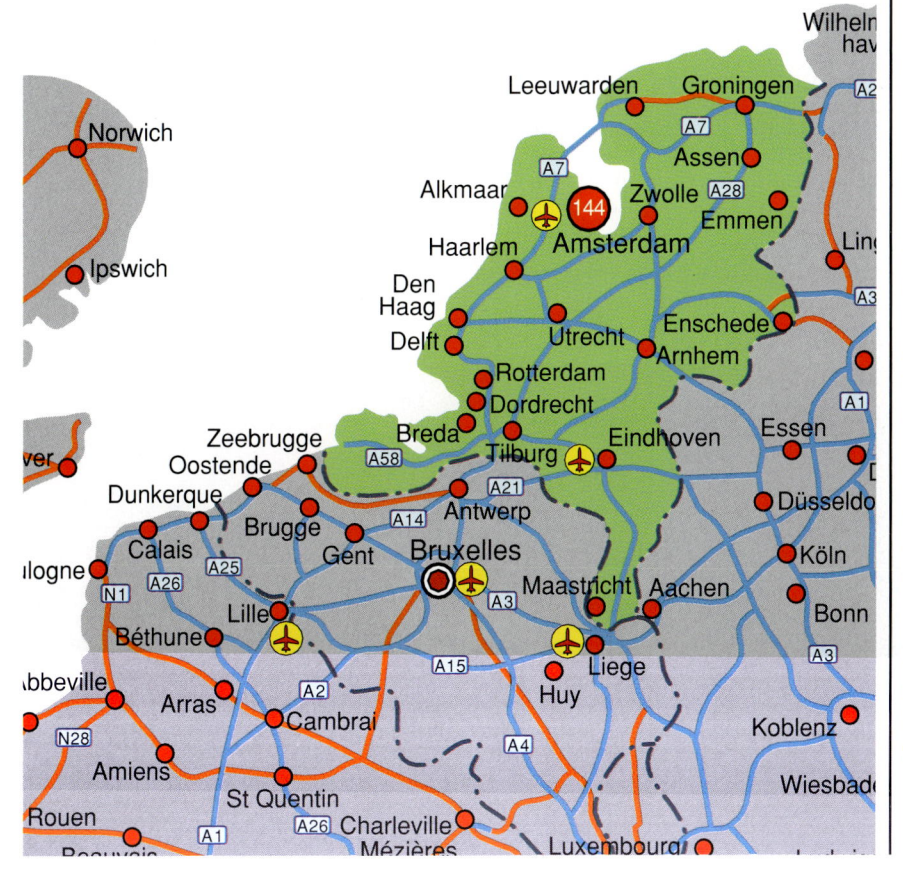

THE NETHERLANDS (Amsterdam)

HOTEL AMBASSADE

HERENGRACHT 341, 1016 AMSTERDAM, THE NETHERLANDS
TEL: 31 20 62 62 333 FAX: 31 20 62 45 321

The Ambassade is a most attractive hotel in the heart of Amsterdam. Originally ten separate houses, each the home of a wealthy merchant on the Herengracht (The Gentlemen's Canal), the hotel has been converted into one building which retains all the erstwhile interior architecture and the external façades. No two bedrooms are alike, and each has its own colour scheme in accordance with its style. The graceful furniture complements the history of the building. The five suites are superb and the apartments luxurious. Overlooking the canal are two elegant and spacious lounges, with tall windows, splendid oil paintings on the walls and fine Amsterdam grandfather clocks. Breakfast is served in the traditional dining room, or guests can take advantage of the efficient room service available. There is no restaurant in the Ambassade, but there is a wide choice of places to eat in the city, among them the historic Vijff Vlieghen, and many small bistros along the canal-sides. Amsterdam has wonderful museums and art galleries to visit – the famous Rijksmuseum, Rembrandt's House and the Van Gogh Museum. Anne Franks' House is very special. After seeing the flower market and fantastic shops, visitors can sample the lively nightlife. **Directions:** Parking is not easy. 20 minutes by taxi from Schipol Airport. Price guide: Single Fl 230; double/twin Fl 285; suites Fl 390–Fl 450.

Portugal

Eating is taken seriously in Portugal, and, not surprisingly, seafood is a staple diet. Freshly caught lobster, crab, prawns, tuna, sole and squid are prepared in innumerable ways, but if you want to sample a bit of everything, try caldeirada, a piquant stew made with whatever is freshest from the sea. In the Algarve, cataplana is the speciality. A mouth watering mixture of clams, ham, tomatoes, onions, garlic and herbs – named from the dish in which it is cooked. There are some excellent local wines, and in modest restaurants even the vinho da casa – house wine – is usually very good. Water is generally safe, but visitors may want to drink bottled water from one of the excellent Portuguese spas.

The country is divided into six historic provinces. Most visitors head for the low lying plains of the southern Algarve or the region around the Lisbon – Estoril coast, but as traditional tourist destinations become more crowded, adventurous travellers are trekking in other directions. The northern and central provinces – Minho, Beiras, and Tras os Montes – are wonderfully unspoilt, full of tiny villages and splendid scenery. In Tras os Montes – literally translating as 'over the hills' – you'll discover sweet chestnut and walnut trees – and in the south, vines on steep terraces fall down to the River Douro providing the grapes for port wine.

Estremadura, running up the coast from Lisbon to Leiria and south to Setubal, is undulating and cultivated, the land nearer to Lisbon supplying most of the fruit and vegetables for the capital. Lisbon's wide boulevards are bordered by black and white mosaic pavements made up of tiny cobblestones called calcada. Modern, pastel coloured apartment blocks vie for attention with Art Nouveau houses faced with decorative tiles. Winding, hilly streets provide scores of miradouros, natural vantage points that offer spectacular views of the Tagus estuary.

Lisbon is not a city easily explored on foot. The steep inclines of many streets present a tough challenge to the casual tourist, and visitors are often surprised to find that, because of the hills, places that appear to be close to one another on a map are actually on different levels. Yet the effort is worthwhile – judicious use of trams, a funicular railway, and the majestic city centre elevator make walking tours enjoyable even on the hottest summer day.

Up river from Lisbon lies the Ribatejo, the fertile plain with rice fields, market gardens and great pastures on which splendid horses and black fighting bulls roam freely. The Alentejo occupies nearly a third of the total land area of the country and lies between the Atlantic Ocean and Spain. The province is flat, with every eminence crowned by a castle-topped whitewashed village or town. Vast wheat fields stretch into the shimmering distance and groves of olive trees and cork oaks provide the only shade.

The Algarve is now the best known part of Portugal for the visitor. The sandy beaches are endless, clean and safe on the southern coast, the few to the west sometimes getting the full force of the Atlantic. Inland there are many interesting and beautiful places and Faro, the capital, is one of the most fascinating cities in Portugal.

Madeira is probably best known for its eponymous fortified wine, originally called malmsey, and its dusty bottles have a compelling history. Among its many devotees none can surpass the pioneering enthusiasm of the Duke of Clarence who, facing execution in the Tower of London in 1478, demanded that he be drowned in a butt of malmsey.

Madeira wine has a variety and distinction that surprise those unfamiliar with it.

The Madeira climate is remarkable for its consistency throughout the year. The weather is invariably warm, wet and sunny with average annual temperatures 61-72 degrees Celsius. March is wet but in the summer there is little rain. The southern coast of Madeira gets the most sun, though Porto Santo, the neighbouring small island being low and exposed, gets even more. Between December and April the temperature steadily increases and the summer months can be humid.

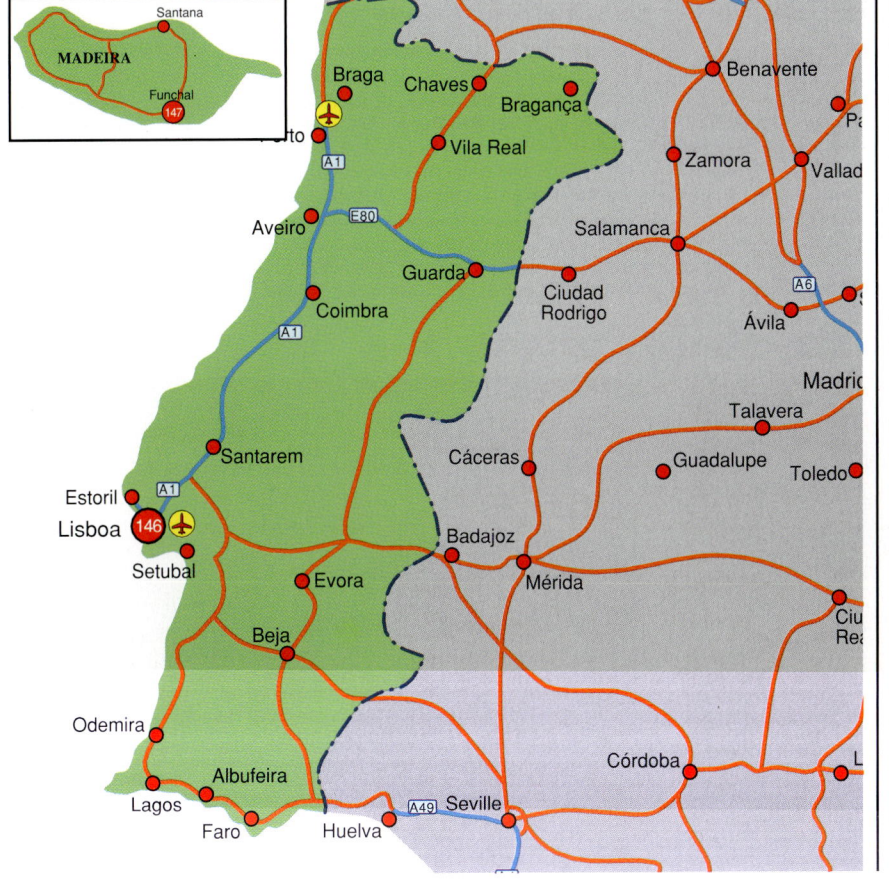

145

PORTUGAL (Lisbon)

In association with MasterCard

AS JANELAS VERDES
RUA DAS JANELAS VERDES 47, 1200 LISBON
TEL: 351 1 39 68 143 FAX: 351 1 39 68 144

Once the home of the famous Portuguese writer, Eca de Queiros, this classical 18th century townhouse in the old part of Lisbon, close to the River Tagus, is now an exquisite small hotel. Graceful archways, a wide staircase with ornate banisters, mahogany woodwork, alcoves filled with pedestals of flowers and warm yellow walls are an appropriate setting for the elegant period furniture, antiques and paintings in the charming salons. The bedrooms are peaceful, all double-glazed and air-conditioned, traditionally furnished and very comfortable. The back of the house is clad in ivy, and there is a delightful patio where guests enjoy breakfast in the summer, and refreshments are served later in the day. In cooler months they retreat to the reading room. The hotel staff will suggest restaurants with national and cosmopolitan menus for dinner at night. Lisbon is a fascinating city to explore, starting at the Museum of Ancient Art right next to the hotel, and there are so many beautiful buildings – cathedrals and palaces – botanical gardens and the castle to visit. Tramcar are in walking distance, and golfers have a choice of good courses nearby. **Directions:** Rua das Janelas Verdes is just off the Avenida Vinte de Quatro de Julho. Price guide: Single 16,900esc–25,000esc; double/twin 18,000esc–27,000esc. American buffet breakfast and taxes included.

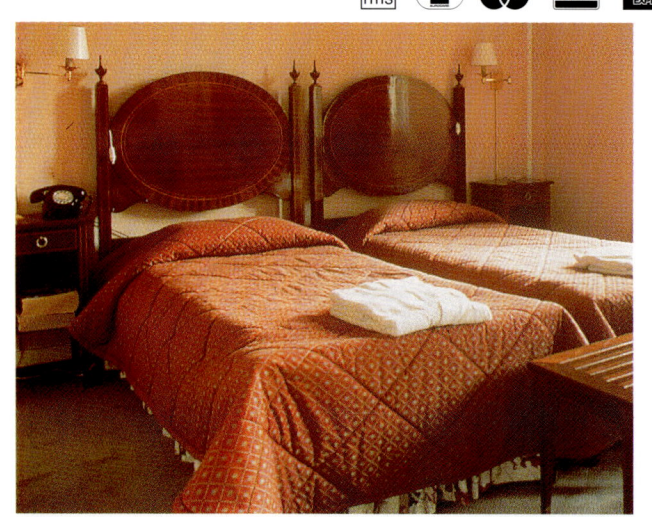

In association with MasterCard

PORTUGAL (Madeira)

REID'S HOTEL

P9000 FUNCHAL, MADEIRA, PORTUGAL
TEL: 44 1256 841155 FAX:44 1256 55226

Over the years this superb hotel has provided a peaceful retreat for many famous personalities. It is the quintessence of comfort and luxury. The bedrooms, which are mostly south facing, have balconies from which to enjoy the lovely sea views. Tropical and sub-tropical flowers, shrubs and trees flourish in profusion throughout the hotel's ten acres of terraced gardens. The Garden Restaurant overlooking the pool is ideal for breakfast, while in the Trattoria Villa Cliff, where meals may be enjoyed alfresco on the terrace, the menu contains a varierty of regional Italian dishes including the fresh catch of the day. Dinner in the elegant Main Dining Room is an experience not to be missed and the hotel's exclusive gourmet restaurant 'Les Faunes' is an option for those seeking the ultimate culinary experience. Irrigation channels known as Levadas cover the island and provide a network of walkways by which to explore the countryside and inland villages. For the less energetic, there are beautiful old houses, gardens, wine lodges, the embroidery factory and museums. Swimming, boat trips, sailing, windsurfing, water skiing, fishing and tennis are readily available. The hotel also offers preferential service at both the spectacular 18-hole Palheiro golf course just 15 minutes away and Santo Antonio da Serra. Price guide: Single £113–£265; double/twin £169–£378; suites £326–£760.

147

Russian Federation

Moscow lies on about the same latitude as Edinburgh in Scotland, although the climate is not similar. Summers are hot, and winters cold by Western European standards, although the dry, often sunny, weather makes them tolerable, if not always pleasurable.

The most popular time to go is in summer, lasting from the beginning of June to mid September. Days and nights are warm and sultry, with heat waves likely during August, when Muscovites leave in droves for their dachas in the country. Culturally, things are rather slack during this period, with the Bolshoi Ballet away from June till early September and many other theatres closed for the duration. Conversely, politics often hot up in August, sometimes boiling over a month or so later. By mid September, autumn is underway, with cloudy skies and falling temperatures, but you can still look forward to a week or two of Indian summer, when Moscow is an impressionist's vision of autumnal colours in the final glow of warmth.

Moscow's festival calendar is brief compared to that of Western European capitals, with just a couple of major events each year, plus the usual religious festivals and anniversary celebrations. The main festival periods are the Russian Winter – December 25 – January 5 and the Moscow Stars festival in May.

Although great parades on Red Square are now a thing of the past, die-hard Communists still celebrate May Day and the anniversary of the October Revolution (November 9) by laying flowers at Lenin's Mausoleum.

For sheer theatricality, Red Square is only surpassed by the Kremlin itself, whose palaces and cathedrals are a concoction of European and Asiatic splendour, echoing Italian Renaissance and the court of Genghis Khan. The name Red Square has nothing to do with communism – it derives from krasniy, the old Russian word for 'beautiful' which probably became 'red' due to people's thirst for bright colours during the long, drab winters.

Russian cooking owes much to the Jewish, Caucasian and Ukrainian influence, but remains firmly rooted to its peasant origins. Most menus start with a choice of zakuski. Zakuski may include salted fish, such as herrings, gherkins, assorted cold meats, salads, hard boiled eggs or blini, the latter served with caviar. Caviar is no longer as cheap as during the Brezhnev era, when people tired of eating so much of it, but still cheaper than in the West.

Main courses are based on meat – beef, pork or mutton, although in Moscow a wide variety of seafood is available. Pickled fish is a popular starter.

The concept of vegetarianism is a vague one for most Russians, so saying you're vegetarian may instil confusion in the waiter. It's often better to ask what's in a particular dish.

Puddings and sweets are not a strong feature of Russian cooking. Ice cream, fruit, apple pie and jam pancakes are restaurant stand-bys, while in Caucasian restaurants you may get a flaky pastry or honey dessert, rather like baklava.

And as for drink. Vodka is the national drink – its name means 'little water'. Drinking small amounts at a time, and eating as you go, it's possible to consume a lot without passing out.

Russians are justifiably proud of their classical music tradition. Moscow has produced some of the world's best known composers – Tchaikovsky, Rimsky Korsakov, Prokofiev and Shostakovich – and their works are played in all the major theatres – especially during the winter season in December and Moscow Stars Festival in May.

The Bolshoi has the largest ballet repertoire of any company in the world. In season, there are performances each day except Mondays, and sometimes a noon matinee on Sunday. Book through an agency and be prepared to pay in hard currency. Avoid touts.

The Puppet theatre is almost a 'must see' and the Moscow Circus is the best in the world – but does use live animals to entertain.

Shopping in Moscow brings home all you've ever heard about the failings of the Soviet economy and the wild capitalism of New Russia. Moscow is a jungle for the consumer, rather than a playground, but infinitely worth a safari.

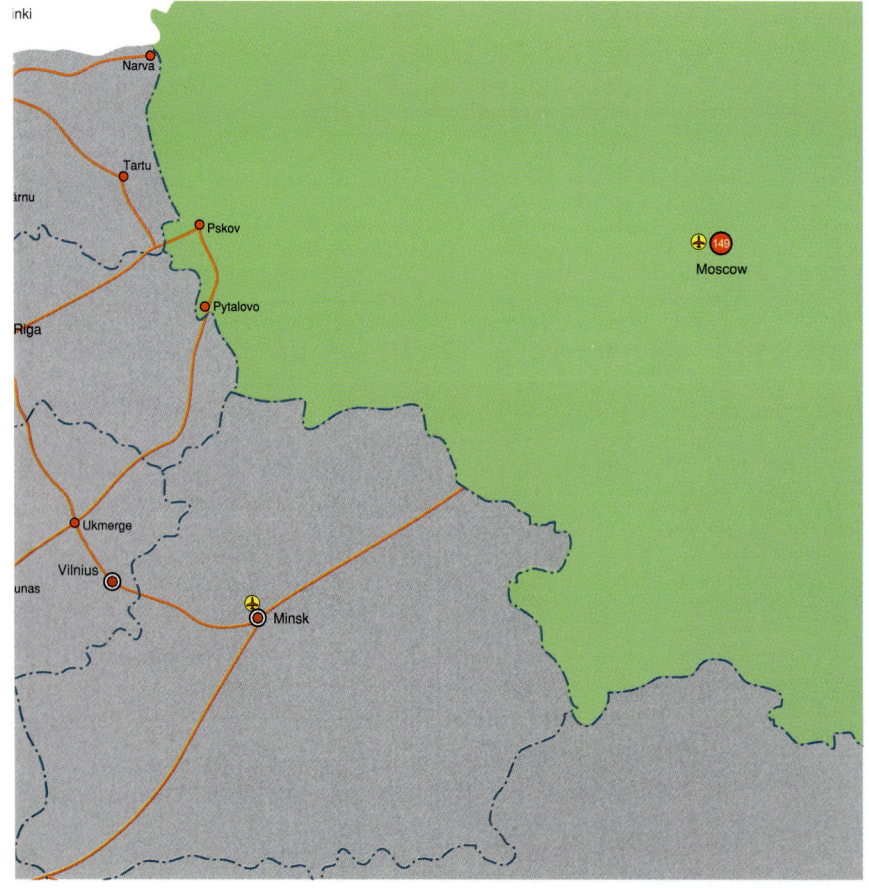

In association with MasterCard

RUSSIAN FEDERATION (Moscow)

KEMPINSKI HOTEL BALTSCHUG MOSKAU

UL. BALCHUG 1, 113 035 MOSCOW, RUSSIAN FEDERATION
TEL: 7 501 230 9500 FAX: 7 501 230 9502

In the heart of the city, on the banks of the Moskva, stands the proud Kempinski Hotel Baltschug Moskau. A five star classic European Grand Hotel, incorporating the graceful architecture of its late 19th century building. Many of its 234 beautifully appointed and air-conditioned rooms and suites invite guests to enjoy magnificent views of the Kremlin and Red Square. In the style of Kempinski Hotels, business travellers will feel at home in this hotel where professional and attentive service by multi-lingual staff comes first. Ample in-room working space and state-of-the-art telecommunication facilities (IDD-telephone, satellite TV, voice mail) guarantee easy and smooth access to business partners worldwide, and family at home. For the leisure traveller, a host of exciting activities are within walking distance: the famous Bolshoi Theatre, the GUM shopping centre on Red Square, the reopened Tretyakov Gallery and the Pushkin Museum of Art. Upon return from a strenuous day outside, you are invited to relax in the fitness centre with indoor pool, whirlpool, health bar, solarium and massage facilities. **Directions:** From airport 20 miles downtown (approx 30 minutes by hotel limousine). Price guide: Single 490DM–540DM; double/twin 540DM–590DM; suites 800DM–2500DM. Excluding taxes. Corporate rates available.

SLOVENIA

The problems of the former Yugoslavia touched Slovenia briefly in July 1991, and since then this independent republic has been a peaceful, safe place to visit. Despite escaping the war, the bad publicity scared off many western travellers, and consequently any visit to Slovenia – at the moment – will be blissfully free of tourists.

Slovenia is a land of contrasts – all of which are beautiful. It is squashed in between Austria, Croatia, Italy and Hungary. About as large as Wales, Slovenia is the smallest country in Eastern Europe. Much of it is mountainous, culminating in the north west at Mount Triglav in the Julian Alps. From this range, the main Alpine chain continues east along the Austrian border, while the Dinaric runs south east along the the coast into Croatia.

As elsewhere in the mediterranean, April to September are the best months to be in Slovenia as the days are long and the weather is warm. Snow lingers on the mountains as late as June, but spring is a good time to be in the lowlands as everything is fresh and in blossom.

The cultural highlights of Slovenia's summer are the International Summer Festival at Ljubljana and the Musical evenings at the Piran and Portoroz, both in July and August. Many events in old Ljubljana accompany the International Wine Fair in late August or early September. In early October there's a festival of Baroque music in Maribor.

In Slovenia you will enjoy some of the best food in Eastern Europe. You'll taste the Germanic flavour in the sausages and sauerkraut, game dishes an meat with mushrooms. Other neighbours have contributed Austrian strudel, layer cake, omelette and burek- a greasy layered cheese or meat pie, which is served at take aways throughout Slovenia.

There are many types of dumplings, of which walnut and cheese are a delicacy. Try the walnut rolls, and gibanica – a pastry filled with apples, cheese and poppy seeds, baked in cream and eaten warm. No Slovene lunch is complete without soup such as goveja juha – beef broth or jota – sauerkraut soup. Goulash is considered a main dish and not a soup. Traditional dishes are most easily found at inns, where the daily menus and specials are advertised on a blackboard on the street outside.

The wine growing regions of Slovenia are Prodravje in the east, Posavje in the south east, and Primorska near Koper. Slovenia is noted for its 'Champagne', Riesling, excellent dry rosé wines, hearty reds.

Ljubljana, capital of Slovenia, is a quaint, compact city – famous for its wonderful architecture and its foggy mornings – which clear mid morning to form brilliant sunshine. The most beautiful part is along the Sava River below the the castle.

Ljubljana enjoys a colourful cultural life, with three or four events each week in old town. From open air and avant garde theatre, to the more traditional symphony orchestra which performs in the Big Hall of ultra modern Cultural and Congress Centre or 'Cankarjev dom' – there's entertainment for all tastes and pockets.

The town of Bled is set on an idyllic, emerald lake which you can walk around in two hours. Trout and carp dance in the crystal clear lake water, which is warm enough to swim in. The climate is also good – and there's no fog at Bled during the summer. To the north east, the Karavanke Range forms a natural boundary with Austria. Bled Castle was the seat of the Bishops of South Tyrol for over 800 years. Set on top of an impressively steep cliff 100 meters above the lake, it offers a magnificent view in clear weather. The castle museum presents the history of the area and allows you to peer into the 16th century chapel.

The other feature of Bled which immediately attracts attention is a tiny island at the west end of the lake. From the massive red and white belfry rising above the forest, the tolling 'bell of wishes' echoes across the still waters. The legend says that all who ring this bell will be successful in love. What better reason could there be for visiting Slovenia?

In association with MasterCard

SLOVENIA (Bled)

HOTEL VILA BLED
CESTA SVOBODE 26, SLO-64260, BLED, SLOVENIA
TEL: 386 64 79 15 FAX: 386 64 74 13 20

This villa has an illustrious past, having been the summer home of the Yugoslavian royal family between the two World Wars. In the late 1940s Tito played host to many world leaders here. Bled is in the Southern Alps, and this lovely now predominantly 1950s style hotel stands in secluded flower-filled parkland overlooking Lake Bled with awe-inspiring mountains on the horizon. The region is famous for its long warm summer, pure air and exhilarating spa waters. Many of the delightful bedrooms and suites have balconies with magical views over the lake at night. The salons reflect the 50s era. Marble and glass are much in evidence in the reception hall and stylish bar-where guests gather while deciding which of the exquisite dishes to eat, either on the romantic terrace watching the lights on the water, or in the traditional restaurant. The wines are Slovenian, the whites from Styria while the reds include the famous 'black' varieties. Relaxation includes rowing, visiting the old castle, enjoying the private beach and strolling in the lovely grounds. Energetic visitors use the hotel tennis court, indulge in water-sports or play golf 2km away. After dark Bled offers discotheques, clubs and its Casino. **Directions:** E55 from Salzburg and at the Karawankentunnel on the Austrian border follow the E61/A1. Price guide: Single £66–£90; double/twin £91–£114; suites £100–£251.

SPAIN

The once common image of Spain as a package holiday destination suffering from over-development and mass tourism has faded. In its place is a Spain of sophisticated European cities, romantic hilltop villages, and a magnificent Moorish legacy.

Most of the Spanish are gathered in the cities, leaving the gaunter inland parts unpopulated. Spain is more mountainous than any European country except Switzerland.

Madrid is one of the highest capitals of the continent. The land climbs quickly up from the narrow strip of the north coast and once across the northern mountains open plains begin.

The beauty of the historic cities surrounding Madrid and the role they have played in their country's history rank them among Spain's most worthwhile sights. Ancient Toledo, the great palace monastery of El Escorial, the sturdy medieval walls of Avila, and the magnificent Plaza Mayor of the old university town of Salamanca all lie within an hour or so of Madrid.

Barcelona, capital of Catalonia and Spain's second largest city, thrives on its business acumen and industrial muscle. Its hard working citizens are almost militant in their use of their own language – with street names, museum exhibits, newspapers, radio programmes, and movies all in Catalan.

And then there is Moorish Spain. Stretching from the dark mountains of the Sierra Morena in the north west to the plains of the Guadalquivir valley, and south to the mighty snow capped Sierra Nevada, Andalucia rings with echoes of the Moors.

In English they are known as the Balearic Islands or the Balearics, in Spanish they are Las Islas Baleares or just Las Baleares. There are three of them, or four if you count little Formentera, next to the island of Ibiza, and they are all distinct from each other. They are geared for the holidaymaker, and they are Ibiza, Menorca and arguably the prettiest, Mallorca.

Mallorca is the biggest island in the archipelago and its capital, Palma de Mallorca, is the main town and administrative centre of the Balearics. The island has a little of everything – wide bays and tiny inlets, fertile, orchard-packed valleys, terraced hillsides and craggy peaks, crowds and concrete high-rises, solitude and lonely, stone farmhouses. Many people leave Mallorca after their holidays without having ventured from the coast. This is a pity because inland Mallorca is delightful.

Ibiza, is not strictly one of the Balearics, but belongs to the Pitiusas, or pine covered isles, and has more in common with North Africa than Spain. Ibiza is hotter, dryer and flatter than Mallorca and Menorca, but also boasts less lush countryside than the other two islands and fewer indigenous species. Parts of the island are extremely unspoilt – with their olive and almond groves, the fig and carob trees and the scented air of wild herbs, they are an authentic showcase for a very specific type of Mediterranean landscape.

The Canary Islands are politically European, being an integral part of Spain. Geographically they are only 60 miles from the north-west coast of Africa. The two biggest islands are Tenerife and Gran Canaria. The climate is excellent with resorts for swimming, golf, night-life and every form of holiday activity, including duty-free shopping.

The islands are pollution-free and the seas are clean. Tenerife has its mountain, Pico de Teide, over 12,000 feet high. Above all it brings water to the lush vegetation in the north. The south is drier and the weather more reliable.

Nelson sailed into the harbour of Santa Cruz and that's where he lost his arm! Nowadays the welcome is more hospitable and the cost of a visit less likely to be as heavy.

Gran Canaria has first-class sandy beaches. Inland there are fertile vineyards, sugar crops and banana groves. Las Palmas once the great port of call en route to South Africa and beyond, remains one of the busiest harbours in the Atlantic.

Columbus visited the Canary Islands on his voyage of discovery. Five hundred years later you should discover the Canaries for yourself!

In association with MasterCard

SPAIN (Ibiza)

PIKES

SAN ANTONIO DE PORTMANY, 07820 ISLA DE IBIZA, BALEARIC ISLANDS, SPAIN
TEL: 34 71 34 22 22 FAX: 34 71 34 23 12

'Informal sophistication' is the rule at this small idyllic hotel standing among olive and citrus groves outside Ibiza Town. Built in natural stone, it blends easily into the countryside, with bougainvillaea and other bright plants adding colour. Graceful archways, olive wood and tiled floors feature in the interior, the perfect background for the rustic furniture and traditional Spanish fabrics. There are more suites than bedrooms, with romantic flower-filled terraces and exotic plants in the luxurious bathrooms. The ambience is relaxing – breakfast is served until noon. The elegant Moorish-style restaurant is renowned throughout the island for its fine cooking and wines. There is a well-equipped meeting room for those combining work with pleasure. Active guests appreciate the large pool, the floodlit tennis court and the extensive gymnasium. Golfers use the practice nets before playing at the new championship course where hotel guests have special facilities. Hotel staff will organise riding, sailing and scuba diving. The lively nightlife in Ibiza Town is five minutes away, and the hotel's Privilege Card gives guests VIP treatment at the many disco clubs and the popular Casino. **Directions:** Pikes is signed off the Camino de sa Vorera. Price guide: 15,000pse–25,000pse; double/twin 15,000pse–25,000pse; suites 22,000pse–90,000pse.

SPAIN (Mallorca)

In association with MasterCard

La Residencia

HOTEL LA RESIDENCIA, DEIÀ, MALLORCA
TEL: 34 71 63 90 11 FAX: 34 71 63 93 70

Situated on the outskirts of the picturesque village of Deià and nestling in 30 acres of olive and citrus groves is La Residencia, a fine hotel which has been lovingly converted from two 16th century manor houses. The bars and salons have terraces where guests can sit under the eucalyptus and linden trees, savouring dramatic views of the nearby mountains and villages. The Olive Press from one of the original manors has been transformed into El Olivo, a delightful candlelit restaurant which has been awarded a Michelin Red Star for excellence. Here, a combination of the finest local produce and the considerable creative skills of the chefs combine to produce memorable cuisine. In the bedrooms breathtaking views and the scent of Jasmine help guests to forget the hustle and bustle of humdrum daily life. Bedrooms are furnished with traditional Spanish furniture and most have four-poster beds. Leisure facilities include a swimming pool fed by mountain spring water, tennis court set amidst the olive groves, gymnasium and a beauty centre. For those seeking sheer relaxation, there is a private cove just three kilometres from the hotel where bathing is safe and the conditions are ideal for snorkelling and diving. Both small and large groups can be catered for in the hotel's conference rooms. Price guide: Single 12,000pse–20,000pse; double/twin 19,500pse–38,000pse; suites 33,000pse–48,000pse.

In association with MasterCard

SPAIN (Salamanca)

RESIDENCIA RECTOR

RECTOR ESPERABÉ, 10-APARTADO 399, 37008 SALAMANCA, SPAIN
TEL: 34 23 21 84 82 FAX: 34 23 21 40 08

This exclusive hotel, with its elegant façade, stands by the walls of the citadel, looking up to the Cathedral – a magnificent golden vision at night when floodlit. Indeed this is a golden city, much of Salamanca being built in a soft yellow stone. The interior looks cool and elegant, with archways between the spacious reception hall and the welcoming bar. Unique features in the main salon, with its big leather furniture and tapestries on the walls, are two exquisite modern stained glass windows. Beyond these there is a courtyard garden. There are just 13 bedrooms, of ample size, all air-conditioned and double-glazed. The furnishings are delightful and facilities in the marble bathrooms include a telephone. The hotel only serves breakfast, but is easy to find restaurants serving traditional Spanish dishes or gastronomic experiences. It is possible to communicate in English in the hotel. There are many wonderful historical buildings in this city, including the Cathedral and the university and the city guide has two recommended routes and the firsts of these starts close to the hotel. **Directions:** Arriving on the main road from Madrid, drive up Avenida De Los Reyes Catolicos, and turn left onto Pa de Rector Esperabe, finding the hotel approximately 300 metres on the left. Price guide: Single 10,000pse; double/twin 16,000pse; suites 20,000pse.

155

SPAIN (Seville)

In association with MasterCard

CASA DE CARMONA
PLAZA DE LASSO, 41410 CARMONA, SEVILLE, SPAIN
TEL: 34 54 14 33 00 FAX: 34 54 14 37 52

Brilliant restoration of the 16th century Lasso de la Vega palace has ensured that today guests, upon entering, feel impressed that they may actually stay in such a fine palace. It is very exclusive, in that it is only open to residents and their friends, not to the casual passer-by. The staff are wonderful, the concierge conducts arrivals to their rooms, explaining how everything works, and the chambermaids will unpack bags and take away laundry. Then it is time to explore the Casa. The exterior is in warm golden stone and the venerable door leads into spacious terracotta-tinted courtyards, the loggia terrace, an Arabian garden and an exchanting pool, surrounded by exotic plants. The salons are very regal, in wonderful harmonising colours and containing many fine antiques. The cool traditional bedrooms are delightful, with pristine linen, and the suites are luxurious. The wines and delicious dishes served in the handsome restaurant are Spanish. Conferences and seminars take place in four meeting rooms, furnished with the latest presentation equipment. Archeologists appreciate Italica, other guests explore Seville, visit Andalucia, taste sherry in Jerez, enjoy the beaches at Cadiz or play golf nearby. **Directions:** From Seville NIV towards Cordoba, take the exit signed Carmona and follow signs to the hotel. Price guide: Single 19,000pse; double/twin 22,000pse–26,000pse; grand suite 80,000pse.

In association with MasterCard

SPAIN (Tenerife)

Gran Hotel Bahia Del Duque
PLAYA DEL DUQUE, FANABE ADEJE, TENERIFE, CANARY ISLANDS
TEL: 34 22 71 30 00 FAX: 34 22 71 26 16

Gran Hotel Bahia Del Duque is a private romantic village created on a gentle hill sloping down to the sea. Nineteen houses in turn-of-the-century Canarian architecture form this prestigious complex in a large estate with sculptured terraces and pools. Corinthian columns flank the entrance, staff in period costume greet guests. There is a well-equipped conference and exhibition area. The bedrooms are in low colour-washed buildings, many with terraces facing the sea. The furniture has been specially designed, the floors are cool Spanish tiles, the bathrooms are luxurious. The Casas Ducales – Manor houses – have a separate reception area, breakfast room and butler service. Descending towards the coast guests find a fountain-filled patio surrounded by several restaurants – French, Spanish, Italian and the à la carte restaurant "El Duque". Two bars and a reading room. Below are four swimming pools, further bars and restaurants. Floodlighting makes these even more spectacular. Leisure activities include strolling among the tropical trees, a beach club, tennis, putting and a fully equipped gym. Golf, windsurfing and diving are nearby. Visiting La Gomera by ferry or the Tenerife National Park is a fascinating experience. **Directions:** The hotel will meet guests at Reina Sofia Airport – there is parking for those hiring a car. Price guide: Single 23,500pse–25,000pse; double/twin 29,800pse–32,000pse; suites 42,300pse–190,000pse.

SWITZERLAND

Like a breath of fresh air, Switzerland revives sagging spirits. Pine forests scale steep mountain sides to the barrier of granite and eternal snow. Wild, thin waterfalls rush to disturb the tranquillity of mirror-still lakes. In the valleys – some scarcely wider than ravines – bells clang as the fat, black and tan cows graze. Medieval castles watch over villages brightened by deep reds and greens in flower pots.

Irascibly devout, manically clean, prompt as their world renowned watches, the Swiss measure liquors with scientific precision into glasses marked for one or two centilitres, and the local wines come in sized carafes that have the look of laboratory beakers. And as for passion – well, the 'double' beds have separate mattresses and sheets tucked firmly down the middle.

Switzerland boasts alpine grandeur, urban sophistication, ancient villages, endless ski slopes, and all round artistic excellence. It's the heart of the Reformation, the homeland of William Tell – and his apple. Its cities are full of historic landmarks, its countryside peppered with castles. The varied cuisine reflects an ethnic mix, with three distinct cultures dominating – French in the south-west, Italian in the south-east, and German – a 70% majority in the north and east.

Because the Swiss are so good at preparing everyone else's cuisine, it is sometimes unkindly said that they have none of their own, but there definitely is a distinct and characteristic Swiss cuisine. Switzerland is the home of great cheeses – Gruyère, Emmentaler, Appenzeller, and Vacherin – which form the basis of many dishes.

Zurich, is not typical of other Swiss cities. Stroll round on a fine Spring day and you'll ask yourself if this can really be one of the great business centres of the world. The lake glistens and an azure blue sky looks down on you, the pavement cafés, the swans gliding in to land on the river, the hushed and haunted old squares of medieval guild houses, the elegant shops.

Draped at the foot of the Juras and the Alps on the western-most tip of Lake Geneva – or Lac Léman, as the natives know it, Geneva is the most cosmopolitan and graceful of Swiss cities and the stronghold of the French speaking territory. Close to the French border and 100 miles or so from Lyon, its grand mansarded mansions stand guard beside the River Rhône, where yachts bob, gulls dive, and Rolls Royces purr beside manicured promenades.

Bern – the Federal capital of Switzerland – is also the geographic and political hub of the country. No cosmopolitan nonsense here – the local specialities are fatback and sauerkraut, the annual fair features the humble onion, and the President takes the tram to work. Walking down broad, medieval streets past squares teeming with farmers' markets and cafés full of shirt-sleeved politicos, you may forget this is the capital of a sophisticated, modern and prosperous nation.

Nearly 200 Swiss towns and villages cater for downhill skiing, among them famous resorts like St Moritz, Zermatt and Gstaad. In most areas the season runs from late November to early April, but conditions vary from year to year and resort to resort. Zermatt also offers summer skiing for those who can't wait until next season.

In spring is the Musical Festival in Neuchâtel, the festival of music and ballet in Lausanne and the Golden Rose Television Festival at Montreux.

Summer welcomes the Rose Week in Geneva, Swiss National Day on August 1st celebrated with fireworks and parades throughout the country and the Yehudi Menuhin Festival in Gstaad.

In autumn, there are torchlit religious processions at Einsiedeln, Garden shows in Geneva, the Italian Opera Festival in Lausanne and vintage festivals in wine-growing regions.

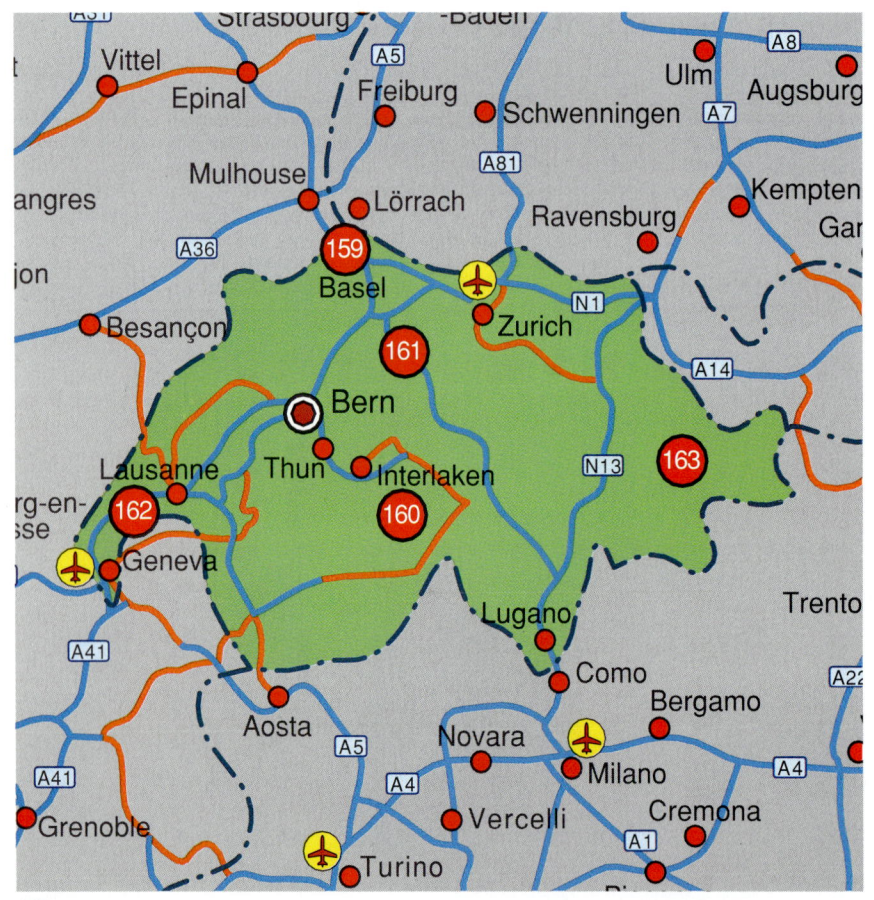

SWITZERLAND (Basel)

Hotel Basel

AM SPALENBERG MÜNZGASSE 12, CH-4051 BASEL, SWITZERLAND
TEL: 41 61 26 46 800 FAX: 41 61 26 46 811

Hotel Basel is a graceful modern hotel, blending easily into the old town. Flowers cascading down from the window boxes add a touch of gaiety. The central location is perfect, both for business people and those exploring this fascinating city. The pristine bedrooms and suites are spacious, modern and very well appointed, with compact bathrooms. The efficient 24-hour room service is a great convenience. The Sperber is a popular bar, with residents and locals alike, who enjoy the convivial atmosphere and frequent jazz concerts. The Brasserie Munz is ideal for informal and quick meals, a boulevard café with a terrace for warm days. The Basler Keller is a very elegant restaurant, serving fabulous French and regional dishes accompanied by superb wines – advance reservations are recommended. Two smart, well equipped conference rooms can be used for private entertaining. Basel has carefully preserved its many mediaeval monuments, the cathedral, the delightful Holbeinbrunnen fountain and the splendid Spalentor city gate. Interesting cruises down the Rhine are available. There are museums, art galleries and concerts galore. The Black Forest is a short drive away. **Directions:** 15 minutes from the Airport by taxi, and private car-parking for motorists who will be sent a detailed city map to assist their arrival. Price guide: Single Sf220-Sf250; double/twin Sf295–Sf350; suites Sf425.

SWITZERLAND (Grindelwald)

In association with MasterCard

ROMANTIK HOTEL SCHWEIZERHOF

3818 GRINDELWALD, SWITZERLAND
TEL: 41 36 53 22 02 FAX: 41 36 53 20 04

This large chalet style hotel, with its bright window boxes and shutters, in the Bernese Oberland, is perfectly situated for skiers in winter and for visitors in the summer as the starting point for alpine tours. Grindelwald is at the foot of the Eiger, and the Schweizerhof is just two minutes from the village centre, close to the mountain railways and chairlifts. The interior of the hotel is in the tradition of the region, with beautiful carved woodwork. The spacious bedrooms, many with terraces facing the Alps, have charming rustic furniture, and modern bathrooms. The lounge and library are peaceful. The dining room caters for all appetites – those who enjoy haute cuisine appreciate the chef's talents and the fine wine list. Those who are really hungry after exercise enjoy the supper menu, while guests just wanting a snack are equally welcome. Ski-ing is superb, and in summer visitors enjoy walking through the alpine flowers or exploring on mountain bikes. A day trip to the Jungfraujoch 'Top of Europe' restaurant will be memorable, whatever time of year. The leisure centre has a heated pool, sauna, solarium, gymnasium and beauty salon. Indoor sports include billiards and bowling. **Directions:** Grindelwald is signed from Interlaken and the hotel has parking. It is also close to the railway station. Price guide: Single Sf170–Sf222; double/twin Sf310–Sf428; suites Sf394–Sf532.

In association with MasterCard

SWITZERLAND (Lucerne)

Hotel Wilden Mann

BAHNHOFSTRASSE 30, CH-6000 LUCERNE 7, SWITZERLAND
TEL: 41 210 16 66 FAX: 41 210 16 29

This elegant hotel, a 16th century townhouse in the Old Town, has been in the same family for 150 years. The attractive façade, with its medieval arched doorway, bright window boxes, pretty blinds and balconies immediately alerts arrivals that the Wilden Mann is special – the lobby is a joy with its fine antiques, and comfortable welcoming furniture. The salon is another delightful room in which to enjoy gorgeous Swiss patisseries. The bedrooms and suites are all different shapes and sizes, as one might expect in such an old building. Charming wallpapers co-ordinate with the bedspreads – even in the single rooms. The intimate bar is ideal for apéritifs before trying one of the three restaurants. The Gourmet is typically French, candle-lit at night, and offers superb food and wines. The light, airy Geranienterrasse is perfect in summer weather, while the rustic Burgerstube is cosy and informal, serving local specialities. There are also handsome private dining rooms which can be used for meetings. Lucerne is fascinating and a pleasant way to see it is from one of the steamers on the historic lake. A day excursion into the mountains to see the glaciers is exciting. Lucerne houses the Swiss National Museum of transport. **Directions:** The hotel is 500 metres from the railway station and has parking. Price guide: Single Sf150–Sf210; double/twin Sf260–Sf320; suites Sf300–Sf420.

161

SWITZERLAND (Morges)

In association with MasterCard

LA FLEUR DU LAC

70 ROUTE DE LAUSANNE, QUAI I, STRAVINSKY, CH-1110 MORGES, SWITZERLAND
TEL: 41 21 80 24 314 FAX: 41 21 80 23 474

This enchanting small hotel is in a perfect setting right on the bank of Lake Geneva, with the soft sound of water lapping on the shore, surrounded by beautiful gardens. The front of La Fleur du Lac is a mass of colour, and at the back landscaped gardens offer peace and shade on warm days. The salons are exquisite, filled with fine antiques. The charming bedrooms contain all modern amenities and, facing south, they look over the lake toward Mont Blanc. Those on the first three floors have balconies. Mobility problems are recognised. The piano bar is convivial and drinks are also served in the gardens. To eat here is a memorable experience, whether in the sophisticated French Restaurant Fleur du Lac, also offering regional specialities, or in the more informal Bistro, with a plat du jour or three course menu, or on the elegant Terrace overlooking the lake, enjoying summer dishes. 35,000 bottles of fine Swiss and French wines are stored in the cellar! Several private dining-rooms and the banqueting hall make handsome well-equipped meeting rooms. Swimming, tennis, golf and sailing nearby, lake cruises, exploring the Old Town, visiting museums and tasting wine soon fill the day. **Directions:** 10 minutes from Lausanne, Morges is signed on the Route de Lausanne. The hotel has parking. Price guide: Single Sf137–Sf207; double/twin Sf172–Sf325; suites Sf436–Sf561.

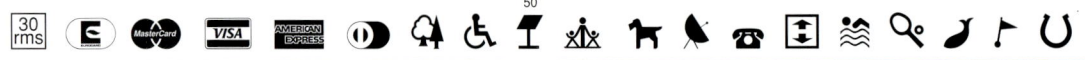

In association with MasterCard

SWITZERLAND (Zuoz)

POSTHOTEL ENGIADINA

VIA MAISTRA, ZUOZ, SWITZERLAND
TEL: 41 82 71 021 FAX: 41 82 73 303 FROM APRIL 1996: TEL 41 81 85 41 021 FAX: 41 81 85 43 303

This traditional Swiss manor house, for over 120 years an immaculate hotel;, is in Zuoz, a village that has kept much of its 16th century architectural charm. In winter the snow-covered Engadine provides superb ski-ing, and in summer it offers wonderful walks among the flower-filled meadows, lakes and forests of the Swiss National Park. The Posthotel reception hall is spacious with graceful vaulted ceilings. The attractive lounges have lovely tiled fireplaces, period furniture and a peaceful ambience. The bedrooms all look across to the Alps. Energetic visitors start the day with a breakfast from the extensive buffets in the colourful Sela Verda and Sela Melna dining rooms, to which they return later in the day for the table d'hôte dinner. Two other handsome restaurants, La Posta Veglia and La Prüveda offer haute cuisine and marvellous Swiss, French and Italian wines. Evenings often end in the La Chamanna bar. In summer the hotel pool, tennis court and bicycles are popular. Europe's highest golf course is nearby, trout fishing can be arranged, and surf boarders go to the Engadine lakes. Winter sports enthusiasts appreciate the sauna to relax their weary muscles. **Directions:** By road or rail, through Chur. Zuoz is signed from St. Moritz, just 15km away. Price guide: Single Sf130–Sf162; double/twin Sf90–Sf152.

Indexes

1996 Johansens Recommended Hotels in Europe listed alphabetically by Country

AUSTRIA

HoteldDorf Grüner Baum	Bad Gastein	10
Thermenhotel Haus Hirt	Bad Gastein	11
Deuring Schlössle	Bregenz	12
Hôtel Der Bär	Ellmar	13
Schlosshotel Igls	Igls	14
Sporthotel Igls	Igls	15
Romantik Hotel Tennerhof	Kitzbühel	16
Hotel Auersperg	Salzburg	17
Hotel Schloss Mönchstein	Salzburg	18
Romantik-Hotel Gasthof Hirschen	Schwarzenberg	19
Hotel Viktoria	Seefeld	20

BELGIUM

Die Swaene	Bruges	23
Hotel De Tuilerieen	Bruges	24
Hotel Prinsenhof	Bruges	25
Relais Oud Huis Amsterdam	Bruges	26
Romantik Pandhotel	Bruges	27
Hostellerie Sparrenhof	De Panne	28
Château Du Lac	Genval	29
Les Ardillières Du Pont D'Oye	Habay-La-Neuve	30
Hostellerie Trôs Marets	Malmédy	31
Château d'Hassonville	Marche-En-Famenne	32

BRITISH ISLES

The Beaufort	London	34
Blakes Hotel	London	35
Cannizaro House	London	36
The Halcyon	London	37
22 Jermyn Street	London	38
The Leonard	London	39
The Milestone	London	40
Number Sixteen	London	41
The Savoy	London	42

CYPRUS

The Annabelle	Paphos	44

CZECH REPUBLIC

Hotel Palace Praha	Prague	46

DENMARK

Steensgaard Herregardspension	Faaborg	48
Strandhotellet	Skagen	49

FRANCE

Le Mas De Peint	Arles – Le Sambuc	52
Auberge de Cassagne	Avignon – Le Pontet	53
Auberge De Noves	Avignon – Noves	54
Hôtel Du Palais	Biarritz	55
Hôtel L'Horset Savoy	Cannes	56
Hôtel Majestic	Cannes	57
Château Hôtel André Ziltener	Chambolle-Musigny	58
Hôtel Albert 1st	Chamonix	59
Château Des Briottières	Champigné	60
Le Prieuré	Chenehutte-Les-Tuffeaux	61
Romantik Hostellerie Le Maréchal	Colmar	62
Le Moulin De Connelles	Connelles	63
Hôtel Annapurna	Courchevel	64
Hôtel Des Trois Vallées	Courchevel	66
L'Hotel Des Neiges	Courchevel	65
Hôtel Royal	Deauville	67
Hostellerie La Briqueterie	Épernay	68
Château Eza	Eze Village	69
Hostellerie Le Phébus	Gordes Joucas	70
Le Castel Marie-Louise	La Baule	71
La Tour Rose	Lyon	72
Château Des Vigiers	Monestier	73
Vista Palace Hotel	Monte Carlo	92
Grand Hotel De La Reine	Nancy	74
Hotel La Pérouse	Nice	75
Château Du Tertre	Normandy	76
Relais Brenner	Paimpol	77
Hôtel Du Roy	Paris	80
Hôtel L'Horset Opéra	Paris	81
Hôtel Lancaster	Paris	82
Hôtel Royal Saint-Honoré	Paris	83
Montalembert	Paris	84
Pavillon De La Reine	Paris	85
Relais Christine	Paris	86
Relais St Germain	Paris	87
Royal Hôtel	Paris	88
Saint James-Paris	Paris	89
Les Suites Saint Honoré	Paris	90
La Chenèvière	Port-en-Bessin	91
Hôtel Château Grand Barrail	Saint-Émilion	93
Saint-Paul Le	Saint-Paul-De-Vence	94
Mas d'Artigny	Saint-Paul-De-Vence	95
Domaine de Valmouriane	St Rémy-de-Provence	97
Château Des Alpilles	St Rémy-de-Provence	96
Hostellerie Du Vallon De Valrugues	St Rémy-de-Provence	98

GERMANY

Hotel Töpferhaus	Alt Duvenstedt	102
Mönchs Posthotel	Bad Herrenbald	103
Hotel Arminius	Bad Salzuflen	104
Der Kleine Prinz	Baden Baden	105
Schlosshotel Bühlerhöhe	Baden Baden	106
Hotel Brandenburger Hof	Berlin	107
Kempinski Hotel Bristol	Berlin	108
Bülow Residenz	Dresden	109
Post-Hotel Garmisch Partenkirchen	Garmisch-Partenkirchen	110
Kempinski Hotel Atlantic Hamburg	Hamburg	111
Schlosshotel Hugenpoet	Kettwig	112
Burghotel Auf Schönberg	Oberwesel/Rhein	113
Pflaums Posthotel Pegnitz	Pegnitz	114
Hotel Alexandra	Plauen	115
Parkhotel Schlangenbad	Schlangenbad	116
Hôtel Stadt Hamburg	Westerland/Sylt	117

GIBRALTAR

The Rock Hotel	Gibraltar	120

HUNGARY

Hotel Gellért	Budapest	122

ITALY

Ripagrande Hotel	Ferrara	125
Hotel Albani	Florence	126
Hotel Regency	Florence	127
Romantic Hotel Oberwirt	Marling/Meran	128
Albergo Miramare	Naples	129
Il Pellicano	Porto Ercole	130
Hotel Farnese	Rome	131
Hotel Lord Byron	Rome	132
Hotel Majestic Roma	Rome	133
Hotel Raphaël	Rome	134
Romantic Hotel Villa Ducale Sicily		135
Hotel Cipriani & Palazzo Vendramin	Venice	137
Hotel Londra Palace	Venice	138
Albergo Quattro Fontane	Venice Lido	136

LUXEMBOURG

Parc Hotel	Berdorf	140

MONACO

Hôtel Mirabeau	Monte Carlo	142

THE NETHERLANDS

Hotel Ambassade	Amsterdam	144

PORTUGAL

As Janelas Verdes	Lisbon	146
Reid's Hotel	Madeira	147

RUSSIAN FEDERATION

Kempinski Hotel Baltschug Moskau	Moscow	149

SLOVENIA

Hotel Vila Bled	Bled	151

SPAIN

Pikes	Ibiza	153
La Residencia	Mallorca	154
Residencia Rector	Salamanca	155
Casa De Carmona	Seville	156
Gran Hotel Bahia Del Duque	Tenerife	157

SWITZERLAND

Hotel Basel	Basel	159
Romantik Hotel Schweizerhof	Grindelwald	160
Hotel Wilden Mann	Lucerne	161
La Fleur Du Lac	Morges	162
Posthotel Engiadina	Zous	163

Alphabetical lists of Johansens recommendations in Great Britain and Ireland – published in full in Johansens guides to Hotels, Inns and Country Houses – see back cover and page 168.

Hotels

LONDON

The Ascott	London	0171 499 6868
The Halcyon	London	0171 727 7288
22 Jermyn Street	London	0171 734 2353
The Basil Street Hotel	London	0171 581 3311
The Beaufort	London	0171 584 5252
Beaufort House Apartments	London	0171 584 2600
Blakes Hotel	London	0171 370 6701
The Cadogan	London	0171 235 7141
Cannizaro House	London	0181 879 1464
Claridges	London	0171 629 8860
The Dorchester	London	0171 629 8888
Draycott House	London	0171 584 4659
Harrington Hall	London	0171 396 9696
The Howard	London	0171 836 3555
The Milestone	London	0171 917 1000
Number Eleven Cadogan Gardens	London	0171 730 3426
Number Sixteen	London	0171 589 5232
The Pembridge Court Hotel	London	0171 229 9977
The Savoy	London	0171 836 4343
The Sloane Hotel	London	0171 581 5757
The Berkeley	London	0171 235 6000
The Leonard	London	0171 493 2055

ENGLAND

The Angel Hotel	Suffolk	01284 753926
The Ardencote Manor	Warwickshire	01926 843111
The Beacon Country House	Somerset	01643 703476
The Borrowdale Gates	Keswick	017687 77204
The Castle At Taunton	Somerset	01823 272671
The Close Hotel	Gloucestershire	01666 502272
The Commodore	Devon	01271 860347
The Edgemoor Hotel	South Devon	01626 832466
The Feathers Hotel	Oxfordshire	01993 812291
The French Horn	Berkshire	01734 692204
The Horn Of Plenty	Devon	01822 832528
The Ilsington House Country Hotel	Devon	01364 661452
The Lygon Arms	Worcestershire	01386 852255
The Manor House	Wiltshire	01249 782206
The Manor House Hotel	Devon	01647 440355
The Mill House Kingham	Oxfordshire	01608 658188
The Old Bell	Wiltshire	01666 822344
The Palace Hotel	Torquay	01803 200200
The Pentire Rocks Hotel	North Cornwall	01208 862213
The Plough	Oxfordshire	013678 10222
The Royal Crescent	Bath	01225 739955
The Victoria Hotel	West Yorkshire	01274 72870
The Webbington Hotel	Somerset	01934 750100
The Well House	Cornwall	01579 342001
The Woolton Redbourne Hotel	Liverpool	0151 428 2152
42 The Calls	West Yorkshire	0113 244 0099
The Alderley Edge Hotel	Cheshire	01625 583033
Alexander House	West Sussex	01342 714914
Alston Hall	Nr Plymouth	01752 830555
Amberley Castle	West Sussex	01798 831992
Angel Hotel	West Sussex	01730 812421
The Angel Posting House	Surrey	01483 64555
Appleby Manor	Cumbria	017683 51571
The Arundell Arms	Devon	01566 784666
Ashdown Park	Ashdown Forest	01342 824988
Bagden Hall	Nr Huddersfield	01484 865330
Bailiffscourt	West Sussex	01903 723511
Balmoral Hotel	Yorkshire	01423 508208
Barnsdale Lodge	Rutland	01572 724678
The Bay Tree Hotel	Oxfordshire	01993 822791
The Bel Alp House	South Devon	01364 661217
Belstead Brook Hotel	Suffolk	01473 684241
Bilbrough Manor	North Yorkshire	01937 834002
Billesley Manor	Stratford-upon-Avon	01789 400888
Bishopstrow House	Wiltshire	01985 212312
Blunsdon House Hotel	Wiltshire	01793 721701
The Boars Head Hotel	North Yorkshire	01423 771888
Bolt Head Hotel	Devon	01548 843751
Brandshatch Place Hotel	Kent	01474 872239
Breamish Country House Hotel	Northumberland	01665 578266
The Bridge Hotel	Cheshire	01625 829326
Briggens House Hotel	Stansted Abbots	01279 792416
Brockencote Hall	Worcestershire	01562 777876
Brookdale House Restaurant	South Brent	01548 821661
The Brookhouse Hotel	Staffordshire	01283 814188
Broomhill Lodge	East Sussex	01797 280421
Broxton Hall Country House Hotel	Cheshire	01829 782321
Buckatree Hall Hotel	Telford	01952 641821
Buckland Manor	Gloucestershire	01386 852626
Buckland-Tout-Saints	Devon	05148 853055
Budock Vean	Falmouth	01326 250288
Buxted Park	East Sussex	01825 732711
Calcot Manor	Gloucestershire	01666 890391
Callow Hall	Derbyshire	01335 343403
Careys Manor Hotel	Hampshire	01590 23551
The Carlton Hotel	Dorset	01202 552011
The Carlton Hotel	Hebden Bridge	01422 844400
Cavendish Hotel	Derbyshire	01246 582311
Charingworth Manor	Gloucestershire	01386 593555
Charnwood Hotel	South Yorkshire	0114 258 9411
The Chase Hotel	Herefordshire	01989 763161
Chedington Court	Dorset	01935 891265
The Chester Grosvenor	Cheshire	01244 324024
Chevin Lodge Country Park	Otley	01943 467818
Chewton Glen	Hampshire	01425 275341
Chilston Park Country Hotel	Nr Maidstone	01622 859 803
Cliveden	Berkshire	01628 668561

164

Combe Grove Manor Hotel	Bath	01225 834644
Congham Hall	Norfolk	01485 600250
Coombe Abbey Hotel	Nr Coventry	01203 450450
Corse Lawn House Hotel	Gloucestershire	01452 780479
The Cotswold House	Gloucestershire	01386 840330
The Cottage In The Wood Hotel	Worcestershire	01684 573487
Crabwall ManorChester	Cheshire	01244 851666
Crathorne Hall Hotel	Cleveland	01642 700398
Crudwell Court Hotel	Wiltshire	01666 577194
Danesfield House	Marlow	01628 891010
Daneswood House Hotel	Nr Winscombe	01934 843145
The Devonshire Arms	Skipton	01756 710441
Dinham Hall	Shropshire	01584 876464
Donnington Valley Hotel	Newbury	01635 551199
Dormy House	Worcestershire	01386 852711
Down Hall	Hertfordshire	01279 731441
Eastwell Manor	Kent	01233 635751
Esseborne Manor	Hampshire	01264 736444
Etrop Grange Hotel	Manchester	0161 499 0500
Ettington Park Hotel	Warwickshire	01789 450123
The Evesham Hotel	Gresham	01386 765566
Farlam Hall Hotel	Cumbria	016977 46234
Fischer's	Derbyshire	01246 583259
Five Lakes Hotel	Malden	01621 868888
Flitwick Manor	Bedfordshire	01525 712242
Foley Lodge Hotel	NewburyBerkshire	01635 528770
Fredrick's Hotel & Restaurant	Berkshire	01628 35934
The Garrack Hotel	Cornwall	01736 796199
The George At Stamford	Lincolnshire	01780 55171
Gibbon Bridge Country House	Lancashire	01995 61456
Gidleigh Park	Devon	01647 432367
Gilpin Lodge	Cumbria	015394 88818
The Glebe At Barford	Warwickshire	01926 624218
Grafton Manor	Worcestershire	01527 579007
The Grange Hotel Clifton	South Yorkshire	01904 644744
Grants Hotel	North Yorkshire	01423 560666
The Grapevine Hotel	Gloucestershire	01451 830344
Graythwaite Manor Hotel	Cumbria	015395 32001
The Greenway	Gloucestershire	01242 862352
Hackness GrangePark	Scarborough	01723 882345
Haley's Hotel And RestaurantLeeds	West Yorkshire	0113 2784446
Halmpstone Manor	Devon	01271 830321
Hambleton Hall	Rutland	01572 756991
Hanbury Manor Hotel	Hertfordshire	01920 487722
Hartwell House	Buckinghamshire	01296 747444
Hassop Hall	Derbyshire	01629 640488
Hatton Court	Gloucestershire	01452 617412
The Haycock At Wansford	Cambridgeshire	01780 782223
Headlam Hall	Darlington	01325 730238
Hintlesham Hall	Suffolk	01473 652268
Hoar Cross Hall Health Spa	Staffordshire	01283 575671
Hob Green Hotel And Restaurant	North Yorkshire	01423 770031
Holbeck Ghyll	Cumbria	015394 32375
Holdsworth House Hotel	HalifaxWest Yorkshire	01422 240024
Hollington House Hotel	Berkshire	01635 255100
Holne Chase Hotel	Devon	01364 631471
Homewood Park	Avon	01225 723731
Hope End Hotel	Hereford & Worcester	01531 633613
Horsted Place	East Sussex	01825 750581
Hotel Du Vin & Bistro	Hampshire	01962 841414
Hotel On The Park	Gloucestershire	01242 518898
Hotel Riviera	Devon	01395 515201
Howfield Manor	Kent	01227 738294
Huntsrete House	Avon	01761 490490
The Ivy House	Wiltshire	01672 515333
Kilhey Court	WiganLancashire	01257 472100
Kirkstone Foot	Cumbria	015394 32232
Lainston House Hotel	Hampshire	01962 863588
The Lake Isle Restaurant And Hotel	Leicestershire	01572 822951
Lakeside Hotel	Cumbria	015395 31207
Langar Hall	Nottinghamshire	01949 860559
Langdale Chase	Cumbria	015394 32201
Langley House Hotel	Wiveliscombe	01984 623318
Langshott Manor	Surrey	01293 786680
Le Maison Restaurant	Essex	01206 322367
Le Manoir Aux Quat'Saisons	Oxfordshire	01844 278881
Linden Hall Hotel	Newcastle Upon Tyne	01670 516611
The Linthwaite House Hotel	Cumbria	015394 88600
Linton Springs Hotel	Wetherby	01937 585353
Little Thakeham	West Sussex	01903 744416
Lords Of The Manor Hotel	Cheltenham	01451 820243
Lovelady Shield	Cumbria	01434 381203
Lower Slaughter Manor	Gloucestershire	01451 820456
Lucknam Park	Wiltshire	01225 742777
The Lugger Hotel	Cornwall	01872 501322
Lumley Castle Hotel	Durham	091 389 1111
The Lynton Cottage Hotel	Devon	01598 52342
Lythe Hill Hotel And Restaurants	Surrey	01428 651251
Madeley Court	Shropshire	01952 680068
Makeney Hall	Belper	01332 842999
The Manor House Hotel	Gloucestershire	01608 650501
The Manor House	North Humberside	01482 881645
The Mansion House	Dorset	01202 685666
Meadow House	Somerset	01278 741546
Meudon Hotel	Cornwall	01326 250541
Michaels Nook	Cumbria	015394 35496
Mickleover Court	Derbyshire	01332 521234
Middlethorpe Hall	Yorkshire	01904 641241
The Millstream Hotel	West Sussex	01243 593234
Monk Fryston Hall	North Yorkshire	01977 682369
Monkey Island Hotel	Berkshire	01628 23400
The Montagu Arms Hotel	Hampshire	01590 612324
Moore Place	Bedfordshire	01908 282000
Moorland Links Hotel & Restaurant	Devon	01822 852245
Mount Royale Hotel	North Yorkshire	01904 628856
Nailcote Hall	Warwickshire	01203 466174
Nansidwell Country House	Cornwall	01326 250340
The Nare Hotel	Cornwall	01872 501279
New Hall	West Midlands	0121 378 2442
New Park Manor	Hampshire	01590 23467
Nidd Hall Country House	North Yorkshire	01423 771598
Normanton Park Hotel	Leicestershire	01780 720315
Northcote Manor	North Devon	01769 560501
Nunsmere Hall	Cheshire	01606 889100
Nutfield Priory	Surrey	01737 822066
Nuthurst Grange	Warwickshire	01564 783972
Oakley Court	Berkshire	01753 609988
Oatlands Park	Surrey	01932 847242
Ockenden Manor	West Sussex	01444 416111
St Olaves Court Hotel	Devon	01392 217736
The Old Bridge Hotel	Cambridgeshire	01480 52681
The Old Vicarage Hotel	Shropshire	01746 716497
The Orestone Manor Hotel	Devon	01803 328098
The Osborne	Devon	01803 213311
Park Farm Hotel	Norfolk	01603 810264
Parkhill Hotel	Hampshire	01703 282944
Passage House Hotel	Devon	01626 55515
Passford House Hotel	Hampshire	01590 682398
Pendley Manor Hotel	Hertfordshire	01442 891891
Pengethley Manor	Hereford	01989 87211
Pennyhill Park Hotel	Surrey	01276 471774
Penrhos Court	Herefordshire	01544 230720
Periton Park Hotel	Somerset	01643 706885
Petersfield House Hotel	Norfolk	01692 630741
Petwood House Hotel	Lincolnshire	01526 352411
The Pheasant	North Yorkshire	01439 771241
Plumber Manor	Dorset	01258 472507
The Polurrian Hotel	Cornwall	01326 240421
Pontlands Park Country Hotel	Essex	01245 476444
Powdermills Hotel	East Sussex	01424 775511
Priest House Hotel	Derbyshire	01332 810649
The Priory Hotel	Avon	01225 331922
The Priory Hotel	Dorset	01929 551666
The Priory Hotel	Buckinghamshire	01296 641239
Puckrup Hall Hotel	Gloucestershire	01684 296200
The Queensberry Hotel	Avon	01225 447928
Quorn Country Hotel	Leicestershire	01509 415050
Rampsbeck Country House Hotel	Cumbria	017684 86442
Ravenwood Hall Hotel	Suffolk	01359 270345
Redworth Hall Hotel	County Durham	01388 772442
Rhinefield House Hotel	Hampshire	015906 22922
Riber Hall	Derbyshire	01629 582795
Richmond Gate Hotel	Surrey	0181 940 0061
Riverside Country House Hotel	Derbyshire	01629 814275
Rookery Hall	Cheshire	01270 610016
Rose In Vale Country House Hotel	Cornwall	01872 552202
Rothay Manor	Cumbria	015394 33605
Rowhill Grange	Kent	01322 615136
Rowton Castle	Shropshire	01743 884044
Rowton Hall Hotel	Cheshire	01244 335262
The Royal Berkshire	Berkshire	01344 23322
Rumwell Manor	Somerset	01823 461902
Salford Hall Hotel	Worcestershire	01386 871300
The Seafood Restaurant	Cornwall	01841 532485
Seckford Hall	Suffolk	01394 385678
Slaley Hall	Northumberland	01434 673350
The Snooty Fox	Gloucestershire	01666 502436
Soar Mill Cove Hotel	Devon	01548 561566
Sopwell House	Hertfordshire	01727 864477
South Lodge Hotel	West Sussex	01403 891711
The Spa Hotel	Kent	01892 520331
The Spread Eagle Hotel	West Sussex	01730 816911
The Springs Hotel	Oxfordshire	01491 836687
Sprowston Manor Hotel	Norfolk	01603 410871
St Michael's Manor	Hertfordshire	01727 864444
The Stanneylands Hotel	Cheshire	01625 525225
Stanton Manor	Wiltshire	01666 837552
Stapleford Park	Leicestershire	01572 787 522
Ston Easton Park	Somerset	01761 241631
Stonehouse Court	Gloucestershire	01453 825155
Studley Priory	Oxfordshire	01865 351203
Summer Lodge	Dorset	01935 83424
Swallow Hotel	West Midlands	0121 452 1144
Swallow Royal Hotel	Avon	0117 925 5100
The Swan Diplomat	Berkshire	01491 873737
The Swan Hotel	Suffolk	01502 722186
Swinfen Hall Hotel	Staffordshire	01543 481494
Talland Bay Hotel	Cornwall	015032 72667
Temple Sowerby House Hotel	Cumbria	017683 61578
The Fernie Lodge	Leicestershire	01858 880551
The Swan Hotel	Gloucestershire	01285 740695
Tillmouth Park	Northumberland	01890 882255
Topps Hotel	East Sussex	01273 729 334
Treglos Hotel	Cornwall	01841 520727
Trelawne Hotel	Cornwall	01326 250226
The Tufton Arms Hotel	Cumbria	017683 51593
Tylney Hall	Hampshire	01256 764881
Tytherleigh Cot Hotel	Devon	01460 221170
Underscar Manor	Cumbria	017687 75000
Washbourne Court Hotel	Gloucestershire	01451 822143
Watersmeet Hotel	Devon	01271 870333
Welcombe Hotel And Golf Course	Warwickshire	01789 295252
Wentbridge House Hotel	West Yorkshire	01977 620444
Wentworth Hotel	Suffolk	01728 452312
West Lodge Park	Hertfordshire	0181 440 8311
Whatley Manor	Wiltshire	01666 822888
The White Hart	Essex	01376 561654
White Lodge Country Hotel	East Sussex	01323 870265
Whitechapel Manor	North Devon	01769 573377
Whitehall	Essex	01279 850603
Whitley Hall Hotel	South Yorkshire	0114 245 4444
Willington Hall Hotel	Cheshire	01829 752321
The Wind In The Willows	Derbyshire	01457 868001
Wood Hall	West Yorkshire	01937 587271
Woodland Park Hotel	Cheshire	061 928 8631
Woodlands Manor	Bedford	01234 363281
Woodlands Park Hotel	Surrey	01372 843933
Woolacombe Bay Hotel	Devon	01271 870388
Woolley Grange	Wiltshire	01225 864705
The Wordsworth Hotel	Cumbria	015394 35592
The Worsley Arms Hotel	South Yorkshire	01653 628234
Wrea Head Country Hotel	North Yorkshire	01723 378211
Wroxton House Hotel	Oxfordshire	01295 730777
Wyck Hill House	Gloucestershire	01451 831936
Ye Olde Bell Hotel	Berkshire	01628 825881

SCOTLAND

The Townhouse Hotel	Glasgow	0141 332 3320
Allt-Nan-Ross Hotel	Inverness-shire	01855 821210
Ardanaiseig	Argyllshire	01866833 333
Ardsheal House	Argyllshire	01631 740227
Arisaig House	Inverness-shire	01687 450622
Balcary Bay Hotel	Dumfries & Galloway	01556 640217
Ballathie House Hotel	Perthshire	01250 883268
Barons Craig Hotel	Kirkcudbrightshire	01556 630 225
Borthwick Castle	Mid Lothian	01875 820514
Bunchrew House Hotel	Inverness-shire	01463 234917
The Cally Palace Hotel	Kirkcudbrightshire	01557 814341
Cameron House	Dunbartonshire	01389 755565
Castleton House Hotel	Angus	01307 840340
Channings	Mid Lothian	0131 315 2226
Cringletie House Hotel	Peebleshire	01721 730233
Cromlix House	Perthshire	01786 822125
Culloden House Hotel	Inverness-shire	01463 790461
Dalhousie Castle Hotel	Edinburgh	01875 820153
Dalmunzie House	Perthshire	01250 885224
Darroch Learg Hotel	Aberdeenshire	013397 55443
Ednam House Hotel	Roxburghshire	01573 224168
Enmore Hotel	Argyllshire	01369 702230
Farleyer House Hotel	Perthshire	01887 820332
Gleddoch House	Strathclyde	01475 540711
Greywalls	East Lothian	01620 842144
The Howard	Edinburgh	0131 557 3500
Invercreran Country House Hotel	Argyllshire	01631 730414
Isle Of Eriska	Argyll	01631 720371
Johnstounburn House Hotel	East Lothian	01875 833696
Kildrummy Castle Hotel	Aberdeenshire	019755 71288
Kingsmills Hotel	Inverness-shire	01463 237166
Kinloch House Hotel	Perthshire	01250 884237
Kinnaird	Perthshire	01796 482440
Kirroughtree Hotel	Wigtownshire	01671 402141
Knipoch Hotel	Argyllshire	01852 316251
Knockie Lodge	Inverness-shire	01456 486276
Knockinaam Lodge	Wigtownshire	0177681 471
Letham Grange Hotel	Angus	0124189 0373
Loch Torridon Hotel	Inverness	01445 791242
Malmaison	Glasgow	0141 221 6400
Malmaison	Edinburgh	0131 555 6868
Mansion House Hotel	Inverness-shire	01343 548811
Montgreenan Mansion House Hotel	Ayrshire	01294 557733
Murrayshall Country House Hotel	Perthshire	01738 551171
Nivingston House	Kinross-shire	01577 850216
The Norton House Hotel	Midlothian	0131 333 1275
One Devonshire Gardens	Glasgow	0141 3392001
Parklands Hotel And Restaurant	Perthshire	01738 622451
Piersland House Hotel	Ayrshire	01292 314747
Roman Camp Hotel	Perthshire	01877 330003
Rufflets Country House	Fife	01334 472594
Shieldhill House	Lanarkshire	01899 20035
Summer Isles	Ross-shire	01854 622282
Sunlaws House Hotel	Roxburghshire	01573 450331
Uig Hotel	Isle Of Skye	0470 542205
Western Isles Hotel	Argyllshire	01688 2012

WALES

The Cawdor Arms Hotel	Dyfed	01558 823500
The Curt Bleddyn Hotel	Gwent	01633 49521
Allt Yr Ynys	Hereford	01873 890307
Bodysgallen Hall	North Wales	01492 584466
Bontddu Hall	Gwynedd	01341 430661
Bron Eifion Country House Hotel	Gwynedd	01766 522385
Bryn Howel Hotel	Clwyd	01978 860331
Celtic Manor Hotel	Gwent	01633 413000
Coed-Y-Mwstwr Hotel	Mid Glamorgan	01656 860621
Conrah Country Hotel	AberystwythDyfed	01970 617941
Crown At Whitebrook	GwentWales	01600 860254
Egerton Grey Country House Hotel	South Glamorgan	01446 711666
Gliffaes Country House Hotel	Powys	01874 730371
Hotel Maes-Y-Neuadd	Gwynedd	01766 780200
The Hotel Portmeirion	Gwynedd	01766 770228
Kinsale Hall Hotel	Clywd	01745 560001
The Lake Country House	Powys	01591 620202
Lake Vyrnwy Hotel	Powys	01691 870692
Llangoed Hall	Powys	01874 754525
Miskin Manor Country House	Mid Glamorgan	0443 224204
Norton House Hotel & Restaurant	West Glamorgan	01792 404891
Pale Hall	Gwynedd	01678 530285
Penally Abbey	Dyfed	01834 843033
Penmaenuchaf Hall	Gwynedd	01341 422129
Peterstone Court Hotel	Powys	01874 665387
Porth Tocyn Country House Hotel	Gwynedd	01758 713303
Seiont Manor Hotel	Caernafon	01286 673366
Soughton Hall Country House Hotel	Clwyd	01352 840811
Trearddur Bay Hotel	Anglesey	01407 860301
St Tudno Hotel	Gwynedd	01492 874411
Tyddyn Llan Country House Hotel	Clwyd	0149084 264
Tynycornel Hotel	Gwynedd	01654 782282
Warpool Court Hotel	Dyfed	01437 720300
Ynyshir Hall Country House Hotel	Powys	01654 781209

IRELAND

The Hibernian Hotel	Dublin	353 1668 7666
Adare Manor	Co Limerick	353 61 396566
Aghadoe Heights Hotel	Co Kerry	353 64 31766
Ashford Castle	Co Mayo	353 92 46003
Dromoland Castle	Shannon Area	353 61 368144
Galgorm Manor	Co Antrim (NI)	01266 881001
Glenlo Abbey	Galway	353 91 526666
Kelly's Resort Hotel	Co Wexford	353 533 2114
Kildare Hotel & Country Club	Co Kildare	3531627 3333
Marlfield House	Co Wexford	353 552 1124
Mount Juliet	Co Kilkenny	353 562 4455
Nuremore Hotel	Co Monaghan	353 42 61438
Park Hotel	Co Carey	353 64 41200
Renvyle House	Co Galway	353 95 43511
Tinakilly House Hotel	Co Wicklow	353 404 69274

CHANNEL ISLANDS

The Atlantic Hotel	Jersey	01534 44101
Chateau La Chaire	Jersey	01534 863354
Hotel L'Horizon	Jersey	01534 43101
Hotel La Place	Jersey	01534 44261
Longueville Manor	Jersey	01534 25501
St Pierre Park Hotel	Guernsey	01481 728282

GBI Country Houses

ENGLAND

The Bauble	Suffolk	01206 337254
The Beeches Hotel	Norfolk	01603 621167
The Brakes	Shropshire	01584 856485
The Country House At Winchelsea	East Sussex	01797 226669
The Countryman At Trink	Cornwall	01736 797571
The Crown Hotel	Somerset	01643 831554
The Eastbury Hotel	Dorset	01935 813131
The Gordleton Mill Hotel	Hampshire	01590 682219
The Grange Country House Hotel	Cumbria	017687 72500
The Great House Restaurant	Suffolk	01787 24731
The Lodge	Dorset	01308 863468
The Lord Haldon Hotel	Devon	01392 832483
The Manor	Surrey	01483 222624
The Mill At Harvington	Worcestershire	01386 870688
The Old Rectory	Worcestershire	01386 853729
The Old Rectory	Norfolk	01328 820597
The Parsonage Hotel	North Yorkshire	01904 728111
The Peacock Hotel At Rowsley	Derbyshire	01629 733518
The Priory	Lincolnshire	01780 720215
The Stower Grange	Norfolk	0603 860210
The Thatched Cottage	Hampshire	01590 23090
The White House	West Yorkshire	01423 501388
The Wind in the Willows	Derbyshire	01457 868001
The Woodville Hall	Kent	01304 825256
4 South Parade	North Yorkshire	01904 628229
Abbotts Oak	Leicester	01530 832328
Allhays Country House	Cornwall	01503 72434
Appleton Hall Hotel	North Yorkshire	01751 417227
Apsley House Hotel	Avon	01225 336966
Aynsome Manor Hotel	Cumbria	015395 36653
Bath Lodge Hotel	Bath	01225 723040
The Beeches Farmhouse	Derbyshire	01889 590288

GBI Country Houses continued

Beechleas Hotel	Dorset	01202 841684
Beechwood Hotel	Norfolk	01692 403231
Beryl	Avon	01749 678738
Bessemer Thatch	North Devon	01271 882296
Bibury Court	Gloucestershire	01285 740337
Biggin Hall	Derbyshire	01298 84451
Biggin Mill House	Derbyshire	01335 370414
Blagdon Manor Country House	Devon	01409 211224
Bloomfield House	Avon	01225 420105
Bovey House	Devon	01297 680 241
Box House	Wiltshire	01225 744447
Bradfield House	Suffolk	01284 386301
Broom Hall	Norfolk	01953 882125
Burleigh Court	Gloucestershire	01453 883804
Burpham Country Hotel	West Sussex	01903 882160
Catton Old Hall	Norfolk	01603 419379
Chapel House	Warwickshire	01827 718949
Charlton Kings Hotel	Gloucestershire	01242 231061
Chase Lodge	Surrey	0181 943 1862
Chelwood House	Avon	01761 490730
Chequers Hotel	West Sussex	01798 872486
Chippenhall Hall	Suffolk	01379 588180
Collin House Hotel	Worcestershire	01386 858354
Coombe Farm	Cornwall	01503 240223
Cotswold Park	Gloucestershire	01285 831414
Crosby Lodge Country House Hotel	Cumbria	01228 573618
Cross Lane House Hotel	Shropshire	01746 764887
Dale Head Hall	Cumbria	017687 72478
Dannah Farm Country House	Derbyshire	01773 550273
Delbury Hall	Shropshire	01584 841267
Dial House Hotel	Gloucestershire	01451 822244
Down House	East Sussex	01825 712328
Dunsley Hall	North Yorkshire	01947 893437
Duxford Lodge Hotel	Cambridgeshire	01223 836444
Eagle House	Avon	01225 859946
East Lodge Country House Hotel	Derbyshire	01629 734474
Easton Court Hotel	Devon	01647 433469
Eastwrey Barton Hotel	Devon	01647 277338
Fallowfields	Oxford	01865 820416
Farthings Hotel & Restaurant	Somerset	01823 480664
Fayrer Garden House Hotel	Cumbria	015394 88195
Foxdown Manor	Devon	01237 451325
Frogg Manor	Chester	01829 782629
Glencot House	Somerset	01749 677160
Glenview	Northumberland	01661 843674
Glewstone Court	Herefordshire	01989 770367
Halewell	Gloucestershire	01242 890238
Harrop Fold	Lancashire	01200 447600
Higher Huxley Hall	Chester	01829 781484
Hinton House	Gloucestershire	01285 740233
Hipping Hall	Cumbria	015242 71187
Hockley Place	Essex	01206 251703
Hooke Hall	East Sussex	01825 761578
Irondale House	Wiltshire	01373 830730
Kemps Country House Hotel	Dorset	01929 462563
Kingston House	Devon	01803 762235
Langtry Manor	Dorset	01202 553887
Laurel Villa	Cumbria	015394 33240
Leasow House	Worcestershire	01386 584526
Leusdon Lodge Hotel	Devon	01364 631304
Lions Court Restaurant	Hampshire	01425 652006
Little Offley	Hertfordshire	01462 768243
Lower Bache	Herefordshire	01568 750304
Lower Brook House	Gloucestershire	01386 700286
Maison Talbooth	Essex	01206 322367
Malt House	Gloucestershire	01386 840295
Marsh Hall Country House Hotel	Devon	01769 572666
Melbourn Bury	Hertfordshire	01763 261151
Middle Lypiatt House	Gloucestershire	01453 882151
The Millers House Hotel	North Yorkshire	01969 622630
Monkshill	Avon	01225 833028
Moor View Hotel	Devon	0182 2820 220
Nanny Brow Hotel	Cumbria	015394 32036
Nansloe Manor	Cornwall	01326 574691
New House Farm	Cumbria	01900 85404
Newbridge House	Avon	01225 446676
Newstead Grange	North Yorkshire	01653 692502
The Old Rectory	Norfolk	01379 677575
The Old Rectory	Worcestershire	01527 523000
The Old Vicarage	Cumbria	015395 52381
Orchard House	Gloucestershire	01989 720417
Otley House	Suffolk	01473 890253
Paradise House	Avon	01225 317723
Pen-Y-Dyffryn Country Hotel	Shropshire	01691 653700
Periton Park Hotel	Somerset	01643 706885
Peterstow Country House	Herefordshire	01989 562826
Petty France	Avon	01454 238361
The Pheasant Hotel	Somerset	01460 240502
Rectory House	Dorset	01935 83273
Rock's Place	Herefordshire	01531 660218
Romney Bay House	Kent	01797 364747
Rookhurst Country House Hotel	North Yorkshire	01969 667454
Salisbury House	Norfolk	01379 644738
Simonsbath House Hotel	Somerset	01643 831259
St Peter's House	Suffolk	01502 713203
Stanhill Court Hotel	Surrey	01293 862166
The Steppes	Herefordshire	01432 820424
Swinside Lodge Hotel	Cumbria	01767 72948
Tanyard	Kent	01622 744705
The Thatched Cottage	Devon	01566 784224
Trebrea Lodge	Cornwall	01840 770410
Tregildry Hotel	Cornwall	01326 231378
Twitchill Farm Cottages	Derbyshire	01433 621426
Tye Rock Hotel	Cornwall	01326 572695
Underleigh House	Derbyshire	01433 621372
Upper Court	Gloucestershire	01386 725351
Wallett's Court	Kent	01304 852424
Waren House Hotel	Northumberland	01668 214581
Wark Farmhouse	Northumberland	01890 883570
Washingborough Hall	Lincolnshire	01522 790340
White Moss House	Cumbria	015394 35295
White Wings	Leicestershire	01827 716100
Whitley Ridge Country House Hotel	Hampshire	01590 22354
Widbrook Grange	Wiltshire	01225 864750
Wigham	Devon	01363 877350
Yalbury Cottage	Dorset	01305 262382

SCOTLAND

The Manor House	Oban	01631 562087
Altamount House Hotel	Perthshire	01250 873512
Ardfillayne Hotel	Argyllshire	01369 702267
Ardvourlie Castle	Isle Of Harris	01859 502307
Balgonie Country House	Grampian	013397 55482
Conchra House	Ross-shire	01599 555233
Corrour House Hotel	Inverness-shire	01479 810220
Craigmhor Lodge	Perthshire	01796 472123
Culcreuch Castle Hotel	Stirlingshire	01360 860228
Culdearn House	Morayshire	01479 872106
Culduthel Lodge	Inverness	01463 240089
Dunfallandy House	Perthshire	01796 472648
Dupplin Castle	Perthshire	01738 623224
Harlosh House	Isle Of Skye	01470 521367
Killiechronan	Argyll	01680 300403
The Killiecrankie Hotel	Perthshire	01796 473220
Knockomie Hotel	Morray	01309 673146
The Lake Hotel	Perthshire	01877 385258
Polmaily House	Inverness-shire	01456 450343
Sciberscross Lodge	Sutherland	01408 641246
Well View Hotel	Dumfriesshire	01683 220184

WALES

Berthlwyd Hall Hotel	Gwynedd	01492 592409
Bodfach Hall Country House Hotel	Powys	01691 648272
Dolmelynllyn Hall Hotel	Gwynedd	01341 440273
Glangrwyney Court	Powys	01873 811288
Llanwenarth House	Gwent	01873 830289
Mynydd Ednyfed	Gwynedd	01766 523269
Old Gwernyfed Country Manor	Powys	01497 847376
The Old Rectory Conwy	Gwynedd	01492 580611
Parva Farmhouse	Gwent	01291 689411
Penyclawdd Court	Gwent	01873 890719
Plas Bach	Gwynedd	01341 281234
Plas Glyn Y Mel	Dyfed	01348 872296
Stone Hall	Dyfed	01348 840212
Tan-Y-Foel	Gwynedd	01690 710507
Tower	Clwyd	01352 700220
Ty'n Rhos	Gwynedd	01248 670489
Tyddyn Llan Country House	Clwyd	0149084 264
Waterwynch House Hotel	Dyfed	01834 842464

IRELAND

Beech Hill	Co Down (NI)	01232 425892
Edenvale House	Co Down (NI)	01247 814881
Portaferry Hotel	Co Down (NI)	012477 28231
The Old Rectory	Wicklow	353 404 67048
Barberstown Castle	Co Kildare	353 16288157
Belcamp Hutchinson	Dublin	353 1 846 0843
Castlegrove House	Co Donegal	353 745118
Coopershill House	Co Sligo	353 71 65108
Kinnity Castle	Co Offaly	353 509 37318
Liss Ard Lake Lodge	Co Cork	353 28 22365
Markree Castle	Co Sligo	353 71 67800
St David's Country House	Co Tipperary	353 67 24145

CHANNEL ISLANDS

Almorah Hotel	Jersey	01534 21648
La Favorita Hotel	Guernsey	01481 35666
Les Embruns Hotel	Guernsey	01481 64834

GBI Inns with Restaurants

ENGLAND

The Acorn Inn Hotel	Dorset	01935 83228
The Anchor Inn	Nr Ely	01353 778537
The Anchor Inn	Somerset	01398 23433
The Anchor Inn	Suffolk	01502 722112
Arrow Mill	Warwickshire	01789 762419
Baraset Barn Restaurant	Stratford-Upon-Avon	01789 295510
The Barn Owl Inn	Newton Abbot	01803 872130
Barnacles Restaurant	Leciestershire	01455 633220
The Barton Angler Country Inn	Nr Wroxham	01692 630740
The Bell Hotel	Gloucestershire	01684 293293
Bird In Hand	Nr Twyford	0162882 6622
The Black Horse Inn	Lincolnshire	01778 591247
Blue Bell Hotel	Belford	01668 213543
The Blue Boar Inn	Warwickshire	01789 750010
The Blue Lion	North Yorkshire	01969 24273
Boars Head Hotel	Derbyshire	01283 820344
The Boathouse Brasserie	Near Arundel	01798 831059
Boulters Lock Hotel	Berkshire	01628 21291
The Castle Inn	Wiltshire	01249 783030
The Chequers At Slaugham	West Sussex	01444 400239
The Chequers Inn	Derbyshire	01433 630231
The Christopher Hotel	Windsor	01753 852359
Cotswold Gateway Hotel	Burford	01993 822695
The Countrymen	Suffolk	01787 312356
The Cricketers	Essex	01799 550442
The Cridford Inn	Devon	01626 853694
The Crown At Hopton	Nr Kidderminster	01299 270372
East Ayton Lodge Country Hotel	Scarborough	01723 864227
The Falcon Hotel and Restaurant	Northamptonshire	01604 696200
The Feathers Hotel	Ledbury	01531 635266
The Feversham Arms Hotel	North Yorkshire	01439 770766
Fox Country Hotel	Buckinghamshire	01491 638289
Freshmans Restaurant	Near Stowbridge	01562 730467
The Garden House Hotel	Norwich	01603 720007
The George & Dragon	Kirkbymoorside	01751 433334
The George Hotel	Dorchester	01865 340404
The George Hotel	Somerset	01963 350761
The George Hotel	Basingstoke	01256 702081
The George Hotel	Hatherleigh	01837 810454
The Golden Lion	Warwickshire	01788 832265
Green Farm Restaurant And Hotel	Norfolk	01263 833602
The Green Man	North Yorkshire	01653 600370
The Greyhound	Leicestershire	01455 553307
The Harbour Inn	Nr Helston	01326 573876
Hare & Hounds	Lincolnshire	01400 272090
The Harrow At Warren Street	Kent	01622 858727
The Highwayman	Berkshire	01491 682020
The Holcombe Hotel	Oxfordshire	01869 338274
Home Farm Hotel	Devon	01404 831278
The Horse & Groom Inn	Wiltshire	01666 823904
The Hoste Arms	Norfolk	01328 738777
Hotel Des Clos	Nottinghamshire	0115 986 6566
The Hundred House Hotel	Nr Shifnal	01952 730353
The Inn At Whitewell		01200 448222
The Inn On The Lake	Surrey	01483 415575
The Jersey Arms	Oxfordshire	01869 343234
Jubilee Inn	Cornwall	01503 220312
The Kings Arms Hotel	Wensleydale	01969 650258
The Kings Arms Inns Hotel	Somerset	01935 822513
The Kings Head Inn & Restaurant	Nr Kingham	01608 658365
Kingshead House Restaurant	Birdlip	01452 862299
The Lamb Inn	Oxon	01993 823155
The Lamb Inn	Shipton	01993 830465
Leatherne Bottel Riverside Inn	Berkshire	01491 872667
Longview Hotel	Knutsford	01565 632119
Mallyan Spout Hotel	North Yorkshire	01947 86486
Manor Hotel	Dorset	01308 897616
Manor House Hotel	Dronfield	01246 413971
Marston Farm Hotel	Warwickshire	01827 872133
The Masons Arms	Gloucestershire	01285 850164
Maynard Arms Hotel	Derbyshire	01433 630321
The Mermaid Inn	East Sussex	01797 223065
The Milburn Arms Hotel	North Yorkshire	01751 417312
The Milford Hall Hotel	Wiltshire	01722 417411
The Mill & Old Swan	Oxfordshire	01993 774441
Mole And Chicken	Aylesbury	01844 208387
The Monckton Arms Hotel	Rutland	01572 822326
The Morritt Arms Hotel	Durham	01833 267232
The Mortal Man Hotel	Cumbria	015394 33193
The New Dungeon Ghyll Hotel	Cumbria	015394 37213
The New Inn	Gloucestershire	01285 750651
The Nobody Inn	Devon	01647 52394
The Noel Arms	Gloucestershire	01386 840317
The Old Beams Restaurant	Staffordshire	01538 308254
The Old Bell Inn Hotel	Saddleworth	01457 870130
The Old Custom House Inn	Cornwall	01841 532359
The Old Manse Hotel	Gloucestershire	01451 820082
The Old Tollgate Restaurant	Bramber	01903 879494
The Old Vicarage	Burton Upon Trent	01283 533222
Old White Lion Hotel	West Yorkshire	01535 642313
The Oxenham Arms	Devon	01837 840244
Panos Hotel Restaurant	Cambridgeshire	01223 212958
The Pheasant Inn	Cumbria	015242 71230
The Pheasant	Chester	01829 770434
Poppies At The Roebuck	Shropshire	01584 711230
Port Gaverne Hotel	North Cornwall	01208 880244
Quorn Grange	Leicestershire	01509 412167
Quy Mill Hotel	Cambridge	01223 293383
The Ragged Cot Inn	Stroud	01453 884643
Red Lion Inn	Hawkshead	015394 36213
The Red Lion At Adderbury	Near Banbury	01295 810269
The Redfern Hotel	Shropshire	01299 270395
Rhydspence Inn	Nr HayOnWye	01497 831262
Ringlestone Inn	Kent	01622 859900
The Rising Sun Hotel	Devon	01598 753223
The Rising Sun	St Mawes	01326 270233
Riverside Hotel	Worcestershire	01386 446200
The Rock Inn Hotel	West Yorkshire	01422 379721
The Royal Oak Hotel	Berkshire	01635 201325
The Royal Oak Inn	Cumbria	017683 51463
The Royal Oak Inn	Winsford	01643 851455
The Royal Oak Inn	Withypool	01643 831236
Royal Wells Inn	Kent	01892 511188
The Royalist	Gloucestershire	0151 830670
Sculthorpe Mill	Norfolk	01328 856161
The Sea Trout Inn	Devon	01803 762274
The Shaven Crown Hotel	Oxfordshire	01993 830330
The Snooty Fox	Cumbria	015242 71308
The Starr	Essex	01371 874321
Stonor Arms Hotel	Henley-On-Thames	01491 638345
The Swan Hotel Newby Bridge	Cumbria	015395 31681
The Tempest Arms	North Yorkshire	01282 842450
The Talkhouse	Stanton-St-John	01865 351648
Thatchers Inn	Nr Oxford	0184421 2146
Thelbridge Cross Inn	Devon	01884 860316
Three Horseshoes Inn	Near Leek	01538 300296
Treetops Country House Restaurant	Nr Southport	01704 879651
Trengilly Wartha Country Inn	Falmouth	01326 40332
Tyacks Hotel	Cornwall	01209 612424
The Walnut Tree	Somerset	01935 851292
The Waltzing Weasel	Derbyshire	01663 743402
The Wensleydale Heifer	North Yorkshire	01969 622322
Wesley House	Gloucestershire	01242 602366
The Wheatsheaf Inn	North Yorkshire	01947 85271
The Wheatsheaf Inn At Onneley	Staffordshire	01782 751581
Wheelbarrow Castle	Herefordshire	01568 612219
The White Hart	Wiltshire	01249 782213
The White Hart Hotel	Cornwall	01726 72100
The White Horse Inn	West Sussex	01798 869221
White Lion Hotel	Worcestershire	01684 592551
The White Swan	North Yorkshire	01751 472288
Whoop Hall Inn	Carnforth	015242 71284
The Windmill Inn Hotel	Nr Daventry	01327 702363
The Woodfalls Inn	Fordingbridge	01725 513222
The Woolpack Inn	Somerset	01373 831244
Wykeham Arms	Hampshire	01962 853834
Ye Horns Inn	Lancashire	01772 865230
Ye Olde Nags Head	Derbyshire	01433 620248
Ye Olde Salutation Inn	Herefordshire	01544 318443

SCOTLAND

The Winnock Hotel	Stirlingshire	01360 660245
Cairnbaan Hotel	Argyll	01546 603668
Comrie Hotel	Perthshire	01764 670239
Glenisla Hotel	Perthshire	01575 582223
Hotel Eilean Iarmain	Scotland	01631 720 371
Kylesku Hotel	Sutherland	01971 502231
Potarch Hotel	Kincardineshire	013398 84339

WALES

The Dragon Hotel	Wales	01686 668359
Castle View Hotel	Gwent	01291 620349
George III Hotel	Gwynedd	01341 422525
The Lion Hotel And Restaurant	Powys	01686 640452
The Plough Inn	Dyfed	01558 823431
The West Arms Hotel	Clwyd	01691 600665

GUEST SURVEY REPORT

Name and location of hotel: _____ Date of visit: _____

Name and address of guest: _____

_____ Postcode: _____

Please tick one box in each category below:	Excellent	Good	Disappointing	Poor
Bedrooms				
Public Rooms				
Restaurant/Cuisine				
Service				
Welcome/Friendliness				
Value For Money				

PLEASE return your Guest Survey Report form!

Occasionally we may allow other reputable organisations to write with offers which may be of interest.
If you prefer not to here from them, tick this box ☐

To: Johansens, FREEPOST (CB264), 175-179 St John Street, London EC1B 1JQ

Your own Johansens 'inspection' gives reliability to our guides and assists in the selection of Award Nominations

---

GUEST SURVEY REPORT

Name and location of hotel: _____ Date of visit: _____

Name and address of guest: _____

_____ Postcode: _____

Please tick one box in each category below:	Excellent	Good	Disappointing	Poor
Bedrooms				
Public Rooms				
Restaurant/Cuisine				
Service				
Welcome/Friendliness				
Value For Money				

PLEASE return your Guest Survey Report form!

Occasionally we may allow other reputable organisations to write with offers which may be of interest.
If you prefer not to here from them, tick this box ☐

To: Johansens, FREEPOST (CB264), 175-179 St John Street, London EC1B 1JQ

Your own Johansens 'inspection' gives reliability to our guides and assists in the selection of Award Nominations

---

GUEST SURVEY REPORT

Name and location of hotel: _____ Date of visit: _____

Name and address of guest: _____

_____ Postcode: _____

Please tick one box in each category below:	Excellent	Good	Disappointing	Poor
Bedrooms				
Public Rooms				
Restaurant/Cuisine				
Service				
Welcome/Friendliness				
Value For Money				

PLEASE return your Guest Survey Report form!

Occasionally we may allow other reputable organisations to write with offers which may be of interest.
If you prefer not to here from them, tick this box ☐

To: Johansens, FREEPOST (CB264), 175-179 St John Street, London EC1B 1JQ

Your own Johansens 'inspection' gives reliability to our guides and assists in the selection of Award Nominations

Order Coupon

To order Johansens guides, simply indicate which publications you require by putting the quantity(ies) in the boxes provided. Choose you preferred method of payment and return this coupon (NO STAMP REQUIRED). You may also place your order using FREEPHONE +44 990 269397 or by fax on +44 171 490 2538.

❏ I enclose a cheque for £_____ payable to Biblios PDS Ltd (Johansens book distributor).
❏ I enclose my order on company letterheading, please invoice me. (UK companies only)
❏ Please debit my credit/charge card account (please tick)
❏ MASTERCARD ❏ VISA ❏ DINERS ❏ AMEX

Card Number _____

Signature _____ Expiry Date _____
Name (Mr/Mrs/Miss) _____
Address _____
_____
_____ Postcode _____
(We aim to despatch your order with 10 days, but please allow 28 days for delivery)

Occasionally we may allow reputable organisations to write to you with offers which may interest you. If you prefer not to hear from them, tick this box ❏

CALL THE JOHANSENS CREDIT CARD ORDER SERVICE FREE ☎ **+44 990 269397**

	PRICE	QTY	TOTAL
WHEN YOU BUY A SET OF ALL THREE 1996 UK JOHANSENS GUIDES	£35.80		
Boxed presentation set of three 1996 UK Johansens guides with slip case	£39.00		
Johansens Recommended Hotels in Great Britain & Ireland 1996	£21.90		
Johansens Recommended Inns with Restaurants in Great Britain 1996	£11.95		
Johansens Recommended Country Houses and Small Hotels in Great Britain & Ireland 1996	£11.95		
Johansens Recommended Hotels in Europe 1996	£11.95		

ALL PRICES INCLUDE HANDLING AND UK POSTAGE ONLY   48J
Outside the UK add £3 for each single guide ordered, or £5 for a set or boxed set to cover additional postage.   PRICES VALID UNTIL 31/12/96

Post free to:
JOHANSENS, FREEPOST (CB264), HORSHAM, WEST SUSSEX RH13 8ZA

Order Coupon

To order Johansens guides, simply indicate which publications you require by putting the quantity(ies) in the boxes provided. Choose you preferred method of payment and return this coupon (NO STAMP REQUIRED). You may also place your order using FREEPHONE +44 990 269397 or by fax on +44 171 490 2538.

❏ I enclose a cheque for £_____ payable to Biblios PDS Ltd (Johansens book distributor).
❏ I enclose my order on company letterheading, please invoice me. (UK companies only)
❏ Please debit my credit/charge card account (please tick)
❏ MASTERCARD ❏ VISA ❏ DINERS ❏ AMEX

Card Number _____

Signature _____ Expiry Date _____
Name (Mr/Mrs/Miss) _____
Address _____
_____
_____ Postcode _____
(We aim to despatch your order with 10 days, but please allow 28 days for delivery)

Occasionally we may allow reputable organisations to write to you with offers which may interest you. If you prefer not to hear from them, tick this box ❏

CALL THE JOHANSENS CREDIT CARD ORDER SERVICE FREE ☎ **+44 990 269397**

	PRICE	QTY	TOTAL
WHEN YOU BUY A SET OF ALL THREE 1996 UK JOHANSENS GUIDES	£35.80		
Boxed presentation set of three 1996 UK Johansens guides with slip case	£39.00		
Johansens Recommended Hotels in Great Britain & Ireland 1996	£21.90		
Johansens Recommended Inns with Restaurants in Great Britain 1996	£11.95		
Johansens Recommended Country Houses and Small Hotels in Great Britain & Ireland 1996	£11.95		
Johansens Recommended Hotels in Europe 1996	£11.95		

ALL PRICES INCLUDE HANDLING AND UK POSTAGE ONLY   48J
Outside the UK add £3 for each single guide ordered, or £5 for a set or boxed set to cover additional postage.   PRICES VALID UNTIL 31/12/96

Post free to:
JOHANSENS, FREEPOST (CB264), HORSHAM, WEST SUSSEX RH13 8ZA

Order Coupon

To order Johansens guides, simply indicate which publications you require by putting the quantity(ies) in the boxes provided. Choose you preferred method of payment and return this coupon (NO STAMP REQUIRED). You may also place your order using FREEPHONE +44 990 269397 or by fax on +44 171 490 2538.

❏ I enclose a cheque for £_____ payable to Biblios PDS Ltd (Johansens book distributor).
❏ I enclose my order on company letterheading, please invoice me. (UK companies only)
❏ Please debit my credit/charge card account (please tick)
❏ MASTERCARD ❏ VISA ❏ DINERS ❏ AMEX

Card Number _____

Signature _____ Expiry Date _____
Name (Mr/Mrs/Miss) _____
Address _____
_____
_____ Postcode _____
(We aim to despatch your order with 10 days, but please allow 28 days for delivery)

Occasionally we may allow reputable organisations to write to you with offers which may interest you. If you prefer not to hear from them, tick this box ❏

CALL THE JOHANSENS CREDIT CARD ORDER SERVICE FREE ☎ **+44 990 269397**

	PRICE	QTY	TOTAL
WHEN YOU BUY A SET OF ALL THREE 1996 UK JOHANSENS GUIDES	£35.80		
Boxed presentation set of three 1996 UK Johansens guides with slip case	£39.00		
Johansens Recommended Hotels in Great Britain & Ireland 1996	£21.90		
Johansens Recommended Inns with Restaurants in Great Britain 1996	£11.95		
Johansens Recommended Country Houses and Small Hotels in Great Britain & Ireland 1996	£11.95		
Johansens Recommended Hotels in Europe 1996	£11.95		

ALL PRICES INCLUDE HANDLING AND UK POSTAGE ONLY   48J
Outside the UK add £3 for each single guide ordered, or £5 for a set or boxed set to cover additional postage.   PRICES VALID UNTIL 31/12/96

Post free to:
JOHANSENS, FREEPOST (CB264), HORSHAM, WEST SUSSEX RH13 8ZA

North American Order Coupon

To order Johansens guides in North America, simply indicate which guide(s) you wish by entering the quantity in the boxes provided. Select your preferred method of payment and forward whole Order Coupon by mail to Johansens at the address given at the bottom of this coupon.

PLEASE PRINT

Your Name

Street Address

Town/City

State/Province   Zip/Post Code

☐ I enclose a check for US $ _____ payable to JOHANSENS.

☐ Please debit my credit/charge card account the amount of US $ _____ in favor of JOHANSENS.

☐ MasterCard   ☐ Diners   ☐ Amex   ☐ Visa   ☐ Discover   ☐ Carte Blanche

Card No

Signature   Expiry date   Date

SAVE $5 When you buy all three 1996 UK Johansens guides — US$49.75 + $8.25 s&h

Boxed presentation set of three 1996 UK Johansens guides — US$58.75 + $8.75 s&h

Johansens Recommended Hotels in Great Britain & Ireland 1996 — US$24.95 + $6.00 s&h

Johansens Recommended Inns with Restaurants in Great Britain 1996 — US$14.95 + $4.75 s&h

Johansens Recommended Country Houses in Great Britain & Ireland 1996 — US$14.95 + $4.75 s&h

Johansens Recommended Hotels in Europe 1996 — US$14.95 + $4.75 s&h

Qty   US$ Total

All items shipped UPS Ground Service. Canadian customers or for experdited delivery details telephone 1-800 213 9628 (24 Hours). New Jersey customers, please add appropriate sales tax. Please allow 21 days for delivery.

BILLING ADDRESS OF CREDIT/CHARGE CARD, IF DIFFERENT FROM ABOVE

Street Address

Town/City

State/Province   Zip/Post Code

Mail to: JOHANSENS, 30 Edison Drive, Wayne, New Jersey 07470

North American Order Coupon

To order Johansens guides in North America, simply indicate which guide(s) you wish by entering the quantity in the boxes provided. Select your preferred method of payment and forward whole Order Coupon by mail to Johansens at the address given at the bottom of this coupon.

PLEASE PRINT

Your Name

Street Address

Town/City

State/Province   Zip/Post Code

☐ I enclose a check for US $ _____ payable to JOHANSENS.

☐ Please debit my credit/charge card account the amount of US $ _____ in favor of JOHANSENS.

☐ MasterCard   ☐ Diners   ☐ Amex   ☐ Visa   ☐ Discover   ☐ Carte Blanche

Card No

Signature   Expiry date   Date

SAVE $5 When you buy all three 1996 UK Johansens guides — US$49.75 + $8.25 s&h

Boxed presentation set of three 1996 UK Johansens guides — US$58.75 + $8.75 s&h

Johansens Recommended Hotels in Great Britain & Ireland 1996 — US$24.95 + $6.00 s&h

Johansens Recommended Inns with Restaurants in Great Britain 1996 — US$14.95 + $4.75 s&h

Johansens Recommended Country Houses in Great Britain & Ireland 1996 — US$14.95 + $4.75 s&h

Johansens Recommended Hotels in Europe 1996 — US$14.95 + $4.75 s&h

Qty   US$ Total

All items shipped UPS Ground Service. Canadian customers or for experdited delivery details telephone 1-800 213 9628 (24 Hours). New Jersey customers, please add appropriate sales tax. Please allow 21 days for delivery.

BILLING ADDRESS OF CREDIT/CHARGE CARD, IF DIFFERENT FROM ABOVE

Street Address

Town/City

State/Province   Zip/Post Code

Mail to: JOHANSENS, 30 Edison Drive, Wayne, New Jersey 07470

North American Order Coupon

To order Johansens guides in North America, simply indicate which guide(s) you wish by entering the quantity in the boxes provided. Select your preferred method of payment and forward whole Order Coupon by mail to Johansens at the address given at the bottom of this coupon.

PLEASE PRINT

Your Name

Street Address

Town/City

State/Province   Zip/Post Code

☐ I enclose a check for US $ _____ payable to JOHANSENS.

☐ Please debit my credit/charge card account the amount of US $ _____ in favor of JOHANSENS.

☐ MasterCard   ☐ Diners   ☐ Amex   ☐ Visa   ☐ Discover   ☐ Carte Blanche

Card No

Signature   Expiry date   Date

SAVE $5 When you buy all three 1996 UK Johansens guides — US$49.75 + $8.25 s&h

Boxed presentation set of three 1996 UK Johansens guides — US$58.75 + $8.75 s&h

Johansens Recommended Hotels in Great Britain & Ireland 1996 — US$24.95 + $6.00 s&h

Johansens Recommended Inns with Restaurants in Great Britain 1996 — US$14.95 + $4.75 s&h

Johansens Recommended Country Houses in Great Britain & Ireland 1996 — US$14.95 + $4.75 s&h

Johansens Recommended Hotels in Europe 1996 — US$14.95 + $4.75 s&h

Qty   US$ Total

All items shipped UPS Ground Service. Canadian customers or for experdited delivery details telephone 1-800 213 9628 (24 Hours). New Jersey customers, please add appropriate sales tax. Please allow 21 days for delivery.

BILLING ADDRESS OF CREDIT/CHARGE CARD, IF DIFFERENT FROM ABOVE

Street Address

Town/City

State/Province   Zip/Post Code

Mail to: JOHANSENS, 30 Edison Drive, Wayne, New Jersey 07470

MAIL TO:

JOHANSENS
30 EDISON DRIVE
WAYNE
NEW JERSEY 07470

MAIL TO:

JOHANSENS
30 EDISON DRIVE
WAYNE
NEW JERSEY 07470

MAIL TO:

JOHANSENS
30 EDISON DRIVE
WAYNE
NEW JERSEY 07470